W0113976

THE
National ⚾ Pastime
A REVIEW OF BASEBALL HISTORY

This year we have the longest piece we've ever published in *The National Pastime*, Dick Thompson's cover story on Wes Ferrell, which you'll find sturdily anchoring the issue, just before Dan Zamudio's pair of closing verses. You can also savor the first long poem we've ever run, B.H. Fairchild's "Body and Soul," which you'll find when you turn this page. These two unique offerings sandwich an especially chewy issue. Don't miss George Thompson's historic discovery of a baseball reference in the New York press of 1823; our three grouped pieces relevant to the hundredth anniversary of the American League; or Jim Smith's pictorial appreciation of Hall-of-Fame Chicago sportswriter Ed Munzel. You'll find other offerings that incorporate medieval art (p. 41), the American Civil War (p. 17), a president (p. 67), a player who just doesn't want to talk about it (p. 9), dignity and incivility (p. 23), a pitching professor (p. 11), and a Battalion of Death (p. 44). And there's more: on ballparks, on tours, on forgotten players and their forgotten feats. On what-ifs and how-comes. Looking down the bench, a pretty strong lineup for today's game.

—Mark Alvarez

THE NATIONAL PASTIME Number 21. Published by The Society for American Baseball Research, Inc., 812 Huron Rd., Suite 719, Cleveland, OH 44115. Postage paid at Birmingham, AL. Copyright 2001, The Society for American Baseball Research, Inc. All rights reserved. Reproduction in whole or in part without written permission is prohibited.
Printed by EBSCO Media, Birmingham, AL.

Editor
Mark Alvarez

Copy Editor
A.D. Suehsdorf

Designated Reader
Dick Thompson

The Society for American Baseball Research

History

The Society for American Baseball Research (SABR) was founded on August 10, 1971, by L. Robert "Bob" Davids and fifteen other baseball researchers at Cooperstown, New York, and now boasts more than 6,600 members worldwide. The Society's objectives are to foster the study of baseball as a significant American institution, to establish an accurate historical account of baseball through the years, to facilitate the dissemination of baseball research information, to stimulate the best interest of baseball as our national pastime, and to cooperate in safeguarding proprietary interests of individual research efforts of members of the Society.

The National Pastime

The Society published its first issue of **The National Pastime** in 1982. The present volume is the twenty-first. Many of the previous volumes are still available for purchase (see page 128). The editorial policy is to publish a cross section of research articles by our members which reflect their interest in history, biography, statistics and other aspects of baseball not previously published.

Interested in Joining the Society?

SABR membership is open to all those interested in baseball research, statistics or history. SABR membership runs on a calendar year basis; if you join after October 1, you will be rolled over into the next calendar year. Membership dues are $50 US, $60 Canada & Mexico and $65 overseas (US funds only). Students and seniors can join for $30 ($40 in Canada & Mexico and $45 overseas). Members receive the **Baseball Research Journal**, **The National Pastime**, *The SABR Bulletin*, a Membership Directory and other special publications. To join SABR, send the appropriate amount and your name and address to the address below . Feel free to contact SABR for more information at the address below as well.

SABR
Dept. TNP
812 Huron Rd E #719
Cleveland, OH 44115
216-575-0500
www.sabr.org
info @ sabr.org

Body and Soul

B. H. Fairchild

Half-numb, guzzling bourbon and Coke from coffee mugs,
our fathers fall in love with their own stories, nuzzling
the facts but mauling the truth, and my friend's father begins
to lay out with the slow ease of a blues ballad a story
about sandlot baseball in Commerce, Oklahoma decades ago.
These were men's teams, grown men, some in their thirties
and forties who worked together in zinc mines or on oil rigs,
sweat and khaki and long beers after work, steel guitar music
whanging in their ears, little white rent houses to return to
where their wives complained about money and broken Kenmores
and then said the hell with it and sang *Body and Soul*
in the bathtub and later that evening with the kids asleep
lay in bed stroking their husband's wrist tattoo and smoking
Chesterfields from a fresh pack until everything was O.K.
Well, you get the idea. Life goes on, the next day is Sunday,
another ball game, and the other team shows up one man short.

They say, we're one man short, but can we use this boy,
he's only fifteen years old, and at least he'll make a game.
They take a look at the kid, muscular and kind of knowing
the way he holds his glove, with the shoulders loose,
the thick neck, but then with that boy's face under
a clump of angelic blonde hair, and say, oh, hell, sure,
let's play ball. So it all begins, the men loosening up,
joking about the fat catcher's sex life, it's so bad
last night he had to hump his wife, that sort of thing,
pairing off into little games of catch that heat up into
throwing matches, the smack of the fungo bat, lazy jogging
into right field, big smiles and arcs of tobacco juice,
and the talk that gives a cool, easy feeling to the air,
talk among men normally silent, normally brittle and a little
angry with the empty promise of their lives. But they chatter
and say rock and fire, babe, easy out, and go right ahead

and pitch to the boy, but nothing fancy, just hard fastballs
right around the belt, and the kid takes the first two
but on the third pops the bat around so quick and sure
that they pause a moment before turning around to watch
the ball still rising and finally dropping far beyond
the abandoned tractor that marks left field. Holy shit.
They're pretty quiet watching him round the bases,
but then, what the hell, the kid knows how to hit a ball,
so what, let's play some goddamned baseball here.
And so it goes. The next time up, the boy gets a look
at a very nifty low curve, then a slider, and the next one
is the curve again, and he sends it over the Allis Chalmers,
high and big and sweet. The left fielder just stands there, frozen.
As if this isn't enough, the next time up he bats left-handed.
They can't believe it, and the pitcher, a tall, mean-faced
man from Okarche who just doesn't give a shit anyway
because his wife ran off two years ago leaving him with
three little ones and a rusted-out Dodge with a cracked block,
leans in hard, looking at the fat catcher like he was the sonofabitch
who ran off with his wife, leans in and throws something
out of the dark, green hell of forbidden fastballs, something
that comes in at the knees and then leaps viciously towards
the kid's elbow. He swings exactly the way he did right-handed,
and they all turn like a chorus line toward deep right field
where the ball loses itself in sagebrush and the sad burnt
dust of dustbowl Oklahoma. It is something to see.

But why make a long story long: runs pile up on both sides,
the boy comes around five times, and five times the pitcher
is cursing both God and His mother as his chew of tobacco sours
into something resembling horse piss, and a ragged and bruised
Spalding baseball disappears into the far horizon. Goodnight,
Irene. They have lost the game and some painful side bets
and they have been suckered. And it means nothing to them
though it should to you when they are told the boy's name is
Mickey Mantle. And that's the story, and those are the facts.
But the facts are not the truth. I think, though, as I scan
the faces of these old men now lost in the innings of their youth,
I think I know what the truth of this story is, and I imagine
it lying there in the weeds behind that Allis Chalmers
just waiting for the obvious question to be asked: why, oh
why in hell didn't they just throw around the kid, walk him,
after he hit the third homer? Anybody would have,
especially nine men with disappointed wives and dirty socks
and diminishing expectations for whom winning at anything
meant everything. Men who knew how to play the game,
who had talent when the other team had nothing except this ringer
who without a pitch to hit was meaningless, and they could go home
with their little two-dollar side bets and stride into the house
singing *If You've Got the Money, Honey, I've Got the Time*
with a bottle of Southern Comfort under their arms and grab
Dixie or May Ella up and dance across the gray linoleum
as if it were V-Day all over again. But they did not.
And they did not because they were men, and this was a boy.
And they did not because sometimes after making love,
after smoking their Chesterfields in the cool silence and

listening to the big bands on the radio that sounded so glamorous,
so distant, they glanced over at their wives and noticed the lines
growing heavier around the eyes and mouth, felt what their wives
felt: that Les Brown and Glenn Miller and all those dancing couples
and in fact all possibility of human gaiety and light-heartedness
were as far away and unreachable as Times Square or the Avalon
ballroom. They did not because of the gray linoleum lying there
in the half-dark, the free calendar from the local mortuary
that said one day was pretty much like another, the work gloves
looped over the doorknob like dead squirrels. And they did not
because they had gone through a depression and a war that had left
them with the idea that being a man in the eyes of their fathers
and everyone else had cost them just too goddamned much to lay it
at the feet of a fifteen year-old boy. And so they did not walk him,
and lost, but at least had some ragged remnant of themselves
to take back home. But there is one thing more, though it is not
a fact. When I see my friend's father staring hard into the bottomless
well of home plate as Mantle's fifth homer heads toward Arkansas,
I know that this man with the half-orphaned children and
worthless Dodge has also encountered for his first and possibly
only time the vast gap between talent and genius, has seen
as few have in the harsh light of an Oklahoma Sunday, the blonde
and blue-eyed bringer of truth, who will not easily be forgiven.

B. H. Fairchild *was born in Houston, Texas and grew up there and in small towns in west Texas, Oklahoma, and southwest Kansas. He attended the University of Tulsa and University of Kansas, working part-time as technical writer for a nitroglycerin plant and English tutor to the Kansas basketball team.* The Arrival of the Future *was his first full-length book of poems, originally published by Swallow's Tale Press in 1985 and recently republished in a new edition by Alice James Books. His third book,* The Art of the Lathe, *won the 1996 Capricorn Award, and the Beatrice Hawley Award at Alice James Books in 1997, and was subsequently a Finalist for the National Book Award, also receiving the Kingsley Tufts Poetry Award, the William Carlos Williams Award, the PEN West Poetry Award, the California Book Award, the Natalie Ornish Award from the Texas Institute of Letters, and an Honorable Mention for the Poet's Prize. His poems have appeared in* Southern Review, Poetry, Hudson Review, Yale Review, TriQuarterly, Sewanee Review, *and many other journals and in several anthologies, including the forthcoming* The Best American Poems of 2000. *He has been the recipient of fellowships and grants from the National Endowment for the Arts, the Guggenheim Foundation, and the Rockefeller Foundation and is the author of* Such Holy Song, *a study of William Blake. Fairchild now lives with his wife and daughter in Claremont, California and is Professor of English at California State University.*

New York Baseball, 1823

George A. Thompson, Jr.

For these past few years I have been browsing through New York City newspapers from the 1820s and 1830s, looking for whatever might present itself in the way of glimpses of everyday life on the streets of the city. One of the fruits of this reading was a collection of material on an all-black theater group active in the city primarily during the years 1821 to 1823, and the subsequent performing career of its leading actor, James Hewlett.[1]

Recently, as I was working my way through the *National Advocate* of 1823, what to my wondering eyes should appear but the following paragraph:

COMMUNICATION.

I was last Saturday much pleased in witnessing a company of active young men playing the manly and athletic game of "base ball" at the Retreat in Broadway (Jones'). I am informed they are an organized association, and that a very interesting game will be played on Saturday next at the above place, to commence at half past 3 o'clock, PM. Any person fond of witnessing this game may avail himself of seeing it played with consummate skill and wonderful dexterity. It is surprising, and to be regretted that the young men of our city do not engage more in this manual sport; it is innocent

amusement, and healthy exercise, attended with but little expense, and has no demoralizing tendency.

A SPECTATOR[2]

This notice offers the earliest reference found so far in the United States to the game of baseball, predating the previous earliest known reference by two years. This is also the earliest occurrence of the word "base ball" in the United States, and the earliest reference— by more than twenty years—to baseball being played in New York City.[3]

In addition, it suggests the following interesting points:

- The games referred to were played by young men, rather than by boys.
- The young men had formed an "organized association."
- They played games on a regular basis, or, at least, they planned games for a specific place and time, a week or more in advance, and
- Spectators interested in witnessing a display of "consummate skill and wonderful dexterity" would attend their games.

The same letter was sent to at least one other city newspaper, which printed a summary of it:

We have received a communication in favor of the manly exercise of base ball; stating that an organized company, who are in the habit of taking this exercise at the Retreat, will play a

---

George A. Thompson *passes the dreary evenings when there is no baseball on the radio by reading newspapers from the early decades of the nineteenth century. He was delighted to find that he now lives about half a block from the site where the game dealt with in this note was played in 1823. He has been a Yankees fan since Whitey Ford was a rookie.*

great match there on Saturday next, to commence at half past 3 o'clock.[4]

"The Retreat in Broadway (Jones')" was on the west side of Broadway between what nowadays is Washington Place and Eighth Street. It had been the residence of William Neilson from the very late eighteenth century until nearly the end of 1820. In 1821 the house and its several acres of grounds were opened to the public under the name of "Retreat Garden." In 1822, a William Jones took the lease on the house and opened a restaurant called "Jones's Retreat." By 1823 the house had reverted to being a residence, reclaimed by William Neilson, Jr.[5] Evidently, Neilson allowed the extensive grounds to be used for baseball games.

Who was "A Spectator"? We will never know, of course. He may have been what he offered himself to be: a spectator who enjoyed seeing baseball played with skill and dexterity, and who wanted to encourage the young men who had given him pleasure. Perhaps he was a member of the association who wanted to publicize its games, in the hope of also encouraging other young men to form baseball associations, so that he and his friends would never lack for opponents. (This would be my guess.) Or he might have been the proprietor of a tavern near the Retreat, who wanted to encourage people to trudge out to see the games, supposing that they would stop by his place for a drink or two afterwards.

The newspapers of that era did not routinely publish information about the weather. The editors had no better ability to predict the weather than anyone else: "red sky at night," and so forth, and they supposed that if their readers had really been interested in the weather yesterday they would have looked out the window. They made an exception, however, for weather that was astonishingly awful, or, occasionally, astonishingly nice. The weather during the spring of 1823, when these young men were establishing their baseball association, was of the awful variety. There had been a great storm at the very end of March that dumped a deep blanket of snow on the city.

> "...the snow, being remarkably wet and heavy, was driven horizontally through the atmosphere; and immense masses gradually accumulating on roofs and sides of buildings, at times thundered down with a tremendous motion, and a sound resembling an earthquake. ...The snow fell to a great depth, and completely enveloped the city, covering not only the roofs, but the walls and windows of buildings looking towards the east."[6]

It hardly seems likely that such a snowfall could have melted sufficiently to permit playing a game of baseball by Saturday, April 5. Even the following week seems early. Probably the game on Saturday, April 19, which "A Spectator" had been so pleased to watch, had been the first of the season. Then the weather turned hot. On Tuesday, the *Advocate* referred to the "powerful July sun" of the previous day.[7] But this weather may not have lasted until the game on Saturday, for on May 1 an editor complained:

> *The Season.*—We have seldom or never known a more bleak, gloomy, and inhospitable May day than the present. For the last week, the weather has been unusually cold and inclement; and to-day the city is visited with a piercing east wind, accompanied with rain. This paragraph is written before a winter fire, which is necessary to comfort, while from the window, fruit trees are seen in full blossom.[8]

Two weeks later, this editor was still complaining about the unseasonably "chilly, dreary and unpleasant" weather, which he blamed on the numerous icebergs to be found in the ocean offshore.[9] But in another week or so, the editor of the *Advocate* remarked "the weather is immoderately hot for the season, and the streets are moderately dirty," while the *Gazette* noted that the 3 PM temperature at the Bowling Green, Monday, May 19 through Wednesday, May 21 had been 82°, 86°, and 84°.[10] But this was not to last either; in mid-June an editor complained "Our teeth are chattering with the cold this morning, but we presume it will be warm enough in a few days."[11] All in all, not a good time to play baseball, and especially not a good time to hope to attract spectators to stand and watch the games.

There were eight daily newspapers published in New York City during 1823. Of these, the *Mercantile Advertiser* seems to be available for 1823 only at the Library of Congress, having never been microfilmed. Of the others, I have read through the news columns of the New-York *Gazette and General Advertiser* and the New-York *Daily Advertiser* for April through June. Neither paper paid attention to local happenings, although, as already noted, the Gazette printed a summary of Spectator's letter. I have also read through the news columns of the *National Advocate*, the New-York *Evening Post*, the *Commercial Advertiser*, the *American*, and the *Statesman* from March to the Fall, without finding any other references to baseball or to the association.

None of the papers made much effort to gather city news (the editors aparently supposing that New York was still small enough that citizens would learn of local happenings without having to read about them in a newspaper), so the absence of any further mention of the association does not necessarily mean that it was not active. If "A Spectator" had been, in fact, a spectator who had written his letter in a burst of enthusiasm, then he might well never have written another. But if he had been a member of the association trying to publicize its existence, I expect that he would have continued to try to get notices of their games into the paper. Perhaps the adverse weather that spring discouraged other young men from forming opposing associations, and caused this one to break up.

A final note: complaints about boys desecrating the Sabbath by playing games were pretty common in the newspapers at that time. The editor of the *Commercial Advertiser* was a particular bear for Sabbath-keeping. But when I reviewed my notes from the 1820s, I was surprised to find that I had only four that complained specifically of boys playing *ball* on Sunday, and all but one were from the winter months. For instance, the *Commercial Advertiser* wrote in February, 1824:

> A correspondent of ours calls the attention of the proper officers to the numerous boys who collect on the Sabbath, in the Park. They were last Sabbath quietly permitted to "play ball," and to amuse themselves in other exercises, without any interposition of the city authorities.[12]

Other papers carried other such complaints.[13] The only complaint not from the winter was in a September number of the New-York *Evening Post*.[14] In 1823, in fact, only a few days after berating the authorities for allowing boys to play their ball games, the *Commercial* had remarked that the weather was so cold that the Hudson River had frozen so solid that men had walked across from Powles Hook (Jersey City), and that the harbor was choked with drift ice, making it impossible to cross from Staten Island by boat.[14]

Whatever sort of ball these wicked boys were playing, it hardly seems that it could have been any form of baseball.

Notes:

The *National Advocate* (published in 1812-1829) is a different newspaper from the *New-York National Advocate*, (published 1824-1826).

1. George A Thompson, Jr., *A Documentary History of "The African Theatre,"* Evanston: Northwestern University Press, 1998.

2. *National Advocate*, April 25, 1823, p. 2, col. 4.

3. See *Early Innings: A Documentary History of Baseball, 1825-1908*, Dean Sullivan, ed., Lincoln: The University of Nebraska Press, 1995, pp. 1-2 (for baseball in 1823) and 11-13 (for baseball in New York in 1845).

4. *New-York Gazette & General Advertiser*, April 25, 1823, p. 2, col. 2.

5. Thomas M. Garrett, "A History of Pleasure Gardens in New York City, 1700-1865," Ph.D. dissertation, School of Education, Health, Nursing and Arts Professions, New York University, 1978, pp. 487-89.

6. *New-York Statesman*, March 31, 1823, p. 2, cols. 4-5.

7. *National Advocate*, April 22, 1823, p. 2, col. 2.

8. *New-York Statesman*, May 1, 1823, p. 2, col. 6.

9. *New-York Statesman*, May 14, 1823, p. 2, col. 4.

10. *National Advocate*, May 23, 1823, p. 2, col. 4 & *New-York Gazette & General Advertiser*, May 22, 1823, p. 2, col. 1.

11. *Commercial Advertiser*, June 12, 1823, p. 2, col. 3.

12. *Commercial Advertiser*, February 4, 1823, p. 2, col. 3.

13. *Commercial Advertiser*, January 28, 1828, p. 2, col. 4; *New-York Evening Post*, December 22, 1828, p. 2, col. 2 & *Commercial Advertiser*, December 23, 1828, p. 2, cols. 2-3.

14. New-York *Evening Post*, September 18, 1823, p. 2, col. 4.

15. *Commercial Advertiser*, February 8, 1823, p. 2, col. 3.

One ball is usually enough...
(Wilmington *Every Evening*, August 14, 1884)
The strenuous exertions of the police alone prevented a serious difficulty at a game of baseball in Portsmouth (VA) yesterday afternoon between the Baltimore Unions and the Athletic club of that city. Up to the sixth inning the Baltimores had shut out the Athletics when it was discovered that they were playing with two balls, a live one for themselves and a dead ball for their competitors. Intense excitement and confusion prevailed. Four or five hundred men and boys rushed to the diamond, and the Baltimore [sic] would have been roughly handled but for the police and the cooler spectators.
—A. D. Suehsdorf

Elmer Valo: Four-Decade Man?

Jim Charlton

At the start of the 2000 baseball season, three players—Rickey Henderson, Mike Morgan, and Jesse Orosco—joined the list of major leaguers appearing in four decades. The multitalented and inscrutable Henderson, almost certainly headed to the Hall of Fame, showed his skills immediately in 1979 when he first played. The much-traveled Morgan broke in a season earlier, and in 2000 pitched for his twelfth team, the most any player has suited up for in the last hundred years. The veteran Orosco, a left-handed reliever and therefore consistently in demand, has pitched steadily if unspectacularly since 1979.

Adding these three, the ranks of players who have toiled in four different decades is twenty-five. Two of these—Nick Altrock and Minnie Minoso—played in five decades, coming back for token publicity appearances. The four-decade list begins with two players, Jim O'Rourke and Dan Brouthers, who started their careers in the 1870s, and represents thirteen decades worth of big league baseball through the year 2000. Just twenty-five players. But should the number read twenty-six? Missing from this short list is Elmer Valo.

A glance at the baseball encyclopedias shows that Valo started his major league career in 1940 with Connie Mack's Philadelphia A's, playing six games at the end of the season after hitting .364 at Wilmington to lead the Inter-State League. In 1939 he had had equal success at Federalsburg (Eastern Shore), hitting .374 in thirty-four games. A native of Czechoslovakia,

Valo was a solid contact hitter and a fearless competitor, hitting over .300 five times. In his later years, he became an outstanding pinch hitter, setting several major league records and prolonging his career. He retired after the 1961 season and became a coach for the Indians and later a scout and coach for the Phillies. Nice long run, but just three decades. Or so I thought.

In November, 1972, Pulitzer Prize-winning writer Anthony Lukas wrote an article for the *Saturday Review* about that year's World Series between the Cincinnati Reds and Oakland A's. Lukas's chatty first-hand account described the weather, the other writers, hotels, the players, and only in passing discussed the games. He mentioned that before one game he was standing near the batting cage with two venerable New York newspaper writers, Red Smith and Art Daley, as the two swapped baseball stumpers. "'Darold Knowles [an injured A's pitcher] just caught me with one,' says Red. 'Which four players had careers spanning the four decades of the Thirties, Forties, Fifties and Sixties?' Daley doesn't know. "'Ted Williams, Early Wynn, Mickey Vernon, and Elmer Valo,' Smith reveals."

When I read the piece back in 1972, I had no idea how Darold Knowles came up with that one, since baseball players often have no interest in any trivia or history. Especially a question like that. But the record showed that Elmer Valo didn't play in 1939. At the time, I was working for Doubleday, Red Smith's publisher, so I wrote to him on company stationery saying he was wrong. Only three men played in those four decades, I corrected. And by the way, did he know the player who pitched to both Babe Ruth and Mickey Mantle? The good-hearted guy wrote back:

Jim Charlton *is the author of more than three dozen books, including several on baseball. His most recent books are* The Writer's Quotation Book *and* The Who, What, When, Where and Why of Baseball. *He lives in New York City.*

December 26, 1972

Dear Jim Charlton:

As anybody in your business should, you believe that if it appears between hard covers, it must be so. However, the hard-cover reference books have never published and, I hope, never will publish the sordid truth about Elmer Valo.

On the last day of the 1939 season in Philadelphia, Elmer was a kid from the country who had been getting a look-see from the Athletics. Connie sent him up as a pinch-batter and he walked, getting no official time at bat.

When the official scorer learned that Connie Mack had used a player who was not under contract, he left the player's name out of the official score—since he had no time at bat—in order that St. Cornelius escape a possible fine. This piece of perfidy came to light only last October when Elmer told me about it at the World Series and I told Tony Lucas, who didn't work it into his Saturday Review piece.

I haven't proper research material at hand for the Pitcher vs. Ruth & Mantle question but just for fun I'm going to guess Ted Lyons, who may have been too late for one and too soon for the other.

By the way, the official scorer who falsified the record in 1939, and forgot about it until last October, was Red Smith, of the Philadelphia Record. Thanks for writing.

Yours,
Red Smith

Red's recollection about the contract was probably correct. In 1939, Mack did not have to get approval from the league before signing a player. That freedom was reined in by the American League in 1951 after Bill Veeck, the imaginative and fun-loving owner of the St. Louis Browns, inked a contract with the midget Eddie Gaedel and put him in a game. The appearance of Gaedel caused such an uproar that subsequently all player contracts went through the league offices.

Besides the spelling of Tony Lucas's (sic) name, Red was wrong on his answer to my baseball question: "Who pitched to both Babe Ruth and Mickey Mantle?" Ted Lyons did not, as Red had guessed, but journeyman Al Benton did. But was Red right about his official scorer's role in 1939?

Jump forward to the late 1980s. I was no longer working for Doubleday, and Mike Shatzkin and I had just sold a large baseball biographical encyclopedia entitled *The Ballplayers* to Arbor House publishers. The formidable task called for the research and writing, mostly by a team of talented SABR members, of more than 5,000 biographical profiles of players, managers, owners, and others. It included Elmer Valo,

Darold Knowles, and, incidentally, Red Smith.

Recalling Smith's note to me, I wrote to Valo and told him what I was working on, and I asked him about his appearance in the last game of the 1939 season. Six months went by with no response and by then I had forgotten about it. Then one day the phone rang and Shep Long, a young editor working on the project with us, answered it. He handed the phone to me and whispered, "It's Elmer Valo." I said hello and thanked him for responding. I then asked him about the game.

"Listen, just forget about it," he rasped. Taken aback, I said that, though it was a long time ago, it was at least of interest to baseball historians and was it true? "Just forget about," he repeated. I tried a third time. "Are you saying that Red Smith is lying or that he was mistaken?" Elmer was nothing if not consistent. "Fuhgeddaboudit." I thanked him again for calling. And that was that.

Since he didn't deny it or call Smith a liar in our odd conversation, I took it to be true. As historians know, some oldtime ball players are reluctant to change things—years after the fact they'll deny ever having played pro ball under an assumed name when they were eighteen-year-old amateurs. Possibly he thought he was protecting the image of Connie Mack, the longtime owner and venerable manager of the Philadelphia Athletics. So Valo must've had his own reasons.

Valo later became a good friend of Darold Knowles when both worked for the Phillies. When I asked Knowles about it recently, the former reliever told me that he had always dabbled a bit with trivia questions, but, alas, doesn't recall where he first heard the story. But he says that while he never asked Elmer about the story, he also never doubted it.

That long ago game was played in Philadelphia on September 30, 1939 with the Washington Senators winning, 9-5. It drew a Ladies Day crowd of 6,000. The scheduled doubleheader the next day was rained out, so this was the last game of the year for the two also-rans. The winning pitcher for Washington was rookie Joe Haynes, who later married the owner's daughter. The A's managed eleven hits off Haynes, including a homer by Philadelphia native Al Brancato, his first in the majors. The A's were credited with two walks. While there is no sign in the box score of the eighteen-year-old Valo, he might've pinch hit in the fourth inning for starter Lynn "Line Drive" Nelson, who was hammered for six runs in four frames. Nelson had one at bat and his replacement, Chubby Dean, had two; every other position in the order had at least four at bats. Possibly Valo appeared there.

So should we Fuhgeddaboudit? Or is Valo the fourth name to play in the 30s, 40's, 50s and 60s? The two principals in the story, Valo and Smith, are dead now, and the issue is unresolved. But, if you believe Red Smith, the game's official scorer, Valo played.

The Pitching Professor

Rory Costello

Williams College is best known in baseball circles for two nonplaying alumni: the last independent commissioner, Fay Vincent '60, and the blustery Boss himself, George Steinbrenner '52. There hasn't been an Ephman in the majors since 1934, but Ted Lewis, Class of 1896, was not just the finest ballplayer Williams ever produced—like Sir Thomas More he was a man for all seasons. Educator, elocutionist, and natural leader: Lewis embodied an array of talents but always retained a winning humility.

Horatio Alger could not have conjured up a life story like this, which has the power to make the most hardened cynic believe in ideals again. Edward Morgan Lewis was born on Christmas Day, 1872, in Machynlleth, Wales. When the boy was eight years old, his family moved to Utica, New York, where they lived on the banks of the Erie Canal. Little Ted earned his first quarter delivering groceries for the local corner store (though he was docked if he broke a ketchup bottle) and scouted out other odd jobs, supplementing the immigrants' straitened budget.

It is an article of faith that Welshmen have wonderful voices and a love of poetry, and the Lewis family reinforced this tradition. The great American poet Robert Frost was a crony of Ted Lewis for twenty years—even into their sixties, they played "singles" baseball or softball in the back yard whenever they got together. Frost read from Tennyson and Whitman at

Since writing the history of baseball in the Virgin Islands, **Rory Costello** *(Williams 1984) has been investigating the sport in Hawaii with several other SABR colleagues. Williams College was named after Col. Ephraim Williams, hence the terms Ephmen, Ephwomen, and Eph. Acknowledgment to fellow Eph, Martin Kohout '81, who "passed the torch" on Ted Lewis.*

his friend's funeral, and his address showed the profound influence of culture on character:

> He told me once—I was afraid that the story might not be left for me to tell—that he began his interest in poetry as he might have begun his interest in baseball—with the idea of victory—the "Will to Win."
> He was at an Eisteddfod in Utica, an American-Welsh Eisteddfod, where the contest was in poetry, and a bard had been brought in from Wales to give judgment and to pick the winner; and the bard, after announcing the winner and making the compliments which judges make, said he wished the unknown victor would rise and make himself known and let himself be seen. (I believe the poems were read anonymously.) The little "Ted" Lewis sitting there beside his father looked up and saw his father rise as the victor. So poetry to him was prowess from that time on, just as baseball was prowess, as running was prowess. And it was our common ground.

Lewis worked as a bundle boy in a department store and as a surveyor's helper, studying borrowed textbooks by lamplight. With $50 in personal savings he managed to put aside, the youth entered Marietta College in Ohio, which gave him the opportunity to meet his tuition payments by working as a letter carrier, hotel clerk, and janitor.

In the fall of 1893, sophomore Ted Lewis transferred to Williams, the small liberal arts school nestled in the

Berkshire Mountains of western Massachusetts. He made a tremendous impression on his classmates, becoming president of the elite Gargoyle Society and winning the class cup in a walkover, receiving thirty-two votes while no one else got more than four. Ted's accomplishments on the mound were certainly a part of his status. In 1895, he won all eight games in the Triangular League (which then consisted of Williams, Amherst, and Dartmouth rather than Wesleyan), and he followed up with six more in his senior year.

Baseball was the most popular sport at the college in those days, and the *Williams Weekly* was full of manly exhortations to give full voice while cheering. The souvenir scorecard from the 1896 Commencement Game against Amherst is another charming curio, with captain Ted's photo on the front cover and official yells (Osky-wow-wow, Skimmy-wow-wow, Jimmy-wow-wow, W–O–W) on the back.

Lewis faced some most intriguing opponents besides Yale and Harvard. These included the original black pro team, the Cuban Giants. In the Purple Valley, "the Cubans outplayed the Williams men at every point, their coaching and tricky plays having a demoralizing effect…but when Captain Lewis went into the box, he succeeded in hoding the visitors down to two hits."

Another opponent was Louis Sockalexis, then the star center fielder for Holy Cross. A year before his briefly spectacular run with Cleveland, the Penobscot Indian "played a phenomenal game, catching and batting balls, whenever and wherever he pleased."

During his college days, Ted also won the heart of hometown girl Margaret Hallie Williams with a move that would have left Sir Walter Raleigh in the dust. At a local game in Richfield Springs, New York, Ted had promised his friend that he would meet her at the grounds and usher her in. But Margaret arrived a little late, while Ted was facing the first batter. Yet when he spied his wife-to-be, he calmly dropped the ball, walked off the hill (making the captain think Lewis had gone "bughouse") and saw to his escort duties. The gallant then returned to a huge hand from the crowd.

Seeking money to further his studies, the graduate commenced his major league career with Boston. Frank Selee's club was the class of the National League in the 1890s, winning five pennants with numerous Hall of Famers and near-greats. Lewis was a key part of the last two titles, especially in 1898, when he led the league in winning percentage at 26-8.

The "good guy" Beaneaters had an ongoing battle with John McGraw's Baltimore Orioles, notorious for their ruffian tactics. "Parson" Lewis prefigured the fictional Yalie Galahad, Frank Merriwell, and McGraw's Mr. Clean with the Giants, Christy Mathewson. His close friend Damon Hall '97 said:

One might have supposed in those earlier days of professional baseball that a college graduate who did not drink, who refused to play Sunday ball, who said his prayers and read his Bible daily, who even asked his teammates to go to prayer meetings with him, would have been esteemed somewhat of a prig by the other members of the squad. Instead, they took him to their hearts.

Indeed, Ted had seriously considered entering the ministry but decided he could reach more young people through the classroom. While with Boston, he found time to coach the Harvard nine, and after jumping to the new American League in 1901 and playing with the very first Red Sox team (a.k.a. the Pilgrims or Puritans), Lewis retired from baseball to devote his full energies to teaching. His lifetime record was 94-64, with an ERA of 3.53.

The Professor had earned his masters from Williams in 1899, and from 1901 to 1903 he taught elocution at Columbia. His alma mater then lured him back to teach oratory for eight years, during which he also lectured at the Yale Divinity School. In 1910, the Welsh community of Berkshire County formed a society, acclaiming Lewis as president. For many years he returned to

---

On Ted Lewis

"Teddy Lewis will pitch good ball for the Boston Americans no matter how many others may croak."
— Wilbert Robinson

"When at concert pitch there are few better than Lewis."
— Tim Murnane, Boston *Globe*

"Lewis was steady as a minister should be …Chicago's heaviest hitters went down before his speedy deliveries like corn stalks before a gale."
— Jake Morse, Boston *Herald*

"Parson Lewis is closing his career in a blaze of glory."
— Boston *Globe* after Lewis beat Nixey Callahan with a two-hitter in his final game

Compiled by UNH alum Rich Eldred for his Lewis sketch in Nineteenth Century Stars, *(SABR 1988).*

North Adams on St. David's Day, March 1, to address his leek-waving brethren. (The only other Welsh-born major-leaguer was Jimmy Austin, who was one of Lawrence Ritter's subjects in *The Glory of Their Times*.) Also in 1910, Lewis ran for Congress as a Democrat in a staunch Republican district, and missed pulling off an upset by just 865 votes.

The next year, however, Massachusetts Agricultural College in Amherst beckoned. Lewis soon proved how capable an administrator he was, being pressed into service as acting president in 1913-14 (when he made another unsuccessful bid for Congress, supported by pioneering muckraker Ray Stannard Baker). The dean of languages and literature again stepped into the breach in 1918-19 and 1924, finally accepting the position officially in 1926. It was through his efforts that the modest "Aggie" school was transformed into today's UMass. He felt uncomfortable with the political pressure there, however, and moved to the University of New Hampshire in 1927.

Under the aegis of President Lewis, UNH established a graduate school and broadened its infrastructure considerably, building its first women's dorm. In Durham, Lewis received many of his famous friends, including Robert Frost. He had first met the then-unknown poet at Amherst College in 1916—and the Eisteddfod veteran delivered the first public reading of Frost's verse. Forty years later, by then a grand American institution, Frost wrote about the 1956 All-Star Game for *Sports Illustrated*, also reminiscing about his pitching lessons from Lewis.

Ted Lewis passed away in May 1936 at the age of 63. His health had begun to fail about two years before, but even though the beloved "Prexy" was suffering greatly from liver cancer, he summoned up his old athletic reserves to climb the stairs to his office. In February he underwent an operation, and he rallied enough to make an appearance at the Opening Day ballgame versus Bates. The students again took heart, but Lewis relapsed shortly thereafter. He was laid to rest in the Durham Community Cemetery, with former Boston teammate Fred Tenney serving as one of the pallbearers.

This is the centennial of Ted Lewis' last year as a ballplayer. The UNH sports teams still play today at the Lewis Fields, but this man's most fitting memorial might be the measured question he always posed to his colleagues:

"Well…what can we do to better the situation?"

LEWIS.   MOSELY.   IDE.   STREET.   GOODRICH.   ROOT.   ASHTON.
DRYSDALE.   FITCH.   BRADLEY.   DRAPER.   DEWEY.   CORY.

The 1896 Williams College Ephmen, featuring captain Ted Lewis, the future Pitching Professor (upper left).
"By his magnificent work in the box, it needed but a few games to show we had a man among a thousand."

Rance Pless Gets Tough

Gaylon H. White

In fourteen seasons as a professional baseball player, Rance Pless was never kicked out of a game. If an umpire missed a call, Pless might protest by saying, "That was close." He practiced what his father, Garfield, a tobacco farmer and semipro baseball player, preached to him as a youngster: "Go up there, swing the bat, and keep your mouth shut." According to a sportswriter who covered hundreds of games involving Pless, he was a "high-class gent" who "would be an odds-on favorite to win any popularity contest among his fellow gladiators."

So it's ironic that forty years after Pless hung up his bat and glove to return to his roots in Greeneville,Tennessee, he is often remembered for striking the first blow in a free-for-all in September, 1957, when he was a star third baseman for the Denver Bears of the American Association.

Memories of the "basebrawl for the ages" started by Pless were conjured up when the Detroit Tigers and Chicago White Sox squared off in a fight early in the 2000 season that got eleven members of the two teams ejected from the game. Sixteen players, managers, and coaches were subsequently suspended a total of 82 games—the harshest penalty for fighting in baseball history. The true test for the Tigers–White Sox fight, however, will be if anybody remembers it forty years from now.

"When I think of Rance Pless, I think of that fight," says Ralph Houk, who managed Pless at Denver in

1957 and is now retired and living in Winter Haven, Florida. "It turned out to be quite a fight."

Frank Haraway, a former sportswriter for the Denver *Post*, gives this account of the fight, which took place during the ninth inning of a game in Denver between the Bears and the St. Paul Saints:

"No one in the ballpark could believe it when Pless, playing third base, simply laid his glove on the ground and went after St. Paul manager Max Macon, who had been needling him from the third-base coaching lines following a bean-ball episode. Other players got Pless pulled away from Macon but by this time Houk had decided to take on Macon. He backed Macon clear over to the railing along the leftfield line. I remember especially that Macon, having trouble enough defending against the whirlwind fighting tactics of Houk, suddenly was struck on the side of the head, almost in the face, by the handbag of an aroused woman fan who reached over the railing and swung the bag like a lethal weapon."

As Houk recalls, the woman fan was wearing high-heel shoes. "She hit Macon in the head with one of her shoes," he says.

"I went crazy," Pless says today, chuckling over the images of Houk, an ex-Marine, and the high-heeled fan pummeling Macon as players from both teams pushed, shoved, and flailed away at each other. "They tore my shirt off trying to hold me."

Macon taunted opposing hitters by yelling "Stick it in his ear!" to his pitchers. Stan Williams, pitching for the Saints, would eventually star for the Dodgers, where he continued to claim the inside of the plate—and a bit more—as his own. "He'd hit at least two batters a

Gaylon H. White *is a former Denver* Post *sportswriter. He is working on a book about the 1956 Los Angeles Angels and their legendary slugger, Steve Bilko.*

game," Pless says. "And four or five more would hit the dirt."

In the fourth inning Williams drilled Denver's Jim Pisoni in the back. Moments later, Williams fired a pitch over Pless' head. "I didn't say anything," Pless points out. Denver pitcher Ed Donnelly retaliated in the seventh inning by hitting St. Paul's Granny Gladstone. But for Pless, revenge would not be complete until Macon, the chief architect of this and earlier bean-ball wars, was silenced. Houk says: "Rance told me before he went out to third base in the ninth that if Macon said one more thing, he was going to get him."

Macon knew trouble was brewing. During Denver's eighth-inning turn at bat, he called his bullpen pitchers and catchers into the Saints' dugout along the third-base line. And he went to the third-base coaching box wearing a helmet under his cap. Then Pless swung into action—literally—"I hit that helmet and the thing popped. I didn't know he was wearing a helmet. The fight was on after that."

Players from both teams stormed the field, "pushing, shoving, throwing uppercuts and everything else," remembers Pless. Where was Williams? "He was dodging bullets," Pless jokes. "He was out there but, really, I don't remember seeing him. I had my hands full."

The two managers staged the main event and were the last combatants to be separated by Denver policemen who came down from the stands to restore order. Houk "scored a clear-cut decision" over Macon, the Denver *Post* reported the next day. Says Pless, who wound up near the left-field stands where the managers were going at it: "Ralph threw a couple of good punches, I tell you. He nailed him good."

Career—Pless knew what it was like to be hit in the head by a professional fastball. At Nashville in 1952, he suffered a double fracture of the left cheekbone when Jerry Lane of the Atlanta Crackers beaned him after he had slammed a three-run homer off Lane in his previous at bat. The beaning ended a season in which he hit for a .364 average, best in the Southern Association.

Pless's performance in Nashville earned him a trip to the New York Giants' spring training at Phoenix, Arizona, in 1953. Then 27, he was up against the Giants' starting third baseman, Hank Thompson.

"Through the long weeks at Phoenix, he had been probably the biggest single disappointment," *The Sporting News* reported when the Giants assigned him to their top farm team in the Class AAA American Association, the Minneapolis Millers. "He hadn't done any hitting to speak of and there was no sign of the quick, sure hands he was supposed to have in the field. He'd never smiled from the day he reported and he'd kept to himself. He'd looked like a kid who was scared to death."

The story goes on to report that Giants manager Leo Durocher was puzzled by "the kid's inability to live up to his advance notices" until he learned of the beaning at Nashville. "I never knew it until the kid told me the day he left," Durocher explained. "He said he'd been gun-shy at the plate and jittery and uncertain in the field. But he said he'd be able to shake it off in a few weeks and that he'd be back. It wouldn't surprise me if he gets back before too long. He was working under a heavy handicap this spring. Remember Joe Medwick after he was beaned? It took him a long time to get over the jitters, too."

Of his early days in Minneapolis, Pless recalls: "The pitchers knew I'd been hit in the head and they didn't let me forget it for a while." He overcame his fears to become one of the most feared hitters in the league. "He was poison to the Bears when he played against them for Minneapolis," notes Haraway, the Denver sportswriter. In three seasons at Minneapolis (1953-55), he batted .322, .290 and .337. That last was good enough to win the batting title and, combined with 26 home runs and 107 runs batted in, earned Pless the league's 1955 Most Valuable Player award.

Despite the MVP year at Minneapolis and his reputation as "the best hitter in the minors," the Giants still had no room for Pless on their roster. They traded him to Kansas City. "It would be unfair to take him up and keep him on the bench," a Giants official said.

On hearing about the trade, Frank Hiller, a former Giants pitcher and teammate of Pless on the '53 Millers, said: "Pless could be the finest third baseman in the American League. He's the kind of fellow who has to play every day to do the kind of job he's capable of doing."

After watching the 1956 Athletics at spring training, sportswriter Jimmy Cannon wrote: "This is an awful ballclub. We all cherish small victories. Old men are proud when they run after a bus and catch it. Guys with sons who play tennis in the sun across summer afternoons believe it is evidence of vitality when they take the stairs two at a time. They still don't belong on the same field with the Yankees, Red Sox, Indians, White Sox, or Tigers. They have a private tournament, involving Washington and Baltimore." True to form, the Athletics lost 102 games to finish last in the American League.

The thirty-year-old Pless saw little action behind Hector Lopez at third and Vic Power at first, appearing mostly as a pinch-hitter. He batted only 85 times, getting 23 hits for a .271 average. "I felt like I deserved a better chance," Pless says, adding that A's manager Lou Boudreau "made up his mind in the spring who was going to play and that's the way it went."

In 1957 Pless was back in the minors where he finished his career three years later. In fourteen seasons—half in the American Association and International League, the highest of the minor leagues—Pless posted a batting average of .303, with 2,014 hits, including 153 home runs. He batted in 1,083 runs and scored 1,053 more.

"I'm amazed that Rance was not in the major leagues longer than he was," says Houk, who went on from Denver to manage twenty years in the major leagues for the New York Yankees, Detroit Tigers, and Boston Red Sox. "He was a good defensive third baseman. He was a clutch hitter. He was a winner—the kind of guy you wanted on your team. He'd be playing every day in the big leagues today."

Bob Oldis, a former major-league catcher and teammate of Pless's in Denver and Richmond, says, "You've got to be in the right place at the right time. Rance was in the wrong place when Hank Thompson was coming up with the Giants. If he'd been in another organization, I believe he would've got his time in the big leagues."

Watching major-league baseball on television at his home five miles outside Greeneville makes Pless, now seventy-five, want to pick up a bat and hit again. "There is not enough pitching to go around," he says.

What about the "basebrawl" between the Tigers and White Sox and the suspension a few weeks later of Boston Red Sox pitcher Pedro Martinez for hitting a batter with a pitch?

"If somebody in front of me hit a home run, I knew that I might as well sit my tail on the ground," he says. "But if I went down, you went down the next trip up. Nowadays, the pitcher is protected.

"I know you have to pitch inside to be effective," Pless continues. "But you've got a few pitchers who are headhunters and they should be stopped. They could hurt somebody!"

That's essentially the same message Pless delivered to Edward Doherty, the American Association president, the day after the Denver-St. Paul fight forty-four years ago. "We had a meeting in the clubhouse," Pless recalls. "He said, 'You've never been in trouble. I can't believe this.' I said, 'Somebody is going to get killed if something is not done about this. That guy could kill a man!'"

After a long silence, Doherty said, "Well, I tell you what—Don't do it no more!"

That ended the meeting. Nobody from either team had been kicked out of the game, and Pless, the guy who started the "basebrawl for the ages," was never fined or suspended.

Stealing first...twice

Germany Schaefer is frequently credited with initiating the steal of first from second to distract the pitcher. Others did it with less flair, but earlier. Take for example May 7, 1906, Phillies vs. Braves at Philadelphia in the eighth. Sherry Magee is the baserunner on third and Mickey Doolan is on first. Doolan stole second slowly, trying to draw a throw from pitcher Ed Pfeffer or catcher Jack O'Neill to allow Magee to steal home. Pfeffer bluffed a throw to second but kept Magee on third. Doolan then startled the crowd by running back to first. No throw. On the next pitch to the batter Gleason, Doolan again stole second, but neither the pitcher nor the catcher paid any attention to him. He than again ran back to first base. On the next pitch Gleason was walked and Doolan went to second. The bases were loaded. Pfeffer, visibly upset, then hit batter Red Dooin on the arm with an inshoot, forcing Magee home with the tally the Quakers were working so hard to get.

—L. Robert Davids

"One of the best things in the world to keep up the spirits of the men."

Base Ball in the Civil War

Allison Caveglia Barash

I'm surprised you didn't mention Abner Doubleday," said an attendee at one of my talks on the diversions of Civil War soldiers, including baseball. Her accusatory tone made me feel almost un-American, or at the very least, that I had single-handedly and wrongfully shattered a piece of Americana. I proceeded to explain that my omission was deliberate—that while he was a Union general, present at Fort Sumter, Gettysburg, and other major Civil War battles, he was *not* present in Cooperstown, New York, in 1839 where he was supposed to have invented baseball. I went on to explain that he never claimed to have created the game, and in fact, may never even have attended a game. I don't think she believed me.

The origins of the American game of baseball are unclear, but this we know: the Civil War soldier—Johnny Reb and Billy Yank—played an awful lot of baseball...and therein lies its connection to the Civil War.

Baseball had been growing in popularity in the United States since the 1840s and was becoming something of an obsession. Back in 1846, the poet Walt Whitman, who also served as a nurse during the war, wrote: "In our sun-down perambulations of late, through the outer parts of Brooklyn, we have observed several parties of youngsters playing 'base,' a certain game of ball...Let us go forth awhile, and get better air in our lungs. Let us leave our close rooms...the game of ball is glorious."

Allison Caveglia Barash is a professor of psychology. She is a member of the Vintage Base Ball Association and co-founder of the Greater Pittsburgh Civil War Round Table. An avid Pirates fan, she has been fascinated with baseball and the Civil War since childhood.

By 1860, the National Association of Base Ball Players boasted sixty-two member clubs, and spectators were paying admission to watch the contests. But with the firing on Fort Sumter in Charleston Harbor on April 12, 1861, ballplaying athletes began enlisting by the thousands and it looked like organized baseball was about to meet an early demise. Fortunately, some recruits took their bats and balls along with them in their knapsacks, unknowingly ensuring that the sport they loved would not die of neglect.

Once in camp, the excitement of enlistment wore off, reality sank in, and soldiers soon realized that not only did they have the time to play, they had the psychological need to play. "War," said Captain Oliver Wendell Holmes of the 20th Massachusetts Volunteers, "is an organized bore." Thirty years after the war, Chaplain James H. Bradford of the 12th Connecticut expressed his feelings about war this way: "It seems a strange thing to say, in view of sickness, suffering and death always staring one in the face, but nevertheless it is true—I never saw so much merriment in any other three years of my life as in the army...I am not heartless, but it was necessary to relax one from the stern realities of wounds, hardship, and exposure, and to maintain a cheerful spirit."

Fortunately for the soldiers, most officers approved of ballplaying and other organized games, as they lifted spirits, reduced stress, encouraged teamwork, promoted camaraderie, and improved physical fitness. And the officers themselves were clearly not immune to baseball fever.

In April, 1863, Captain Patrick H. "True Blue" Sullivan of the 140th New York Volunteers, who had played for Rochester's Lone Stars Club before the war and was obviously hopelessly addicted to the game, left many written accounts of Civil War ballgames. He writes of an engagement between the officers of his regiment and officers of the 13th New York Volunteers: "We played nearly all day yesterday, our gallant Colonel looking on…with quite a large number of spectators assembled on our parade ground to witness the expertness of our officers, as they were practicing a match-game with the commissioned officers of the veteran 13th…It may appear that we should be engaged in something else beside playing base ball, but I tell you it is one of the best things in the world to keep up the spirits of the men, and not only that, but it is of vast importance to their health…Amusements are becoming the order of the day, and no sooner is drill over than you see the boys flocking together to commence their sports."

Private Alpheris B. Parker of the 10th Massachusetts wrote on April 21, 1863: "The parade ground has been a busy place for a week or so past, ball-playing having become a mania in camp. Officers and men forget, for a time, the differences in rank and indulge in the invigorating sport with a school-boy's ardor."

In another account, Captain Sullivan wrote that "the tedium of a soldier's life was somewhat relieved a few days since by a holiday given us by our Colonel, who believes that the health of a regiment is benefited by amusement and change of labor." The holiday was celebrated "by a match-game of baseball…the game commenced after dinner, the officers of the left wing contending against those of the right. We played but three innings, the right wing being the victors, by a score of 3 to 8…the game was to be renewed on Friday, but the amount of disabled arms, sprained ankles & lame backs prevented the second appearance of the contestants…."

Lieutenant Charles P. Klein documented an engagement between officers on January 10, 1863: "Saturday afternoon is allotted the men for necessary washing and cleansing, at which time the commissioned officers of the regiment indulge in a game of base ball on the parade ground." The score was 32-14 "up to the fifth innings, other duty then interfering."

So whether it was for the pure love of the game, to relieve boredom, or to distract themselves from the gruesomeness of warfare, baseball served both a therapeutic and recreational purpose for these young men so far away from home.

Because playing fields and proper equipment weren't readily available, baseball-playing soldiers often improvised by constructing rudimentary grounds and primitive equipment for their games. The bat may have been a barrel stave, and the ball a walnut wrapped with twine or yarn.

Thanks to the portability of the game and its equiment, it could be played just about anywhere. Legend holds that soldiers played behind the White House, and that sometimes President Abraham Lincoln and his son Tad came to watch. Lincoln himself is purported to have played the game back in Springfield. The story goes that in 1860, when notified by a messenger that the Committee of the Chicago Convention had arrived at his home, Lincoln responded: "Tell the gentlemen that I am glad to know of their coming; but they'll have to wait a few minutes till I make another base hit."

Determined baseball-playing soldiers literally risked their lives to play the game they loved: "It is astonishing how indifferent a person can become to danger," an Ohio private wrote home from Virginia in 1862. "The report of musketry is heard but a very little distance from us…yet over there on the other side of the road is most of our company, playing Bat Ball and perhaps in less than half an hour, they may be called to play a Ball game of a more serious nature."

George Putnam, a Union soldier, recounted playing between the lines when "suddenly there came a scattering fire of which the three outfielders caught the brunt; the center field was hit and captured, the left and right field managed to get back into our lines. The attack…was repelled without serious difficulty, but we had lost not only our center field, but…the only baseball in Alexandria…."

Even back in the 1860s there were potential All-Stars—early day Nolan Ryans, Tom Seavers, or Randy Johnsons, perhaps. Private James A. Hall of the Texas Rangers (the regiment, not the major league team!) remembered: "Frank Ezell was ruled out of the game. He could throw harder and straighter than any man in the company. He came very near knocking the stuffing out of three or four of the boys, and the boys swore they would not play with him."

Surprisingly, baseball was even permitted in certain Union and Confederate prison camps. At Johnson's Island, Ohio, Confederate prisoners learned the New York Game from their Northern captors. Union soldiers in Confederate prisons, like the one in Salisbury, North Carolina, taught the game to their Southern guards. Boys from the western states of Ohio, Illinois, and Wisconsin watched and learned.

The coming of the Civil War did not portend the end of baseball. In fact, it may have been the direct catalyst that caused it to flourish. The men brought it with them, played it in camp, learned from each other, and then brought it back home again after the war. Those who fought against each other on battlefields during the war played with and against each other on baseball fields after the war. Some speculate that baseball may actually have played a role in helping to heal sectional wounds during Reconstruction.

No one claims that baseball was the solution to all of

the problems produced during and after the Civil War, but it unquestionably served a very important purpose for the individual soldier. One soldier wrote that the game totally "erased from their minds the all absorbing topic of the day."

Bibliography

Burns, Ken, *Baseball: A Film by Ken Burns*, Turner Broadcasting Systems, Inc., 1994 ("The First Inning: Our Game).

Kirsch, George B., "Bats, Balls and Bullets: Baseball and the Civil War," *Civil War Times Illustrated*, May, 1998.

Maryniak, Benedict R., "Baseball in the War," *The Civil War Courier*, May, 1996.

Spalding, Albert G., *Baseball, America's National Game*, 1911.

Ward, Geoffrey, and Burns, Ken, *Baseball: An Illustrated History*, Alfred A. Knopf, 1994.

Ward, Geoffrey, Burns, Ric, and Burns, Ken, *The Civil War*, Random House, 1990.

To Help Batsmen
(Sporting Life, 1908)

Pittsburg, September 22.—Claiming that the foul strike rule, as interpreted today, is interfering with good batters of both leagues, George L. Moreland, the well-know base ball statistician of Pittsburg, will appear before the Committee of Rules of the major leagues the coming winter and submit an amendment to the rule, which if adopted he thinks will go far toward improving hitting. His idea is to have a line drawn parallel with the foul lines just six feet outside, and a drive which lands between these two lines shall not be scored as a strike against the batsman. Mr. Moreland said , in explaining the diagram tonight: "The foul strike rule was made for the purpose of preventing scientific batsmen from making the game look foolish by fouling off all the good balls. It was never meant to handicap the real hard batter, who does his best to hammer the ball out hard, and who often hits what would have been good for three bases had it been a few inches further in, but the best he gets out of this honest effort is a strike called on him. My idea now is to begin at third base and draw a line parallel with the foul line only six feet outside clear to the fence. Do the same on the first-base side of the field, and call every ball which lands inside those two lines neither foul nor strike, but a dead ball. This will give such batters as Lajoie, Donlin, Cobb, Leach, Crawford, Wagner, Lumley, and Lobert a better chance. My idea is that the foul-strike rule was made for those who intentionally fouled off balls. There can be no intent to foul if a ball is driven beyond either first or third base before hitting the ground. So my idea would not interfere with the real intent of the foul-strike rule and would encourage batting."

—Joe Murphy

The Sunset Years of Joe McGinnity

Joe Murphy

For most Hall of Famers, their playing career concludes with a final season in the majors. Many of them go on to managerial, coaching, or scouting affiliations thereafter. Only a relative few have descended to the minor league level after leaving the Big Show, and then rarely for more than a year or two. This is the story of Joe McGinnity, whose ten-year Hall of Fame pitching career in the majors was merely a prelude to a lengthier fourteen-year minor league span that took him from coast-to-coast. During those years he won 207 games. He finally retired from active duty at the age of fifty-four.

Joe McGinnity was twenty-eight years old when he first appeared in a major league uniform. He joined the Baltimore Orioles in 1899, after three undistinguished minor league seasons, during which he had won 28 games and lost 32. In the next ten years, with Baltimore, Brooklyn, and the New York Giants, he won 246 games. In a four-year span between 1903 and 1906, he averaged 28 wins a season. In 1903, he pitched three doubleheaders in August, hurling six complete games and winning all of them. He more than earned his nickname "Iron Man."

However, at the end of the 1908 season McGinnity was thirty-eight years old. He won only eleven games that year, with seven losses. Hooks Wiltse had emerged as a 23-game winner for the Giants, complementing Christy Mathewson's 37 victories. Perhaps Joe's most memorable accomplishment that year occurred at the conclusion of the "Merkle Game" on September 23, when he reputedly seized the ball hit by

Al Bridwell, and, attempting to thwart Johnny Evers, hurled the ball out of the ball park. Evers resourcefully obtained a different ball from an unknown source (perhaps the Cubs dugout?) and umpire Hank O'Day ruled that Merkle should have touched second base.

During the 1908 season, Giant owner John T. Brush had been anxious to unload the Iron Man and his $4,000 salary, but John McGraw resisted, perhaps out of loyalty. It appeared, however, that Joe's major league days were numbered, and he looked about for new opportunities. He learned that the Newark club, then in the Eastern League, was up for sale, and he and an old friend, H. Clay Smith, described in *Sporting Life* as "a capitalist of Chicago," purchased the franchise for a reported $30,000. This venture into ownership was McGinnity's first, but it established a pattern that he was to follow in each of his succeeding moves.

In the next four years as Newark's playing manager, McGinnity won 87 games, setting all-time league records for innings pitched (422 in 1909), and shutouts (11 in 1909). On August 27, 1909, he pitched and won both games of a doubleheader against Buffalo, and repeated this achievement on July 23, 1912, against Rochester. Joe pitched in the 1912 season despite a wrist that he had injured while "cranking an auto."

As the 1912 season concluded, Smith wanted out, and his shares were purchased by Charles H. Ebbets, the owner of the Brooklyn club in the National League. McGinnity, who held a 20 percent ownership interest, asked $9,000 for his holdings. The sale was completed about a week later, and the Iron Man had to survey the baseball scene.

In November, he attended the annual meeting of the

Joe Murphy *is the owner and manager of the Grapestompers, perennial contenders in the Fantastic Baseball League.*

Joe McGinnity

National Association in Milwaukee, and actively pursued several possibilities. He wound up purchasing the Tacoma club in the Class B Northwestern League for $3,500. The *Sporting News* correspondent reported that "McGinnity was in great demand at the Milwaukee meeting. The former National League star received flattering offers from Terre Haute and Topeka, but neither appealed to the 'Iron Man' like the Tacoma proposition."

He was Tacoma's playing manager, and asserted himself at spring training by barring cigarettes, explaining that "their use is bad for the eyes." In the next three years, he won 22, 20, and 21 games, appearing in a total of 162 games and 1,117 innings. In mid-1914 he turned over the managerial role to Russ Hall. Friction was reported between the two in the following year, and in September, in what was described as "an unpopular local move," Hall resigned.

The Tacoma venture had apparently not been entirely positive. In July, 1915, *Sporting Life* reported an act of self-sacrifice of a kind that has not survived to the present day: "The Tacoma club was saved from financial embarrassment by the voluntary and cheerful submission of the players, unanimously, to a ten percent reduction of salaries." Nonetheless, McGinnity claimed that he had lost $27,000 in his three years of ownership. In 1916, he purchased an interest in the Butte club in the same league, and racked up another 20-victory season, almost a third of his team's 68 wins. Perhaps of equal importance, the franchise showed a profit of $3,677.39. In 1917, at the age of forty-six, he pitched and won both games against Vancouver in a May 12 doubleheader.

The Northwestern League was experiencing shaky times, and in June McGinnity sold his interest in Butte and finished the short season (the League folded on July 17) with Great Falls. In wartime 1918, only one minor league, the International League, played a full schedule. The Pacific Coast International League chose that inauspicious moment to play its inaugural season, and it suspended operations on July 7. McGinnity appeared in nine games with Vancouver, winning two and losing six. He then took a four-year vacation from organized baseball, pitching in semipro games in Illinois. He lived in Danville, and in 1922 appeared in 16 games with the local Three-I League team, winning one and losing six. In midseason, he learned of an opportunity to acquire an interest in Dubuque of the Class D Mississippi Valley League, and finished the season with them. In 1923, as a fifty-two-year-old player-manager, he appeared in 42 games, pitching 206 innings, winning 15 and losing 12. Even the New York *Times*, which did not lightly record sports happenings in Dubuque, saw fit to recognize his accomplishments: "Dubuque, Iowa. June 3. Manager Joe McGinnity, 52 years old, former New York Giant pitcher, shut out Waterloo this afternoon, 2 to 0. It was his fourth victory in eleven days. McGinnity held Waterloo to five hits, one a misjudged fly, and issued no passes."

Then, on September 5 in far-off New York, where the Yankees and the Giants were gearing up for a renewal of their 1922 World Series rivalry, the *Times* noted: "Dubuque, Iowa. Sept. 4. The Dubuque team, managed by Joe 'Iron Man' McGinnity of New York Giants fame, has won the championship of the Mississippi Valley League for 1923."

He sat out the 1924 season, but returned to the mound in 1925, thirty-three years after he first appeared in a boxscore, with Montgomery of the Southern League. His preseason expectations were recorded by the New York *Times*: "Iron Man Joe McGinnity, 54 years old, expects to pitch at least thirty-five games this season for the Dubuque club of the Mississippi Valley League, of which he is manager and part owner. He is starting his thirty-third professional year.

"'Occasionally I feel a little wobbly in the legs but I believe my arm is almost as good as ever,' McGinnity said today.

"McGinnity pitches apparently with a minimum of exertion and curves the ball almost everywhere he throws, refuting the popular belief that speed-ball pitchers outlast those who rely on 'twisters.' He says he throws curves without imposing the slightest strain on his wrist."

On May 8, he pitched four innings in relief against Burlington, allowing no hits. He got a hit himself, and recorded two assists. On May 11, he pitched his first full game, winning over eighteen-year-old John Welch, the youngest twirler in the league. He was touched for 13 hits, but allowed Ottumwa only three runs, while his teammates were scoring seven.

Two weeks later, on May 24, McGinnity was pitching, and the score was tied, 3-3, in the tenth inning. Umpire Harmon made what was termed "an unacceptable ruling," and when McGinnity protested vehemently, he was thrown out of the game. He refused to leave, and the game was forfeited to Waterloo. McGinnity was fined $25, but when League President Brenden Hill reviewed the full reports of what had occurred, he sided with McGinnity, and released Harmon from further service.

In mid-July, the Dubuque club was in the cellar (although Joe had won five of the seven games in which he had appeared), and there was friction between McGinnity and partner Johnny Armstrong. McGinnity resigned and sold his ownership interest to Armstrong.

On August 6, *The Sporting News* ran the following item, which was brought to my attention by SABR's Dick Thompson :

> Iron Man Joe McGinnity went back to the scene of his baseball activities of 30 years ago when he essayed a pitching role in Springfield, July 28…He pitched for the old-timers in a two-inning game…He was then given a one-day contract by the Springfield management, and the 54-year-old hurler performed on the mound against Bloomington. He allowed seven hits in four and 2/3 innings and retired.

This was his last official playing appearance in Organized Baseball. He returned briefly to his home in Danville, Illinois, but old teammate Wilbert Robinson called him back to Brooklyn, where he served as a coach for several years. In spring, 1929, he assisted Art Fox, baseball coach at Williams College, but became ill, and returned to his daughter's Brooklyn home, where he died on November 14. He was fifty-eight years old. He was buried beside his wife in McAlester, Oklahoma. In mourning his passing, *The Sporting News* editorialized: "He established a personal fame that will live as long as baseball lives, and he was one of the most unassuming, amiable, and gentle mannered men who ever stood on a pitcher's plate and sailed the ball to that point where the batter most dreaded to swing at it, yet knew he must because it was good."

Batboy

Bob Brelsford

In 1957 the Boston Red Sox sponsored a Class D Midwest League team in Lafayette, Indiana. As part of a contest, I wrote an essay on why I wanted to be batboy and was selected as one of the six finalists. These names were printed on a ballot that ran for three consecutive nights in the local newspaper. Candidates were encouraged to collect ballots from friends and neighbors, mark them, and send them in for counting. With great organizational efforts by my parents, I won and was named home team batboy. My pay for the summer consisted of a U.S. savings bond, a batboy uniform, and a ball autographed by the team players. Two of those players made the majors, and a future Hall of Famer visited Lafayette on a scouting mission that summer, providing me with my most cherished memories of the season.

The team consisted of about twenty players, all about nineteen to twenty-one years old. As a thirteen-year-old, these were "old guys" to me. The manager was Ken Deal, who occasionally pitched. The best-known player now would be Tracy Stallard, who served up Roger Maris's 61st homer in 1961. Catcher Russ Gibson also played in the majors, with the Red Sox and the Giants.

The most memorable occasion for me that summer took place off the field. After a game one evening, my father told me that a friend of his had introduced him to Bobby Doerr, the great second baseman, who was in Lafayette for a few days surveying prospects. Doerr had a ranch or farm in the West and needed some ag-ricultural advice. My father, who taught engineering at Purdue for forty-six years, suggested that Purdue had a strong agricultural school and that he would be glad to take Doerr the next morning to someone who might be able to answer questions. I was invited to go along. In the car we talked about second-base defense, since I was a Little League and summer league second baseman.

When we got to Purdue, Doerr asked the agricultural representative his questions. At one point this man said he would have to make a phone call about a certain issue. The Purdue man said, "I have a man here named Doerr. I guess he played major league baseball, but he doesn't impress me very much." I couldn't believe what I heard. Doerr didn't react. My father, however, lost his temper. He said, "You've just confirmed what those of us in other areas of Purdue have heard. You guys act like a bunch of jerks in front of the public. Mr. Doerr deserves an apology." None was given and we all left. My father and I were embarrassed. Doerr, who was a gentleman through the whole mess, told us he wouldn't judge all of Purdue by this one incident.

After forty-two years, when I read about some Purdue agricultural discovery, I still think of Bobby Doerr. It's probably not fair, but I can't help it. I will never forget my embarrassment that day, nor will I forget what a pleasant person Doerr was and what a thrill I had riding in the same car with a great ball player.

Bob Brelsford *is a retired social services worker and a lifetime Yankees fan.*

Edgar Munzel, BBWAA

James D. Smith III

A Baseball Hall of Fame visit brings lifetime encounters with diamond legends: the Bambino and Rajah, Lefty and Old Aches and Pains, Mr. Cub and Ryan's Express. Secure in this company, also, is their master interpreter: the Mouse.

In the spring of 1929, a knot of Chicago baseball writers traveling east was talking shop. Suddenly, the banter halted: where was the twenty-two-year-old rookie in their company? One veteran, Irving Vaughan, gestured to the slight figure listening in the corner: "You mean the Mouse?" The nickname stuck—and so did Edgar Munzel. Forty-five summers later, when he "hung up" his orange Olivetti typewriter and left the pressbox, this genial man's legacy was coverage of over 8,000 big league games, 34 World Series, and 36 All-Star classics.

In 1977, Munzel was voted the prestigious J. G. Taylor Spink Award (named for long-time publisher of the *Sporting News*) by his peers in the Baseball Writers Association of America (BBWAA). Since then, his plaque has accompanied Grantland Rice's, Ring Lardner's, and others in the "writers' wing" of the Hall of Fame.

How did it all start? "I began as a copy boy for the old Chicago *Herald-Examiner*," he once recalled, "and after two years at Northwestern, my uncle helped me land a job on the sports desk. I didn't start covering baseball until the spring of '29. The regular guy covering the White Sox got into a bit of trouble in spring training—he was boozing it up too much—and they needed a quick replacement. The Sox were considered such a bad team…few people considered it a prestigious assignment. It was intended to be just temporary." Sort of like Wally Pipp being replaced by Lou Gehrig ("very gentlemanly" says the Mouse) a few years earlier.

Edgar Munzel's remarkable life began on Jan. 14, 1907 in Reynolds, Indiana—a small farming town 25 miles south of Lafayette. He was the third of seven children. His father, Edward Herman Munzel, was a dedicated Lutheran parochial school teacher and his mother, Sophia, a busy homemaker. When Eddie was eleven, the family moved to LaPorte. In 1922, uncle Harry Munzel, executive secretary to the *Herald-Examiner*'s managing editor, arranged for his young nephew to summer with him and work as a copy boy. When all went well, Harry offered a four-to-midnight shift and an opportunity to finish high school (1925) while living in his home. Eddie liked the idea, and his parents approved.

While at Northwestern University, he worked part-time for the paper, covering mostly college sports on

Jim Smith *has been a SABR member since 1982. He has contributed to* BRJ, TNP, Baseball's First Stars, *and other SABR works. Most recently, he has contributed to the* Biographical Dictionary of American Sports, *and Bill Swank's* Echoes from Lane Field, *a history of the San Diego Padres of the Pacific Coast League. He would like to acknowledge Tom and Karen Munzel for their help in supplying photos for this article.*

campus. When tuition funds ran low, however, he entered journalism full-time in the summer of 1927. Assignments included golf and tennis tournaments, three-cushion billiards, and skiing. He enjoyed some events more than others, but loved writing, the news business, and his adopted city. Then came the spring of 1929, sports editor Warren Brown's predicament, and those memorable words: "Let's send the kid out." Over the following decade, Edgar Munzel's reputation as a first-rate baseball writer became established.

When the *Herald-Examiner* folded in 1939, the White Sox hired Eddie as their first publicity man (1940-41). When World War II broke out, he received a draft notice, but was classified 4F because of a bout of tuberculosis he had suffered in the early 1930s. Meanwhile, Marshall Field was starting a new paper in Chicago, the *Sun*, which later became the *Sun-Times*.

His old boss, Brown, was named sports editor, and he lured the Mouse back to the pressbox as a baseball beat writer. Covering both the Cubs and White Sox, and contributing to national publications like the *The Sporting News*, he was read from coast-to-coast. As a kid who loved anything baseball in the early 1960s, this writer relished the concise, knowledgeable, and often wise words offered "by Edgar Munzel." Occasional telephone conversations, begun thirty years later, have only deepened the appreciation.

Following retirement and Hall of Fame honors, in 1980 Eddie and Rose (married in 1941) moved to Virginia, close to their loved ones. Today his words are fewer, and in these late innings it's our privilege to glimpse through family pictures some moments in which Edgar Munzel helped generations discover baseball as America's National Pastime.

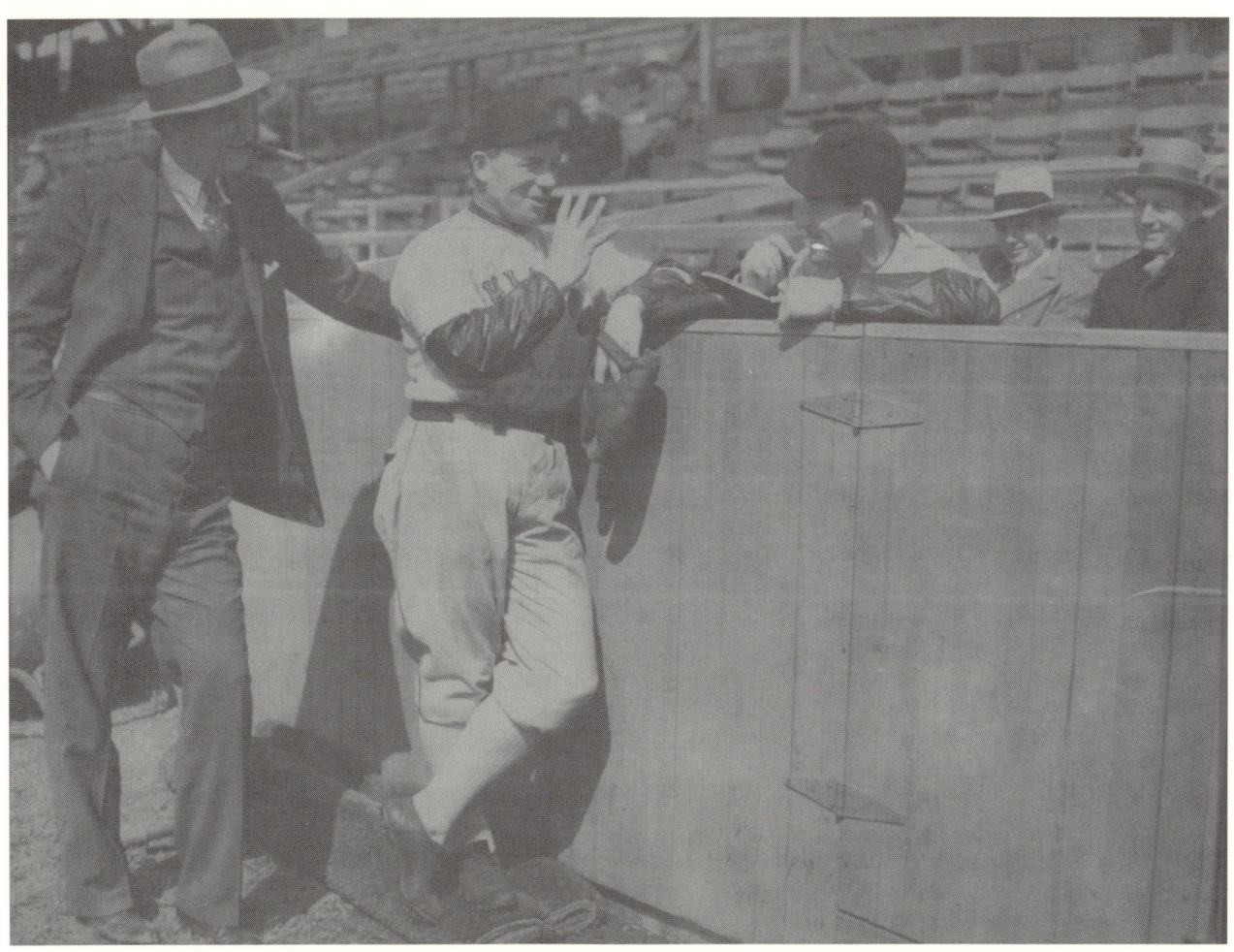

OAKLAND: Oakland Oaks ballpark (early '30s). L to R: Ed Prell, White Sox Jimmie Dykes with Al Simmons (posing as a sportswriter), Munzel, and Skeeter Webb. Not pictured is John Carmichael of Chicago's Daily News, *with whom Eddie sealed an agreement never to write their memoirs. "It was a silly thing," he recalls. "We just said, 'Who'd buy them?'"*

Cubs spring training, Catalina Island, late 1930s. On the bench: Scout Dutch Reuther, batting coach Rogers Hornsby, manager Charlie Grimm. Pressbox: Jim Gallagher, Irving Vaughan, Dave Rush, Roy Brennan, Jim Enright, Bob Lewis, Munzel, and Howard Roberts. "After a great 1929 season, there was conflict on the team. Despite all Joe McCarthy's success, basically Hornsby just moved in and he moved out. Hornsby made a lot of trouble for him, it got to Phil Wrigley and the pressure was on because, as you know, Hornsby was one helluva ball player. A quirky guy, but the greatest right-handed batter ever. So when Joe got the offer from the Yankees, he saw a great opportunity. But that's another story!"

Munzel with White Sox legend Luke Appling in 1943. "What a great, dedicated, all-around player! He was one of a very few who could throw hard from the first day of spring training. And at the plate…he'd just foul off ten or twelve pitches until he got one he liked."

With old-timers Joe McCarthy, Ty Cobb, "Home Run" Baker, and Joe Cronin around 1960. On McCarthy: "Joe was a standout guy—he had great ability to handle players. Those '29 Cubs, who went to the World Series, had Hack Wilson and Pat Malone: playboys at night. He'd personally sit down and appeal to them: 'What is it, don't you guys like me?' They'd be close to tears, and shape up for about two weeks—then start to slide. Hack was a great player." After joining the Hall of Fame Veterans Committee in 1977, Munzel went to bat for him. "I pressed his case for the Hall of Fame, even though some (like Warren Giles) were opposed because of his conduct."

Throwing out the first pitch at the Cubs' 1969 home opener, honoring Munzel's fortieth anniversary covering baseball. "One thing in my favor was my length of service. Plus the fact that I covered both leagues, being in Chicago where they had two teams. It was quite an honorable thing—but I can't say I ever expected to be in the Hall of Fame."

Toward career's end, with Billy Williams and Ernie Banks. "A good hitter in the old days would be a good hitter now, and vice versa. [But] today's batter is always going for the fences, and that has proven costly for the player destined to be no more than a singles hitter." What are the best righty-lefty pitching tandems he ever saw? In the NL, Munzel cites Grover Alexander and Warren Spahn, selecting Bob Feller and Lefty Grove in the AL. "But the most exciting player of all was Babe Ruth. He was a delight to fans and writers both."

Another Look

David Shiner

In the 1999 *Baseball Research Journal*, Joseph M. Wayman contended that the American League should be accorded major league status for the 1900 season. He argued that since the vast majority of the American League players of 1900 spent time in the majors before and/or after that season, the league was of major league quality. It is an interesting analysis, but I believe he missed the crucial issue: whether these players were of major league quality *in 1900*. Would they have been major leaguers even without the new league? Or were they "real" major leaguers in, say, 1894 or 1905, but only playing in the AL in 1900 because players of major league quality were not available?

I'll demonstrate my point with two examples. Ed Abbaticchio, an American League infielder in 1900, later went on to have a solid career in the National League. When the 1900 season began, though, he was what we would nowadays classify as a rookie, having been overmatched in a brief trial with Philadelphia a few years earlier. His next appearance in the majors did not come until 1903, when he batted .227 for the Boston Braves. By 1904 he was a serviceable regular, by 1905 a good one. He was a player of major league quality for a number of years, but 1900 wasn't one of them.

Perry Werden was at the other end of the age/experience spectrum. Werden, a big man with good power by 1890s standards, was a regular major league first baseman for about five seasons. But when he joined

the fledgling American League in 1900 he had played in the majors in only one of the previous six years. He was basically finished by then, and never appeared in the majors again.

Of the players who graced AL rosters in 1900, a considerable number were never of major league quality. Most of the rest were either of the Abbaticchio type or the Werden type—that is, players who weren't of major league quality *at that time*, because they were either not yet ready or over the hill. To study this phenomenon in more detail, let's take a closer look at the players who had the most substantial careers. We'll form an "All-Star" team composed of those 1900 AL players who had the longest major league careers at their respective positions, and take a brief look at each.

Ossee Schreckengost (C) was a rookie regular in 1899. He finished that season with the Cleveland Spiders, an abominable club that won a grand total of 20 games that year. When the Spiders folded, Schreckengost found work in the new league. He remained a first-stringer until 1908, spending most of that period with Connie Mack's Philadelphia A's.

Candy LaChance (1B) came up with Brooklyn in late 1893 and was more or less the team's regular first baseman for five years. In 1899 he went to Baltimore and had a good season both at the plate and in the field. When the team folded, he headed for Cleveland in the AL, for which he played well in 1900 and 1901. He then went to the Boston Red Sox, batting .279 in 1902, .257 in 1903, and .227 in 1904. When he hit .146 in 12 games in 1905, his major league career was over.

David Shiner *is a member of the faculty and administration at Shimer College in Waukegan, Illinois. His book,* Baseball's Greatest Players: The Saga Continues, *the sequel to Tom Meany's* Baseball's Greatest Players *(1953), was recently published by Superior (www.superiorbooks.com).*

Lou Bierbauer (2B) was a regular major league second baseman for about ten years, the last of which was 1895. He appeared in 59 major league games in '96, 12 in '97, four in '98, and none in '99. He was in his mid-thirties in 1900 when the new league gave him another chance. It was to be his last.

Wid Conroy (3B), who did not play in the big leagues in the nineteenth century, had reasonable success with the AL Milwaukee Brewers in 1900 and 1901. The National League champion Pittsburgh Pirates then signed him to play shortstop in 1902. It didn't work out, so after that season Manager Fred Clarke moved Honus Wagner to short and Conroy to the AL New York Highlanders. Conroy played third base and the outfield for New York and Washington over the next nine years, always keeping a regular job although his career batting average was a modest .248.

Germany Smith (SS) was a fine defensive shortstop with Brooklyn and Cincinnati in a major league career that began in 1884. By 1897 his batting average had declined almost to the Mendoza line, at .201. When he hit .159 a year later, at age thirty-five, his major league career was presumably over. Two years later Minneapolis of the AL gave him another shot, his last.

Steve Brodie (LF) was a multitalented outfielder who played for several NL teams in the 1890s. He had a good year for manager John McGraw in Baltimore in 1899, batting .309 although his speed was declining. When the Baltimore club disbanded Brodie, like Candy LaChance and several other ex-Orioles, opted for the AL. He played two more seasons in the majors after 1900, finishing his major league career at age thirty-four.

Dummy Hoy (CF) had a long and impressive major league career as an outfielder in the 1880s and 1890s. In 1899 he batted .306 for the Louisville Colonels in the NL. But the best players of the disbanding Louisville team were to be combined with the Pittsburgh club to form the Pirates in 1900. Ginger Beaumont, who batted .352 as a rookie in '99, was Fred Clarke's choice in center. Hoy, nearly thirty-eight years old at the time, jumped to the new league. His career was over a couple of years later.

John Anderson (RF) had several good seasons with Brooklyn after joining the team in late 1894. In 1899 he had an off year which more or less cost him his regular job. Brooklyn skipper Ned Hanlon had Willie Keeler in right, Joe Kelley in left, and Hughie Jennings at first, the three positions Anderson could handle capably. With all three future Hall of Famers returning to Brooklyn for the '00 season, Anderson headed for the AL club in Milwaukee. He played well for five AL teams over the remaining nine seasons of his career.

These eight All-Stars give us a very clear indication of the upper echelon of the players who performed in the American League in 1900. Some of them were long-time major leaguers who were finished, or nearly finished. Most of the rest were relatively untried youngsters who blossomed sometime after that year. Only one of those listed, John Anderson, was in his late twenties, then as now baseball's prime age for a position player.

Remember, this isn't a group of randomly selected position players. It's the cream of the crop. If we look at the other position players from the 1900 AL season, we find that most of them were far less qualified to be considered major leaguers at that time.

Among pitchers this trend is even stronger, as is clear from a perusal of the ones who tossed over 1,500 innings in their major league careers outside of 1900. These six hurlers will round out our All-Star team.

Rube Waddell is clearly the greatest of the players who appeared on an AL roster in 1900. Waddell was twenty-three; his entire major league career up to that point consisted of twelve games. He lasted just over a month with Connie Mack in Milwaukee, posting a 10-3 record (10-2 according to some sources) before returning to his previous employer, the Pittsburgh Pirates. Waddell went 8-13 in the NL in 1900, 13-17 the following year. Once he returned to the AL in 1902, he won over 20 games four years running on his way to the Hall of Fame.

Red Ehret was a competent although sub-.500 pitcher in an eleven-year career in the late nineteenth century. That career appeared to be over when he went 3-7 with a 5.76 ERA for Louisville in 1898. He was out of the majors in 1899. His poor performance in the AL in 1900 proved that his major league days were behind him.

Tully Sparks, like Rube Waddell, had pitched a handful of games in two different major league seasons before starting the 1900 campaign with Milwaukee. He was a consistent loser until 1905, when he went 14-11 for the Phillies. After that, he enjoyed three more winning seasons before going into his final decline.

Casey Patten was a twenty-four-year-old rookie lefthander without big league experience when he joined the Kansas City club in 1900. When the franchise relocated to Washington the following year, he went along with it and stayed until early 1908. He was a regular starter for all those seasons, although he usually lost more games than he won.

Frank Foreman bounced in and out of the major leagues from 1884 through 1896. He had been out of the majors for three years when he joined the Buffalo team in the AL in 1900 at age thirty-seven. He had good results in the new league in 1900 and 1901, but was gone after a poor start in 1902.

Bill Hart pitched in the majors for parts of seven seasons in the late nineteenth century, losing more games than he won every year. He went 12-29 in 1896, 9-27 in 1897, and 5-9 in 1898 before spending the enitre '00 season in the minors. The AL Cleveland entry gave him a final chance in 1900, and over the next two seasons he proved that he was still capable of losing games. By late 1901 he was out of the majors for good.

Again, the picture given by these six hurlers is much like that of the position players. Three were "old men" who almost certainly would have been out of the majors in 1900 had it not been for the American League. The other three were essentially untried youngsters who eventually made good. Again, these were the most prolific of the pitchers who spent all or part of that year in the American League. In fact, of all the pitchers who spent the entire 1900 season in the AL, Tully Sparks is the only one who more than likely would have spent the whole year in the majors without the new league.

In looking over these fourteen players, we can see how far they were from their peak by pinpointing their best seasons. We'll do this in a quick-and-dirty way, noting the major league season in which each man posted his best earned run average (pitchers) or his highest composite on-base average plus slugging percentage (position players). The results are as follows:

Peak Year	Player
1886	Hart
1887	Smith
1888	Foreman
1890	Bierbauer, Ehret
1894	Brodie, Hoy, LaChance
1901	Anderson
1902	Schreckengost
1905	Conroy, Waddell
1906	Patten
1907	Sparks

Even without analyzing the data, it's clear that few of these players were anywhere near their peak in 1900.

The difference between Rube Waddell's success in the AL and lack of it in the NL says a lot about the relative strength of the leagues at that time. There are many other indicators, which are especially striking among the pitchers. Doc Amole was 4-10 with an ERA close to five in the National League in 1897-8. He was out of the majors in 1899. In the AL in 1900 he pitched a no-hitter on Opening Day and went on to become a 20-game winner. He never won another big league game. Roger Denzer was a similar story: 2-8 with a 5.13 ERA in 1897, out of the majors in '98 and '99, great in the AL in 1900, subpar in the NL in 1901, and gone after that. Denzer's American League teammate, Chauncey Fisher, spent a few seasons as a sub-.500 pitcher in the NL before dropping out of the majors after the 1897 season. He posted 18 victories in the AL in 1900, but was bombed out of the NL in 1901.

Typical of the pitchers who did last a while in the new league was Watty Lee. Lee had an impressive rookie campaign in 1900, going 23-21. In 1901 he slipped to a still-respectable 16-16. In 1902 he was 5-7, in 1903 8-12. He jumped to the National League to pitch for the Pirates in 1904, posted an 8.74 ERA in five appearances, and was out of the big leagues for good before reaching the age of twenty-five. Like many members of the AL class of 1900, his performance declined as the league improved.

Before the 1901 season American League President Ban Johnson declared his circuit a major league, and a number of high-profile major leaguers promptly defected to it. The difference in the quality of play was immediately obvious.

Superstars like Cy Young, Napoleon Lajoie, Jimmy Collins, Joe McGinnity, and Clark Griffith, future Hall of Famers all, dominated the AL in 1901, with many other defectors from the National League chipping in. Of the top ten batters in the league, led by Lajoie and his glittering .422 mark, only two (John Anderson and Socks Seybold) had played in the AL in 1900. Five pitchers won over 20 games in the American League in '01, paced by Young's 33 victories. Only one of them, Roscoe Miller, had pitched in the AL the year before. (Miller lost 20 games the following season and was out of the big leagues within a couple of years.) The AL still wasn't on a par with the NL, but at least it was on its way to justifying its major league status. The reasons for this, though, had little to do with the players who had stocked AL rosters in 1900.

Wayman's auxiliary argument is that the American League in 1900 was as strong or stronger than several other twentieth century teams and leagues that are officially considered "major league." However, if we were to apply this criterion to the teams in the American League in 1900, we would also have to reassess the status of every minor league team that was arguably as good as the worst major league team of the twentieth century. There have been many top-drawer minor league teams that were superior to, for instance, the 1915 Philadelphia A's. Jack Dunn's Baltimore Orioles of the late teens and twenties are a prime example.

As far as leagues are concerned, Wayman contends that the 1900 American League was stronger than the majors during the World War II years. His evidence is that only about 40 percent of the players during the war years were legitimate major leaguers.

But that statistic is deceptive. Very few of the players in the American League in 1900 were "legitimate major leaguers" *at that time*, certainly far less than 40 percent. By contrast, more than fifty men who were of major league quality both before and after the war played regularly throughout at least two of the three World War II seasons. If we were to pick an All-Star team from among those players, again consisting of those who had the longest careers in the majors at their respective positions, it would far outshine the 1900 American League group.

That team would feature Phil Cavaretta at first base, Bobby Doerr at second, Bob Elliott at third, and Lou Boudreau at short. The outfielders would be Stan Musial, Dixie Walker, and Swish Nicholson, with Walker Cooper behind the plate. Five of those eight men were in their late twenties during the war years; two others were close. The six pitchers who pitched the most innings during their major league careers are equally impressive: Early Wynn, Bobo Newsom, Dutch Leonard, Bucky Walters, Hal Newhouser, and Dizzy Trout. That fourteen-man All-Star team includes five Hall of Famers and a multitude of MVPs and other stars.

Failing to make the cut are such luminaries as Mort Cooper, Tommy Holmes, Ken Keltner, Max Lanier, Marty Marion, Frank McCormick, Eddie Miller, Rip Sewell, Vern Stephens, and Rudy York. Every one of those players, like each of the All-Stars, was a full-fledged regular both before and after the war. And that's not even considering a number of others who were stars before the war, regulars throughout it, and semi-regulars afterward, including Doc Cramer, Stan Hack, Ernie Lombardi, Wally Moses, and Claude Passeau.

Of course, we're comparing two leagues in the 1940s with one in 1900. On the other hand, I have considered only those who were regulars both the year before and the year after the period in question. If we were to apply this criterion to the 1900 AL, it would knock out two thirds of the players named, and their replacements would be much weaker. In fact, it's difficult to even *find* six pitchers from the 1900 AL who were major league regulars in both 1899 and 1901. Furthermore, the World War II All-Stars were much closer to their prime years than the stars of the 1900 American League. All things considered, it's clear that the majors during the war years had superior talent, and talent that was much closer to its prime.

Whenever the evidence tells us that the historical record is factually incorrect, as was the case until recently with Hack Wilson's 1930 RBI count, we are honor-bound to change it. In all other cases, those who argue for change must convince the rest of us that justice cannot be done otherwise. It is to Joe Wayman's credit that he has tried to do that for the American League's inaugural season. In light of the evidence presented here, though, I believe that case just isn't good enough.

Maligned Umpire Sues for Libel
(New York Times, September 12, 1895)

PALATKA, Fla. Sept. 11.—As H.H. McCreary, editor of the Gainesville Sun and a member of the Florida Legislature, was passing through here last evening en route to Gainesville, he was arrested on a charge of criminal libel preferred by Dr. Stein. A few days ago the Gainesville and Palatka ball teams played a match game here, and Dr. Stein umpired. Gainesville lost, and they claimed that Stein "robbed" them. The Gainesville Sun, McCreary's paper, was also severe on Stein's umpiring, and the latter resented it by having the editor arrested. McCreary was held in $1,000 to answer.

—Jack Carlson

1901 Openers: The War Is On

Dixie Tourangeau

Byron Bancroft Johnson's renegade American League made its raucous official debut just a century ago amid player franchise jumps, illegal money offers, and constant contract turmoil (see Lajoie sidebar). Johnson had renamed his old Western League in 1900, and for 1901, he dropped Indianapolis, Kansas City, Buffalo, and Minneapolis in favor of the Eastern metro money and population centers of Boston, Baltimore, Philadelphia, and Washington. That left Chicago and Milwaukee as the westernmost clubs in the revamped eight-team circuit, which he proclaimed a major league. The war was on.

What follows is the exact Chicago *Tribune* reprint of the first American League contest, with all its colloquial eccentricities of spelling and punctuation, just as Windy City fans in Michigan Avenue diners and North and South Side neighborhoods read it the next day.

SOUTH SIDE Park, Chicago, Wednesday, April 24—Under the fairest skies the weather clerk could select from his varied stock of April goods; with a championship pennant floating high above them from the proudest pine of all Michigan's forests; with 9,000 fans to cheer them from a pent-up enthusiasm that burst forth at every possible opportunity, the White Stockings opened the American league baseball season on the South Side grounds yesterday with a clean-cut victory over the aggregation from Cleveland. The score was 8 runs to 2.

It was the most auspicious beginning imaginable, without a thing to mar the occasion. The only thing the fans could have asked for, to add to their delight, was a bit more warmth in the atmosphere, and even that was supplied by the spectators when the real rooting began. It was a splendid crowd, both in its proportions and in the elements of which it was composed, and it was a magnificent welcome. It gave the players who fought for, won, and hoisted that pennant and the new men who have joined the champions to help them retain that emblem.

There were cheers for everybody, from Hoy, who couldn't hear them, to Patterson, the hero of many a hard-earned victory last year. There was so much enthusiasm on tap that the visitors came in for a generous share of it, especially Bradley and McCarthy, the two ex-Orphans, who, by the way, cut the greatest figure in the game for the losers, and Wood, who helped the champions so much last season. There were flowers for Brain, the youngest of the White Soxs, and a cane and umbrella for McCarthy from the friends he made at the West Side grounds. And at the end there was so much surplus exuberance that the bleacherites indulged in a merry cushion fight all through the concluding inning by way of celebration.

Hoffer's Costly Bases on Balls

It would have been most discourteous for Cleveland to have won in the face of all that good-natured enthusiasm. It would have been cruelty to have put the slightest damper upon it. But the visitors tried hard enough to be discourteous, and if Bill Hoffer had been able to locate the plate at all in the first two innings

Dixie Tourangeau says this piece is much more about well-timed entertainment than hardcore research. New SABR member Marilyn Miller helped out with the typing of the 1901 Chicago Tribune Opening Day article as well as many other computer adjustments to make this story entertaining.

it would have been an uncomfortably close rub at the best. It was fast, clean baseball. Nine innings were played in an hour and a half, and each team made a single error, on difficult chances in both cases. Dashing base-running gave the White Stockings so wide a margin of scores in comparison to the slight difference in the batting figures, and it was that base-running that made Hoffer's bases on balls costly to his team in the main.

The crowd began to gather long before three o'clock, and the early arrivals were amused by a concert by the First Regiment Rough Riders band. The visiting team was the first to make its appearance and went through its preliminary practice amid the good-natured guying of the bleacherites, while the champions kept modestly out of sight down by the clubhouse. Fifteen minutes later the White Stockings marched out and across the field in a long line of dazzling white, and the spectators arose as if one man to cheer. There was one preliminary burst and then a hush until the advancing line reached the edge of the diamond, then there was another cheer which might have been heard in South Chicago if the wind had been stronger.

Not since 1886 have Chicago fans had such an opportunity as that, not in fifteen years a chance to applaud and feel proud of a team of champions. In that time a new generation of fans has sprung up, and those who can recall Chicago's last previous pennant are in the veteran class of rooters. But old and young seemed bound to make the most of their opportunities on this occasion—and they did.

Greeting the Champions

There was a cheer when the White Stockings took their positions for practice, another when Manager Griffith went out to drive hot liners and grounders to the infield, still another for big Jack Katoll when he began to push long fungoes to the outfielders, and more cheers for each individual player as he handled the ball; for Jones and Hoy and Mertes when they came in under short pop flies; for Hartman, Shugart, and Brain as they scooped up fast bounders with almost mid-season accuracy and shot them over to first; for Isbell when he pulled in the wide throws, and for Billy Sullivan, who stood at the plate and snapped the ball around the different bases with an arm which he says is lame but which showed no signs of it in practice or play.

Then the rival teams congregated at the plate and with the band to lead them marched in two long lines down to the tall flagpole in deepest center field. There was the briefest of delays and then the members of last season's team, to whom belonged the honor of hoisting the pennant, grasped the rope, and, tugging lustily, slowly raised it aloft. The big crowd arose and let out a cheer as the silken banner left the ground, the band played "The Star-Spangled Banner," and everybody hoped the "long may it wave" would come true.

Pennant Is Unfurled

Not until the pennant reached the top of the staff did the breeze seem strong enough to straighten it out, but then, as the long silken folds were slowly and lazily unfurled, disclosing the words so unfamiliar to the eyes of local fans, "Chicago, Champions American League, 1900," cheer followed cheer, and while the teams marched back across the park to the strains of "There'll Be a Hot Time," the spectators settled back into their seats ready for the struggle of 1901 to commence. There was a little delay while the Captains and Umpire Connolly fixed the ground rules made necessary by the crowd on the field and the game was on. And if the "hot time" predicted didn't eventuate it wasn't the band's fault. It was all Hoffer's.

When it was discovered that Roy Patterson, no longer a "boy" in fast company, but still a "wonder," was to pitch the game for the champions, and the crowd once more expressed its delight. Pickering was the first to face him and the first ball of the season was a "ball," but it was closely followed by a "strike," an American league strike, and not the National league brand once known as a foul. Then Pickering raised a high fly which gave Hoy the first putout of the season in pretty nearly the same spot that he made the last putout of last season. McCarthy was next, and, after he had blushed his acknowledgments of the present made him, the West-Sider cracked a sharp hit to Hartman. It bounded off the Dutchman's hands and caromed over to Shugart, who grabbed it and shot it to first just a thousandth of a second too late to catch his man and McCarthy had made the first base hit of the season. Genins flied out to the silent man and La Chance sent an easy one to Brain, forcing McCarthy at second.

Hoy led off for Chicago with a grounder to La Chance and was out. Jones waited with becoming patience and earned his base without even swinging his bat. Mertes shot one at his old teammate, Bradley, who fumbled just an instant and missed a possible double play, then retired Sandow at first. Here Hoffer lost his bearings badly and permitted Shugart and Isbell to walk, filling the bases. Hartman was next, and, after making a half dozen National league "strikes," most of which hit the grand stand, the Dutchman caught a straight squarely and lined it sharply over Hallman's head, scoring the first two runs of the season. Brain flied out to McCarthy, and the score was "two-love, Chicago wins."

Bradley hit to his third-base rival and was out in the second inning, but Beck hit safely. Little Sullivan went back close to the visitors' bench and made a brilliant catch of Hallman's foul and Wood hit to Shugart, forcing Beck for the third out.

Sully's catch of the foul made his welcome at bat one of the warmest of all and he responded with a liner straight over second bag. Patterson struck out trying to sacrifice and Hoy sliced a ball to Bradley, trying to "hit and run" with Sullivan, and was thrown out, but it advanced the runner. Jones once more gave a correct imitation of Job, and was rewarded with another walk. Mertes profited by the example and, after watching four wide balls go by, the bases were filled. Shugart made it three walks in succession, and thereby forced in a run.

Isbell started out to repeat, but changed his mind when he saw one of his favorites coming over the base, and smashed it fast to center field, starting one of the weirdest mixups ever seen at South Side Park, from which the White Stockings emerged with their traditional good luck of last year, without a scar.

Chicago's Good Base Running

Two runs scored on the hit, of course, and when Genins threw the ball to Hoffer, Shugart, thinking it was going to the plate, kept on running for third. Hoffer nailed the throw and relayed it over to Bradley, heading off Shugart, who turned back. Isbell had broken for second on the play and the Clevelanders had two runners trapped, with only one base between them. But those two runners kept pretty nearly the whole Cleveland team busy for a minute, and both of them slipped through the visitors' fingers at that. Shugart dodged, doubled and twisted until he slid into second safely, but that left Isbell at their mercy, and the ball went to La Chance, who ran "Liz" down close to second. Shugart had meanwhile set sail for third again, and La Chance turned his attention that way, chasing Shugart down the line. Just before they reached third, La Chance tossed the ball toward where he supposed Bradley was, but Bradley wasn't there. Shugart had squirmed past him on the line, and the only man at third was Manager Griffith, the coacher. So everybody

was safe, and it cost two runs.

Once more in that inning the White Stockings got away with their traditionally reckless base running. Hartman hit a sharp one at Hallman, who fumbled, then picked the ball up and threw wide of first. La Chance stretched his lanky frame to its utmost and nearly saved the error, but the ball bounded out of his mitt and a few feet away, letting in two runs, for Isbell scored from second on the play and had such a start that La Chance made no attempt to catch him at the plate. Brain was the third out by the way of Bradley.

Visitors' First Score

The third inning was notable only for a brilliant stop by Shugart off Hoffer's hit and for a fast double play by the visitors, retiring both Sullivan and Patterson on a sharp grounder to Hoffer. The visitors accumulated their first tally in the fourth inning, and it was by virtue of a momentary fumble by Brain. La Chance led off with a clean drive to center. Bradley popped a cinch to Shugart, and then Roy Patterson went to the wrong side of the street for a couple of blocks. He gave both Beck and Hallman bases on balls, filling the circuit as full as it would hold without running over. By this time the crowd was willing to see Cleveland do something to make it interesting, and rooted for Wood to hit it out. The ex-champion hit it sharply to Brain, who had an easy double play in front of him, but was in such a hurry to start it that he had to make two grabs for the ball, and that instant was just enough to let Wood beat the relay to first by a step. La Chance scored from third, and then Mertes smothered Hoffer's fly.

In the sixth the White Stockings gave an exhibition of the opposite of team work at bat just by way of contrast to their previous work, evidently. With two out Hoy pushed

out a safe hit. Jones pulled the first ball pitched into right field between La Chance and Beck, but Hoy was not expecting it and failed to get the start that would carry him to third. Then, as if to make amends, the silent man started to steal third on the first ball pitched to Mertes, and neither Jones nor Mertes was expecting it. But Wood made a bad throw, which Bradley stopped only by a miracle, and Hoy landed in safety, slid away over the bag and was touched out.

White Stockings' Only Error

In the next inning the White Stockings made their only error. It was Isbell's muff of a poor throw by Hartman, and it started the inning with a life for Hallman. Wood singled him to second with a jab to left. A faultless double play by Brain, Shugart and Isbell killed Wood and Hoffer on the latter's sharp hit and it looked like another blank, but Pickering bumped one between third and short which Shugart blocked but couldn't stop, and it let in Hallman with Cleveland's last run.

The champions got it back in their half easily enough. It was just a little hit by Mertes into Pickering's preserves, just a little bunt by Shugart toward La Chance, and just a little push by Isbell which sent the ball scurrying past Beck, and Mertes scampered past Bradley to the plate.

Beck opened the ninth with a double—the only one of the day— but he expired on Hallman's grounder to Shugart, who tossed it to third instead of first, and stopped a promising run in its early infancy. A grounder to Hartman and a fly to Mertes did the rest, and the big crowd slowly filed out and faded away with a parting glance over its shoulder at the silken tribute to the prowess of Chicago's White Stockings as it furled itself softly against its support.

The *Tribune* added its traditional notes, which add color to the already bright-hued story. They follow, with a few explanatory editorial additions. I've also modernized and expanded the original boxscore, and added a bit of information about some of the players.

Notes of the Game

Jones handled himself in great shape in the sun field.

Manager McAleer said, "Our men are hardly in shape to play winning ball. This bad weather at Cleveland for the last week [city-stopping blizzard five days before game] in which we had only one day's practice, set us back considerably. I think with a few more games we will round into form. We have a team capable of winning the pennant and it will take a lot of beating to change my mind."

There were no "hurry up" rules in the American Leagues book, but the game ran off in an hour and a half.

Bob Wood received a nasty crack on the end of his little finger yesterday from a foul tip and last night his hand was swollen, but he will take his turn behind the bat on Saturday.

President Kilfoyl of Cleveland watched the game from the press stand for a while, but after a few innings he saw little chance for his team and went down to the ticket office to the pleasant task of counting his share of the receipts.

Mayor Harrison did not attend. He had promised President Comiskey to be present but was kidnapped by William J[ennings]. Bryan, who slipped into town unperceived. Commy's plans for having the Chief Executive start the opening game were shattered.

Bobby Burke occupied a box directly back of the home plate in the midst of a little group of Aldermen. The Mayor's right hand man is extremely fond of baseball and watched the game with interest.

President Ban Johnson was not present to preside at the pennant raising, as is customary. He went East to attend the opening at Philadelphia and it's a 1,000 to 1 shot he was sorry when he found Comiskey was the only magnate who had squared himself with the weather man.

James J. Hart, President of the Chicago National League team, was present, and witnessed the game from a box at the south end of the grand stand. He chatted with President Comiskey for some time and seemed to like the work of the players, but he did not voice his sentiments.

Tom Connolly, the new man on Ban Johnson's staff, is a little fellow, but ran the game without an audible kick from either team. Connolly has had National League experience and resigned because the players were allowed to run the game as they pleased, and his authority was overruled by the magnates several times.

Billy Sullivan nearly upset the ubiquitous photographer when chasing a foul fly in the first inning. For a minute it looked as if either the ball or the photographer's plates would be put out of the business permanently.

Cleveland Bluebirds, manager Jimmy McAleer (55-82, seventh place)

Player	Pos	AB	R	H	RBI	PO	A	E	1901	Yrs.	Teams
Ollie Pickering	RF	4	0	1	1	0	0	0	.309	8	6
Jack McCarthy	LF	4	0	2	0	4	0	0	.321	12	5
Frank Genins	CF	4	0	0	0	1	0	0	.228	3	4
Candy La Chance	1B	4	1	1	0	12	0	0	.303	12	4
Bill Bradley	3B	4	0	0	0	2	5	0	.293	14	4
Erve "Dutch" Beck	2B	3	0	2	0	1	2	0	.289	3	4
Bill W. Hallman	SS	3	1	0	0	1	2	1	.185	14	5
Bob Wood	C	4	0	1	1	2	1	0	.292	7	3
Wizard Bill Hoffer	P	4	0	0	0	1	1	0	.136	6	3
		34	2	7	2	24	11	1			

Hoffer was 31–6 and 25–7 for Baltimore in 1895 and 1896, the National League's best percentage. He was 3–8 for Cleveland in his final major league season in 1901.

Righty-swinging Beck hit the American League's first home run (over the low right field fence) the next day off 7 to 3 Chicago winner, John "Buckshot" Skopec (6–3). Beck was 1900 Interstate League batting champion with the Toledo Mud Hens (.360 on 207 hits).

In 1900, first batter Pickering led the still-minor circuit with 194 hits and 117 runs.

Eleven-year veteran Hallman was dealt to the Philadelphia Phillies after only five games with Cleveland (.211).

McCarthy's career batting high was .321.

In 1901, Genins played the last 26 games of the 149 in his major league career.

Chicago White Stockings, manager Clark Griffith (83–53, first place)

Player	Pos	AB	R	H	RBI	PO	A	E	1901	Yrs.	Teams
Bill Dummy Hoy	CF	5	0	1	0	3	0	0	.294	14	7
Fielder Jones	RF	2	2	1	0	4	0	0	.311	13	2
Sam Mertes	LF	3	2	1	0	4	0	0	.277	10	5
Frank Shugart	SS	1	2	0	1	4	4	0	.251	8	6
Frank Isbell	1B	3	1	2	3	8	0	1	.257	10	2
Fred Hartman	3B	4	0	1	2	0	7	0	.309	6	4
Dave Brain	2B	4	0	0	0	1	4	0	.350	7	6
Billy Sullivan	C	4	1	2	0	2	0	0	.245	14	2
Roy Pat Patterson	P	4	0	0	0	1	1	0	.222	7	1
		30	8	8	6	27	16	1			

Patterson, 20–16 in 1901, was 17–6 in 1900 for Charles Comiskey's champion Chicago club—the best winning percentage in the new (but still considered minor) American League.

Hoy led the American League with 86 walks. He returned to the National League and played for Cincinnati in 1902, his final season.

Hartman's best season was 1901. He ended his career with St. Louis of the National League in 1902.

After his 0-for-4, Brain was 7-for-16 for Chicago in the next four games but didn't play major league ball again until 1903, with St. Louis of the National League. His three errors in one game and a crucial bobble in another contest lost two games for Chicago the first week. Dave had been a poor third baseman for Western League Des Moines in 1900, despite hitting .305. He was shipped back down the minors and Mertes took over second base.

Isbell led the American League with 52 steals. It was his first major league action since he appeared for Chicago's National League club in 1898.

Jones became White Sox manager in 1904.

Runs by innings:
```
Clev  000   100   100   —   2
Chi   250   000   10x   —   8
```

Hits by innings:
```
Clev  111   100   201   —   7
Chi   121   002   20x   —   8
```

Two-base hit Beck. Total bases: Chicago 8, Cleveland 8. Sacrifice hit: Shugart. Struck out: Patterson. Bases on balls off Hoffer, 6; off Patterson, 2.

Double plays: Hoffer–Hallman–La Chance; Brain–Shugart–Isbell.

Left on base: Chicago 5, Cleveland, 5. Passed ball: Wood.

Time: 1:30. Umpire: Tom Connolly. Attendance: 9,000.

There were, of course, other openers in 1901. The National League got a six-day head start on the upstart circuit. Rain postponed three openers on Thursday, April 18, but defending 1900 champion Brooklyn got in its game against Philadelphia.

BAKER BOWL—About 5,000 fans braved a cold, raw wind to see baseball's inaugural game of the twentieth century. Brooklyn pasted Phils starter "Handyman" Jack Dunn (0–1, soon traded) for six first-frame runs and hung on to post a 12–7 win. Dunn, who won 56 games for Brooklyn in the late 1890s (and later owned and managed the Baltimore Orioles minor league powerhouse—see Tom Pendleton's article in this issue), got leadoff batter, rookie right fielder Al "Lefty" Davis (.209, traded in May), but then left fielder Willie Keeler (.355, two runs today) doubled and the rout commenced. Superbas rookie Wild Bill Donovan (25–15), who had a three-year, 3–10 mark coming into 1901, allowed the hosts to close the gap to 7–6 in the fourth, but reliever "Frosty Bill" Duggleby (20–12) could not hold Brooklyn's bats at bay. Jimmy Sheckard (.353, 19 triples), playing only his second game at third base, stroked three triples and scored four runs. Brooklyn first baseman Joe Kelley (.309) also got three hits, as did Frosty Bill (.171). Ned Hanlon's Superbas were said to be in better shape for the opener because of their recent southern exhibition trip. Bill Shettsline's Phillies practiced at home.

Brooklyn	12	16	2
Philadelphia	7	14	2

ROBISON FIELD (April 19)—Crisp, clear weather made for good hitting on the west bank of the Mississippi as the Chicago Orphans defeated Patsy Donovan's St. Louis Cardinals, 8–7, behind veteran first baseman Dirty Jack Doyle's (.232) four singles and two runs, and left fielder Topsy Hartsel's (.335) two triples. Winner "Brakeman" Jack Taylor (13–19, a year away from stardom) and loser Jack Powell (19–19) allowed 32 hits as all eighteen starters got safeties except Taylor. Card center fielder Emmett "Snags" Heidrick (.339) smashed out four hits, including a double and two triples, and scored two runs. Host left fielder Jesse "the Crab" Burkett (.382) added three hits and two runs scored, while right fielder Pat "Cozy" Dolan (.263) had three hits for Tom Loftus's Orphs. About 5,000 witnessed the two hour, seven minute battle. Heidrick whacked a home run and a single in the next day's game, giving him a two-day cycle, the first player to get all four types of hits in the century.

Chicago	8	17	2
St. Louis	7	15	1

SOUTH END GROUNDS (April 19)—Three hundred-plus game winner Charlie "Kid" Nichols (19–16) five-hit the visitors from New York, 7–0, as six Boston batters drilled starter Luther "Dummy" Taylor (18–27) for multiple hits. In his twelfth (and last) season for Boston's National League Beaneaters, Nichols seemed to be recovered from his worst campaign (1900), blanking George Davis's Giants crew. Second baseman Bobby Lowe (.255, his final year with Boston) got three hits and scored twice. New York fifteen-year vet, center fielder George Van Haltren (.342), saved his club from further embarrassment by making two fine running catches in the eighth, turning one into a double play. NY manager Davis (.309) had two safeties as did pitcher Nichols (.282). A crowd of 6,500 was delighted that the hour and half game went to Frank Selee's men.

New York	0	5	2
Boston	7	15	2

LEAGUE PARK [Crosley Field location] April 20—Five thousand fans braved frigid weather to watch the visiting (eventual pennant-winning) Pirates rally to beat the Reds, 4–2. Cincinnati's Frank "Noodles" Hahn (22–19, 315 innings, 239 Ks) battled Sam "the Goshen Schoolmaster" Leever (14–5) for a 2–0 lead after five frames. Then manager-left fielder Fred Clarke (.324), right fielder Honus Wagner (.353, 126 RBIs) and rookie first baseman William "Kitty" Bransfield (.295) all tripled and scored in a four-run outburst aided by two miscues. Bransfield had a near triple crown (.371/17 HRs/115 runs) for the Eastern League's Worcester Farmers in 1900. Host first baseman Jake Beckley (.307) matched Kitty's two hits

with a double and triple of his own. Right fielder Sam Crawford (.330, 16 HRs) also had two hits for the losers. Hahn's triple and run scored came in the fifth. Frozen fans were thankful for a quick 100 minute contest in near wintry conditions. Retired Queen City legend, Bid McPhee, managed his first game.

Pittsburgh	4	6	2
Cincinnati	2	9	4

When the rest of the American League finally got going, it started off with a real bang.

BENNETT PARK, Corktown Neighborhood (April 25)—A record Detroit overflow crowd of 9,000 people not only saw one of the great comeback victories (the city's first official American League game) in history, but had an important part in it. As the final inning began, hordes of Tiger fans spilled onto the left field area and soon made it impossible for rookie left fielder Bill Hallman (.211) to catch would-be fly outs. Detroit scored ten runs for a wild 14–13 finish. The last blow by George Stallings' men was first baseman Frank "Pop" Dillon's (.288) fourth double (five RBIs, three runs) of the game. The home cranks then carried the hero off the diamond. Starting Milwaukee pitcher, Beaver Dam, Wisconsin's native son, Emerson "Pink" Hawley (7–14) had a nice 7–3 lead when he (in his final season of ten) was replaced in the seventh inning. The score mounted to 13–4 as Detroit's last at-bat came due. Reliever Pete Dowling (12–26, mostly with Cleveland) could not hold the margin and neither could rookie finisher Bert Husting (10–15) as ten runners scampered across home plate. Host twirler Roscoe "Roxy" Miller (23–13) was pounded soundly, as was eventual victor Emil Frisk (5–4) but to a lesser degree. Usually positioned in the outfield, Frisk (.313) helped his own cause with three hits and a run, which equaled the output of his veteran second baseman Bill "Kid" Gleason (.274). Rookie shortstop Wid Conroy (.256) was the Brewers' swat star with four singles and four runs. He was backed by three hits each by two rookies: second baseman Billy Gilbert (.270) and third baseman Jimmy Burke (.225). It is a wonder that any of the crowd stayed for the ninth after watching Hugh Duffy's (.308) Brewers get sixteen hits with the Tigers compounding that attack with seven errors. (A little more than a year before, Buffalo slapped Detroit, 8–0, in the first game played at Bennett Park in the Western League. Bison lefty Morris "Doc" Amole threw a no-nitter.) It was Detroit's return to the major leagues after being absent since the close of the National League's 1888 season.

Milwaukee	13	16	4
Detroit	14	19	7

COLUMBIA AVENUE PARK (April 26)—(This is the game that Rober Glenn Weaver details in the next article.) Philadelphia Mayor Ashbridge threw out the ceremonial first ball as 10,547 watched Jimmy Manning's visiting Washington club beat the Athletics, 5–1, in just under two hours. Senator second baseman "Old Reliable" Joe Quinn (.252) in his seventeenth and last season, starred with three hits and two runs behind the twirls of Bill Carrick (14–23) who fooled all Philadelphia batters except second baseman Nap Lajoie (.422, 14 HR, 125 RBIs), who cracked three hits, the only extra-base hit of the game (a double), and scored the A's lone run on a single, steal, an errant throw and a groundout. Hurler Chick Fraser (22–16) was not helped by his team's seven errors. Lajoie seemed unmoved by the legal battles surrounding his playing for Connie Mack's Athletics. Rookie third baseman Bill Coughlin (.278) and first baseman Mike Grady (.285) scored the other Senator runs. Veteran catcher Bill "Boileryard" Clarke (.280) knocked home three with two singles while winner Carrick punched in an insurance tally. SABR retro rookie of the year pick, A's left fielder Ralph "Socks" Seybold, was 1-for-4 and made an error.

Washington	5	8	1
Philadelphia	1	7	7

AMERICAN LEAGUE PARK at York Road (April 26)—Two days of rainouts could not dampen Baltimore's support for its league-switching Orioles, the new American League, and a new ball yard. Manager-third baseman John McGraw's (.349) hard players defeated 1890s National League city rival Boston, 10–6, in bright sun and mild spring air. The teams were led to the park by a parade through Baltimore's streets.

Some 10,370 of the finest fans then saw Boston rookie lefty Win Kellum (2–3) give up three runs in the first inning. Oriole sticks were hot and built a 6–1 margin after seven innings. League-jumper Joe McGinnity (26–20), the National League's top winner in 1899 (Orioles) and 1900 (Brooklyn), coasted the last two innings, as Baltimore made four more runs to Boston's five. In his third stint with a Baltimore team, city native and Oriole shortstop "Wagon Tongue" Bill Keister (.328) smacked a single, a double and the first of his 21 1901 triples, and scored twice to lead the attack. Left fielder Mike Donlin (.347) added two triples and two runs scored, and McGraw and rookie center fielder Jimmy Jackson (.250) each had two doubles and a run. For manager-third baseman Jimmy Collins' (.332) Bostons, catcher Lou Criger (.231) had a single, a double and two runs scored. Collins, also with a double and a single, had a single run scored. Rookie pinch-hitter Larry McLean (.211/9 g) swatted a double and had an RBI and a run scored in the ninth inning rally. Fast play allowed fans to head for home in 1 hour and 45 minutes. A delighted American League president Ban Johnson and vice president Charles W. Somers attended the game after arriving from Philadelphia.

Boston	6	9	1
Baltimore	10	11	3

For the two leagues' combined eight games, the home and road clubs each won four. The Chicago entries took both. Philly lost in each circuit. Boston split. An inning summary of 1901's runs:

NL	9	1	4	10	6	10	2	4	1	—47
AL	5	7	6	5	1	4	7	5	13	—59

The American League Opens in Philadelphia

Robert Glenn Weaver

Bad weather had set in and for two days the opening of the new American League in Philadelphia, scheduled for April 24, had to be postponed. Chicago had managed to open as scheduled, beating Cleveland. Detroit, in a thriller, had conquered Milwaukee. In Philadelphia, while the visiting Washington team lolled around the hotel, fans and players chafed.

The American League. That name had a nice ring to it. It would be almost unpatriotic not to support a team in *that* league. The Philadelphia Athletics. That name had an evocative ring, too. First used by a Philadelphia club in 1860, it was the oldest nickname in baseball. It had also been the name first chosen by the Philadelphia entry in the National League when that organization formed in 1876.

The manager of the new team, stringbean Cornelius McGillicudy, displayed a touch of the talent that would earn him a reputation as a pioneer sports entrepreneur. When he learned that fans had special affection for the white uniforms and blue stockings worn by earlier teams, he chose that combination for his new team, hoping to attract all the fans who had quit in disgust when they felt the Philadelphia National team had given up trying to win. They would come back, he figured, telling each other about the good old days, the exciting games between the old A's and the Cincinnati Reds, the St. Louis Browns, and the New York Metropolitans.

As an added incentive, Mack signed Lave Cross, a

popular bowlegged hustler who had worn the blue and white before. Lave was to be the symbol of the revived winning spirit. Fans had good reason to reunite, to celebrate, and to hope.

Mack's "Babies," as they were called, had spent a few weeks getting ready—a sort of at-home spring training—by playing college teams, amateur teams, and whatever pick-up opposition was available. The A's had done well, but they hadn't looked like world-beaters. (It took them eleven innings to beat Yale, 4-3.) Players and fans were tired of practice. They wanted real competition. Two days of rain only sharpened their interest. When the moon broke out on the night of the 25th and the sun almost came through on the 26th, Philadelphia's baseball cranks really caught the fever.

By game time a reported 15,000 men and women had packed Columbia Park at 29th Street and Columbia Avenue. (The attendance figure was probably inflated. There were probably more like 10,000 to 11,000 at the ballpark.) A few got in without paying the twenty-five cent admission charge. A small group of enterprising men in the left-field bleachers had a rope they threw down to an accomplice selling "hauling tickets" on the street below. About a dozen people had been hauled up this way before police confiscated the rope. Another fan handed the gatekeeper a pass signed by Colonel John I. Rogers. The gatekeeper laughed and waved him in. It was a good gag, worth the price of admission. Colonel Rogers was the owner of the unpopular National League Phillies, who at that very moment were playing Boston before 779 fans. With Columbia Park sold out the ticket taker could afford to feel expansive.

Standing room eventually sold out too, and several

Robert Glenn Weaver, *protegé of Connie Mack, pitcher, Duke Blue Devils, one exhibition game in an A's uniform, minor league ball in Newport News and Hickory, is the author of a baseball novel,* Nice Guy, Go Home, *Harper & Row, 1967.*

---

thousand disappointed fans with 25 cents in their hands were turned away. What was the attraction? It couldn't have been just a game of baseball, or the Phillies would have played to more than 779. It must have been the excitement and promise of a new era.

The First Regiment Band played. Team president Ben Shibe sat in a position of honor. A good showing of politicians and other notables acknowledged the crowd. "Three cheers for the mayor," the crowd yelled as Mayor Ashbridge struggled down the crowded aisle.

At 3:55, Mr. Shibe passed a box to Mayor Ashbridge. Umpire Haskell appeared. The athletes took the field. The mayor tossed the ball, still in the box, to the umpire. Haskell clawed the ball out of the box and tossed it to Fraser, the Philadelphia pitcher. The game began.

The *Inquirer* reported the game as "an entertaining affair," but as a contest it was nothing special. Washington won, 5-1. Chick Fraser of the A's pitched well, but Washington's Bill Carrick pitched brilliantly. Errors made the difference: Philadelphia, 6; Washington, 1. Dave Fultz, the A's shortstop, was the goat with three. Napoleon Lajoie, who had jumped from the Phillies, had the only extra-base hit, a double. (He also had two singles, a good start in what would be a sensational year for him. By season's end he achieved the still-enduring modern batting average record of .422.) He scored the A's only run in the game after a single, a wild throw by Boileryard Clarke, and Socks Seybold's fly out. Playing time: 1:55.

Not much of a game, but the start of a legend. Mack and Lajoie were named to the Hall of Fame in 1937. Mack would take teams to nine pennants and five World Series victories and establish a record for years managing in the big leagues.

WASHINGTON

		AB	R	BH	TB	SH	SB	PO	A	E
Farrell	cf	4	0	0	0	0	0	2	0	0
Everett	1b	1	0	0	0	0	0	4	0	0
Grady	1b	3	1	0	0	0	0	8	0	0
O'Brien	lf	5	0	1	1	0	0	1	0	0
Dungan	rf	5	0	0	0	0	0	3	1	0
Quinn	2b	5	2	3	3	0	1	2	3	0
Clingman	ss	5	0	0	0	0	0	0	5	0
Coughlin	3b	4	2	1	1	0	0	2	4	0
Clarke	c	3	0	2	2	0	0	5	0	1
Carrick	p	3	0	1	1	0	0	0	2	0
Totals		**38**	**5**	**8**	**8**	**0**	**1**	**27**	**15**	**1**

PHILADELPHIA

		AB	R	BH	TB	SH	SB	PO	A	E
Hayden	rf	2	0	1	1	0	1	0	0	0
Geifer	cf	4	0	0	0	0	0	1	0	0
Fultz	ss	4	0	0	0	0	0	4	4	3
Lajoie	2b	4	1	3	4	0	1	3	2	0
Seybold	lf	4	0	1	1	0	0	1	0	1
Cross	3b	4	0	1	1	0	0	2	2	1
Carr	1b	4	0	0	0	0	0	8	1	1
Powers	c	3	0	1	1	0	0	6	3	0
Fraser	p	3	0	0	0	0	0	2	4	0
Totals		**32**	**1**	**7**	**8**	**0**	**2**	**27**	**16**	**6**

INNINGS
Philadelphia (runs)   0 0 0   0 0 0   1 0 0 —1
Base hits   0 1 0   1 1 1   1 1 1 —7
Washington (runs)   0 0 0   1 0 2   1 1 0 —5
Base hits   1 0 0   2 0 3   0 1 1 —8

Runs earned—Washington, 2. Two-base hit—Lajoie. Left on bases—Washington, 10; Philadelphia, 6. Struck out—Clingman, 2; Carrick, 2: Hayden, Seybold, Fraser. Double plays—Dungan and Grady; Carrick, Quinn and Everett. First base on errors—Washington, 4. First base on called balls—Farrell, Everett, Clarke, Carrick, Hayden, 2. Missed grounders and fumbles—Fultz, Seybold, Cross. Wild throws—Fultz, 2; Clarke. Dropped thrown balls—Carr. Umpire—Haskell. Time—1:55.

Baseball's Ancestry

Dr. Joseph A. Baldassarre

Throughout history the ball has been the most common object around which games have been focused. Balls come in a variety of shapes, sizes, and compositions, and they can be thrown, kicked, carried, cradled, balanced, dribbled, racketed, wicketed, or clubbed.

Egyptian children were often buried with clay, leather, or wooden balls. Surviving pictures (below) show balls being juggled or tossed about in dance and play. Some ancients became virtuosi with the ball, but it was an object for all ages and both sexes, not the domain of professionals.

In Greek society, sport and theater were often not separated and there are occasional references to ballplaying in literature and iconography. For instance, in Homer's *Odyssey*, girls are depicted frolicking by passing a ball in rhythm. Odysseus is awakened by the shouting group when the ball is thrown errantly into the stream.

In Sparta, the word for "youth" and "ball player" were the same. Many of their ball games were similar to field hockey, soccer, or simple keepaway. They were played by children and older people, not serious athletes. For the Olympic (or war-oriented) athletes of ancient civilizations, team and ball sports took a back seat to individual and specialized excellence.

Romans took on the Greek values in sports, dividing them into serious and non-serious categories. As in Greece and Egypt, ball games appear occasionally in the literature and iconography of Rome. There are surviving pictures in Rome showing men playing ball. One game named *harpastrum* was played to warm and limber the body before bathing in cold weather. Here again, we see the ball used for fitness and play rather than competition.

Medieval Ball Games—There are many procedural similarities between medieval Europe and modern America. The modern baseball fan cannot separate the hero from his statistics. We cannot divorce stolen bases from Maury Wills, Ty Cobb, and Rickey Henderson; home runs from Hank Aaron and Babe Ruth; or legends from "Shoeless" Joe Jackson and Christy Mathewson. This attention to statistics and story is rooted in medieval English society.

The tendency to keep written records in Medieval England began with William the Conqueror's *Domesday Book* (1089), and continued in Edward I's great survey *quo warranto* (1290). In one session of Edward's court, over 2,000 documents were produced.

Dr. Joseph A. Baldassarre *is professor of classical guitar and music history at Boise State University and a performing musician. He also still plays baseball in the over-forty division of the MSBL.*

The *Registrum antiquissimum* of Lincoln Cathedral contains over 2,800 records. This need for bureaucratic accounting transferred itself to sport in Medieval England.

For instance, William the Marshal (ca. 1200) found glory as a real-life Galahad or Gawain when, through his prowess at tournaments (the "baseball" of the Middle Ages) he was proclaimed the greatest knight who ever lived. His accolades are recounted in records and in a 2,500-line poem, a more ancient style of keeping records, by John the Poet one generation later. Poems at this time were performed like a song or a tale for an audience by professionals, much like the color announcer in modern media.

In France, an ancient ritualistic Gallic ball game was played yearly in honor of the sun in springtime. Centuries later in early Christian France in the year 470, the Bishop of Clermont organized a ball game (similar to keepaway) for an Easter Church festival. It is recorded that a ball was often passed around during processions, and ball games were often played after the Easter meal as part of the tradition.

Other ritualistic games in earlier medieval France featured an animal organ, most often a pig's bladder, which was kicked, thrown, batted, or smuggled into the opponent's goal which was a line, hole, point, or area as much as a mile away. Rules were often localized. Rough-and-tumble play was expected and injuries were common. Many players took this opportunity to settle old scores.

In many European communities, the presence of ball games at religious ceremonies was so common that the games were noted when they *did not* take place—generally due to plague, famine, or war.

On the Iberian peninsula, ritualistic Moslem ball games are virtually indistinguishable from Christian ball games. The early Christians played these games at Easter, and the Moslems, like many ancient and early medieval European peoples, ushered in spring with them.

In medieval Italy, *calcio* was played. In the Florentine version, the ball could be advanced by carrying, kicking, or striking it with the hand or forearm. These methods are the same as those used in rugby. Of course, striking the ball with the hand is not so far removed from advancing it in the air by passing it with a lacrosse stick, batting it in the air with a hurling stick, or advancing it on the ground with a hockey stick.

Medieval bat-and-ball games—There are references to a bat and ball game called *creag* of which there are no extant rules or procedures. King Edward I (1272-1307) dispensed 100 shillings for his son, the Prince of Wales, to play *creag* and other sports at Westminster.

Like *creag*, *club ball* is mentioned, but I have found little concrete procedural evidence of the sport. There are drawings and illuminations showing what we believe to be club ball games in progress, generally like the one in the picture with a batter holding a bat and a ball, and with person or persons waiting with hands outstretched. This game may have been like our modern informal fungo-based games like *five-hundred* and *hit-the-bat*.

Stool ball was undoubtedly the precursor to *cricket* and was played by milkmaids. The object is for the batter to protect an upturned milking stool. At first, the batter used her outstretched arm or hand—this was later replaced with a stick. The bowler (pitcher) tries to throw the ball (which could have been any round object—even a ball of yarn) and hit the stool. If she succeeds, she scores a point. If the batter hits the ball and it is caught before hitting the ground (or before the second bounce), they change positions. If the pitcher cannot catch the ball, the batter scores a point. Thus one precursor of the American, urban, and male game of baseball, had its infancy as an English, rural, and female game.

The game of *hand-in-and-hand-out* was popular in Scotland and England. Played in the forest with upright stumps rooted in the soil, two holes are cut in the ground at opposing positions and the dog (batsman) tries to keep the cat (ball hurled by the bowler) out of

the hole. One variation of the game is not dissimilar to horseshoes: the batter has a stick to bat the ball away from the hole. The players then reverse functions, the batsman becomes the bowler.

Later each hole was marked with a stick so the bowler could better see it. Eventually, the hole was discarded and the ball was thrown at the stick. This being difficult, a second stick was added to give the target breadth, then a third was added in the center since many balls were passing between the sticks. It was in the batter's charge to protect the sticks or lose a point.

King Edward IV outlawed what his scribes wrote as *hande-yn-and-hande-oute* in 1477 because it interfered in both time and space with archery. The penalty for playing the game was set at two years imprisonment—three years for allowing the game to be played on your property. Later times were more tolerant of the game although the laws stayed on the books for many years.

Cricket, of course, is baseball's most closely related professional sport. There is direct evidence of the game of *cricket* in iconography as early as 1344. A drawing in the King's library in London shows a batsman facing a bowler with the bat upside down in a waiting position.

Stool ball, *creag*, and *hand-in-and-hand-out* seem to have been played by different classes: *stool ball* by female manual laborers; *creag* by the youthful aristocracy; *hand-in-and-hand-out* by potentially combatant males. *Club ball* may refer to a more informal game or be an "umbrella term" encompassing any game played with a club and a ball. Certain types of sports were banned from certain classes, but often that same sport with some variation based on facilities, equipment, or skill, existed in a varied form anyway. Nonetheless the upper and lower classes generally did not play together.

Similar distinctions apply to our modern games of . *baseball*, *softball*, *tee-ball*, *stick ball*, and so forth. After all, age, skill, temperament, level of play, playing environment, and available equipment all affect the play of the games and the rules by which they are played.

Later baseball precursors—In the sixteenth through eighteenth centuries, bat-and-ball games survived primarily as children's games, depleted of their religious and ritualistic meanings and structures. They were known by many names and shared few specific rules from community to community. Only general aspects of the games were common: two teams of undetermined (and not necessarily equal) sizes, a pitcher, defensive fielders, a batsman, stations (stakes or bases to be used as "safe" locations by runners), a bat, and a ball.

One such bat-and-ball game is mentioned by William Shakespeare. In *The Tempest* (1611), he refers to *bat-fowling*: a curious sport of the time played by lantern at night which combines baseball with hunting—live birds, attracted by the light of the lantern, substitute for the ball.

Bat and ball games survived Puritan strictures against the play of "silly games" as idle and pointless entertainment. They were shunned in England in the seventeenth century, but in America, Governor William Bradford notes the open play of *stool ball* in 1621. The participants were chastised, but they did not cease and were not punished. On a similar note, John Bunyan's autobiography of 1672 dramatizes his conversion to righteousness at the very moment he wickedly engages in a game of *cat*.

Similarly, Christian moralists of the nineteenth century tried to limit the playing of baseball, which was described as yielding "mindless, and immoral pleasure" on the Sabbath. It is ironic that ball games, once a part of the Christian religious tradition, had developed into pastimes that would attract the ire of religious groups.

American baseball—It is true that station games, and games played with a stick and ball in Europe and America, differ greatly from our present national sport not only in procedure, but also in social context. But baseball's own organic development is clear. All over America, the dimensions of the playing field varied according to the space available. The presence or absence of a fence, a building, trees, or railroad tracks all figured in. The number of players varied, officiating took on new meanings with every play, and equipment was whatever worked. In my personal backyard league, the field resembled a dented triangle more than a diamond, second base was a bare spot on the grounds, foul territory varied depending on where the high grass started, and anything hit into the houses in left or over the second railroad track in right was an automatic out. Your "ball park" was probably similar, and so were tens of thousands around the country.

Bat-and-ball games have been played by both sexes and all ages. They have cut across class lines as well as helped to define them. They appear throughout the Western world with uncounted variations. They have existed in ancient, medieval, and modern times, and in all sorts of cultures. They have been condemned by religious groups and integrated into religious ceremony and ritual. They have often been a reflection of the society itself.

The RBI Record of The Battalion of Death

Viola Owen

In 1934 Charles P. Ward, Detroit *Free Press* baseball writer, christened the Detroit Tigers infield "the Battalion of Death." Other newspapers picked up the name and ran stories and pictures of the "Battalion." That infield consisted of Charlie Gehringer at second base, Billy Rogell at shortstop, Hank Greenberg at first base, and Marv Owen at third base. The four played together from 1933 through 1937, and in 1934 they established an RBI record that no other four men have ever surpassed: 462.

Amost forgotten today, this great infield was also known at the time by other superlatives in the style of its time: "First Line of Defense," "Punch and Protection of Bounding Bengals," "Tigers Million Dollar Infield," "Detroit's Big Guns," and "The Infield of Dreams."

From shaky to dominant—Dan Daniel of the New York *World Telegram* analyzed the four infielders this way, looking back on the previous season:

> In 1933 the Detroit Tigers infield failed to function with more than ordinary brilliance, and only Gehringer was mentioned among the more adroit players of the circuit. Greenberg was just a big, somewhat awkward lad at first base, frankly an experiment. Rogell was tabbed as an uncertain fielder, lacking the arm to make him a winning shortstop. Owen was regarded as a brittle third sacker with tremendous potentialities."

Viola Owen is a SABR member, a retired educator, and a writer. She is the author of Adventures of a Quiet Soul *(1996) and* So You Want to Write a Baseball Book? *(1999). She lives in Aptos, California.*

(Marv was labeled "the sick man from San Jose." He had acute allergies, hay fever, and sinus problems so severe that he had to limit his batting practice to save enough strength for the game. After the 1933 season, through the efforts of specialists, tests, and treatment, Marv was able to return with renewed health.)

The rest of Dan Daniel's column turned his gaze on the same infield in 1934:

> Gaze upon these 1933 also rans now! Greenberg has developed into a dependable, if not altogether graceful workman; Rogell has become a sure shortstop, and Owen ranks with the best third basemen of the majors, disputing the leadership with Frank Higgins, of the Athletics and Pie Traynor, of the Pirates.
>
> GAINED NEW CONFIDENCE
>
> In searching for the reason for this concerted development of Mickey Cochrane's infield, we must yield the top place to winning momentum. Once in front, those Detroit infielders began to believe thoroughly in themselves. They soon discovered that they had something on the other inner fours of their league.
>
> While the Detroit club has been the hardest-hitting team in the American League all year, defensive strength really has been its forte. Standing out in its ability to stop runs has been the work of its brilliant infield, with Greenberg at first, Gehringer at second, Rogell around shortstop and Owen in charge of operations at third.

The Battalion of Death in its prime: Hank Greenberg, Charlie Gehringer, Billy Rogell, Marv Owen.

Ninety-six-year-old Billy Rogell, the last living member of the 1934 Detroit Tiger Infield, told the Santa Cruz *Sentinel* in 1996 that "the infield was the strength." Rogell says his three mates were all quiet, unassuming men. "He made me captain of the infield," Rogell said. Cochrane said 'Hell, Greenberg won't say nothing, Gehringer won't say nothing, Owen won't say nothing, you're the only one who'll fight. You're the captain.'

"It was an exceptional fielding infield, this Battalion of Death," Rogell concluded.

How the infield became airtight—Manager Mickey Cochrane was able to instill fight, hustle, and teamwork into the four infielders in a variety of ways. He urged them to view the veteran Goose Goslin as an example. He pointed to Gehringer's smooth fielding to inspire Rogell. He got Owen to show Greenberg how to position his hands to catch a high fly. He himself, with his magnetism, instilled in Owen the toughness he needed to guard third base.

H. G. Salsinger of The Detroit *News* wrote:

> Detroit's main strength is its infield. If it can continue at its present gait it will be recognized as one of the best infields ever carried by a ranking team.
>
> We cannot remember an infield that included as much batting power and fielding ability. True, there have been infields that were stronger defensively, but there never has been an infield that we remember that produced as many hits as the Detroit infield. All four men on the infield are hitting above .300 and one of them has been hitting above .400 a good part of the season. We do not believe there was ever before an infield on which every man was a .300 hitter; at least no infield with the com-

1934 Detroit Tiger Batting Order			
Player, Position	**BA**	**HR**	**RBI**
Jo Jo White, cf	.313	0	44
Mickey Cochrane, c	.320	2	76
Charlie Gehringer, 2b	.356	11	127
Goose Goslin, lf	.305	13	100
Billy Rogell, ss	.296	3	100
Hank Greenberg, 1b	.339	26	139
Marv Owen, 3b	.317	8	96
Pete Fox, rf	.285	2	45

Major league infields with at least 400 RBIs in a single season

Year	Team	1B	%1B	RBI	2B	%2B	RBI	SS	%SS	RBI	3B	%3B	RBI	Total RBIs
1927	NY-n	Terry	100%	121	Hornsby	100%	125	Jackson	98%	98	**Lindstrom**	63%	58	402
1930	PIT	Suhr	100%	107	Grantham	97%	99	Bartell	98%	75	Traynor	100%	119	400
1930	NY-a	Gehrig	99%	174	**Lazzeri**	53%	121	Lary	97%	52	**Chapman**	66%	81	428
1931	NY-a	Gehrig	99%	184	**Lazzeri**	67%	83	Lary	100%	107	Sewell	93%	64	438
1934	DET	Greenberg	100%	139	Gehringer	100%	127	Rogell	100%	100	Owen	100%	96	462
1935	DET	Greenberg	100%	170	Gehringer	99%	108	Rogell	100%	71	Owen	98%	71	420
1936	CHI-a	Bonura	99%	138	**Hayes**	82%	84	Appling	99%	128	Dykes	98%	60	410
1936	NY-a	Gehrig	100%	152	Lazzeri	99%	109	Crosetti	100%	78	Rolfe	99%	70	409
1937	BOS-a	Foxx	100%	127	**McNair**	84%	76	Cronin	100%	110	Higgins	99%	106	419
1938	BOS-a	Foxx	100%	175	Doerr	100%	80	Cronin	99%	94	Higgins	99%	106	455
1940	BOS-a	**Foxx**	66%	119	Doerr	100%	105	Cronin	98%	111	Tabor	100%	81	416
1948	CLE	Robinson	98%	83	Gordon	100%	124	Boudreau	99%	106	Keltner	100%	119	432
1950	BOS-a	Dropo	99%	144	Doerr	100%	120	Stephens	98%	144	Pesky	91%	49	457
1996	BAL	**Palmeiro**	88%	142	Alomar	92%	94	Ripken	97%	102	**Surhoff**	74%	82	420

bined batting average that the Detroit quartet presents.

When you couple this batting with very good fielding you have a combination that should take any team quite a long way. It has.

Today Cochrane proclaims Owen the best third baseman in baseball.

Rogell has no managerial worries to hamper him. An ultra-aggressive player with a little coaxing, Rogell is strictly in his element in the Cochrane regime.

Greenberg is a winning type of ball player.

Charlie Gehringer is playing the best ball of his scintillating career, which means that Gehringer is the best player in the American League, if not in baseball.

Looking at the 1934 infield RBI record—In 1934 this hard-hitting, beauty-in-motion infield was on its way to an all-time record. The four infielders were com-

At a 1958 reunion: Owen, Rogell, Gehringer, Greenberg.

Detroit Tigers Archives

THE NATIONAL PASTIME

pared to other great infielders: Baker and Steinfeldt at third, Tinker and Barry at shortstop, Evers and Collins at second, and Chance and McInnis at first. But those earlier players could not match the RBI record of the 1934 infield.

The *Baseball Encyclopedia* lists most RBIs by an infield on a year-by-year, team-by-team basis. Only thirteen major league infields of just four players have amassed at least 400 RBIs in a single season. They are listed in chronological order in the table on the next page. (Thanks to Herman Krabbenhoft for supplying this information.)

The top RBI infield remains the 1934 tandem of Greenberg (139), Gehringer (127), Rogell (100), and Owen (96); their total was 462. This crew also topped the 400 mark in 1935, with 420 RBIs).

The closest that any four-man infield has come to the Greenberg-Gehringer-Rogell-Owen 462 pinnacle was the 1950 Red Sox group of Dropo (144), Doerr (120), Stephens (144), and Pesky (49), for a total of 457. (The Boston infield of 1950 drove in 505 runs, but it took eight men to do it, according to research done by Bill Deane. Billy Goodman added 43 of his 68 as an infielder, Lou Stringer had one of his two, and Ken Keltner and Fred Hatfield had two each.)

No infield combination has yet had *each* of four fielders contribute at least 100 RBIs in the same season.

The table shows RBIs for each player for the entire season at all positions played. RBIs at the specified infield position might, in actuality, be less than the number given. Most of the players played more than 98 percent of their games at the specified infield position. Boldface type indicates those players who played fewer than 90 percent of their games at the specified infield position. All the 1934 Tiger infielders played all their games at a single position. They are the only quartet to have done so.

Later Years—Tiger president Frank J. Navin said the 1934 infield was the greatest Detroit had had since he became connected with the club over thirty years before. Some baseball historians claim it was the best infield ever. In 1934, Gehringer, Greenberg, and Owen were nominated for Most Valuable Player award. Gehringer and Greenberg have both been inducted into the Hall of Fame at Cooperstown. (In 1939, on the day of Charlie Gehringer's induction into the Hall of Fame, he was absent. He and his bride-to-be, Josephine Stillen, were in San Jose, California for their June wedding at St. Patrick's Church. Marv and Violet Owen were their wedding attendants. Charlie missed the enshrinement at Cooperstown, but he became a bridegroom and a Hall of Famer on the same day.)

The four infielders, always good friends, had a special respect for each other. Reminiscing in 1999, Billy Rogell wrote, "We thought the world of each other. We four never had a bad thought if one made a bad play. Let me say—four men who got along so well—respect is the answer." For over forty years Bill Rogell and Mr. and Mrs. Charlie Gehringer corresponded regularly with Marv Owen.

In 1984 Owen designed and ordered commemorative Louisville Sluggers and had one sent to each of the members of that '34 infield. On each bat (below) was a listing of their RBI records. Here are the batting statistics of Detroit's 1934 Battalion of Death, holders of the four-man major league infield RBI record, and one of the great infields of all time:

Player, position	BA	HR	RBI
Hank Greenberg, 1B	.339	26	139
Charlie Gehringer, 2B	.356	11	127
Billy Rogell, SS	.296	3	100
Marv Owen, 3B	.317	8	96
TOTALS	**.327**	**48**	**462**

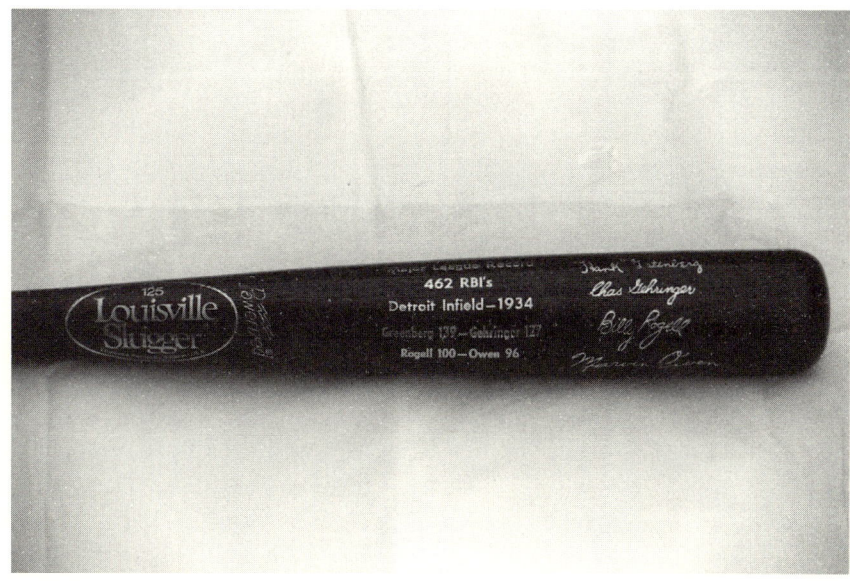

John Kling, Cub Stalwart

David W. Anderson

Fame is a fickle mistress. If you seek it, it will often elude you. If you do not seek it, it may find you despite your efforts to hide. Then there are those who achieve glory but are fogotten by fame. The great John Kling has fallen into this "Who's he?" category.

Kling was a mainstay of the Cub dynasty from 1906 to 1910, a team that won 530 games in a five-year span, more than any other team in history. The Cubs won the pennant each of those years except 1909, a season Kling sat out. Many observers attributed the 1909 second-place finish to Kling's absence.

That hiatus stemmed from his often stormy contract negotiations with Cub owner Charles Murphy. In the days before free agency, owners and players often played a game of chicken, the owner driving a hard bargain with salary and the player threatening to hold out. Few players were in a position to make a credible holdout threat, but Kling had other ways to make a living, so Murphy's negotiations with him were always difficult. As the result of his refusal to sign a contract for 1909, Kling was suspended. Murphy's parting words were harsh. Noting the recent death of Marshall Field, Murphy told Kling that Field's store would go on as if nothing happened and so would the Cubs if Kling sat out.

Universally recognized by his contemporaries as one of the best all-around catchers in the game during the Deadball Era, Kling is now overshadowed by New York Giant Hall-of-Famer Roger Bresnahan, even though

---

David W. Anderson *is author of* More Than Merkle *and lives in the Kansas City Metro area. His book about the 1908 season led him to research John Kling's life.*

Bresnahan played other positions than catcher. Yet those who watched Kling and those who played with and against him marveled at his ability to play defense, handle pitchers, and be part of the psychological warfare that characterized the game during the first decade of the twentieth century.

Johnny Evers described Kling as a "brilliant general who worked perfectly with pitchers and the infield." Evers claimed that Kling could tell a pitcher what his best stuff was during warmups. In *Pitching in a Pinch*, Christy Mathewson said Kling's constant chatter was distracting to rookies and veterans alike. It was no accident his nickname was "Noisy." Finally, Evers said Kling was a "past master of the art of working umpires on balls and strikes." Unlike many of his contemporaries, Kling tried to be friendly with the men in blue, and, according to Evers, tried to support them and even warn them to be on guard if an unusual play or pitch was coming.

Sportswriters Fred Lieb and Hugh Fullerton also praised Kling's ability highly. Lieb said Kling and Bresnahan were the outstanding catchers between the years 1901 and 1925. Fullerton, a Chicago *Tribune* writer, said the only catcher he saw who compared to Kling, in terms of his defensive and batting skills, was Mickey Cochrane.

The man—So Kling was a great player, but what kind of a person was he? His granddaughters, Jonne Kling Rose and Jerre Kling Wiggans, still live in the Kansas City area. They describe Kling as a doting father who could best be described as "strait-laced." During an era when players often smoked, drank, and gambled to ex-

---

John Kling

cess, Kling the family man condoned none of those vices. Both Jonne and Jerre admitted that their mother enjoyed a late-day highball, but she had to sneak it when the Cub backstop was around. This attitude is especially surprising because Kling, an expert billiards player, operated a poolroom in his home town of Kansas City.

Another glimpse into Kling's character comes from Ford Frick, who credits him with firing his interest in baseball as a career. Frick encountered Kling during an exhibition game in Kendallville, Indiana, in 1907. The Cubs had to dress in a tavern due to lack of facilities. In his memoir, *Games, Asterisks, and People*, Frick describes what happened as he saw Kling walk to the ballpark. Kling asked him if he wanted to go the game. Frick picks it up from there: "I gulped, and managed to convey the idea that I would." Kling then asked Frick to carry his shoes and walk into the gate with the team and maybe the gateman would let him in.

Frick wrote, "I did exactly as he told me, and the miracle happened. I walked right into the ballpark with the players. Furthermore, I was permitted to sit on the ground alongside the players' bench. I could see Mordecai Brown and Ed Reulbach in person. I could hear Schulte and Tinker and Chance and Evers and Steinfeldt talking on the bench between innings. What a moment."

Retirement and desegregation—The great Cub dynasty began showing its age in 1910, winning the pennant but losing the World Series to the next great powerhouse, Connie Mack's Athletics. Reflecting unhappiness over Kling's postseason play, the Cubs traded him in 1911 to Boston. He managed the Braves to a last-place finish in 1912. He was sold during the off-season to Cincinnati where he hit a respectable .273 in 1913 before retiring.

Kling went on to a successful career as a businessman and real-estate developer in the Kansas City area. He operated the Pennant Café in the downstairs of the Dixon Hotel. This establishment featured four sidewalk glass windows to honor the four Cub pennants (see the inside front cover), and the billiards room itself featured chandeliers made of bats and balls. Descriptions of the Pennant Café indicate that this establishment was as much a baseball museum as it was a billiards hall. The glass shown on these pages is the only surviving piece from this business.

Kling pursued business interests outside of baseball until 1934 when he bought the American Association Kansas City Blues. He owned the team until 1937, when he sold it to Col. Jacob Ruppert of the New York Yankees. Kling's ownership left what should have been an indelible mark on baseball: he ordered seating at the Blues ballpark, Muehlebach Stadium, to be desegregated. This gesture was not widely reported outside of Kansas City. The stadium served as the site for the Blues and Monarchs of the Negro Leagues, and it may be that during the Great Depression such restrictions were economically counterproductive. But other owners with segregated ballparks did not take this step. Kling's action was bold, if not visionary, during a time when such actions were all too rare.

Reassessment— Kling died in January, 1947, at the age of 72, a successful man whose family never wanted for money, even during the Great Depression. But the Fates dealt him another blow. Because of a newspaper strike, his obituary was not printed in his hometown newspaper. He is buried at Mount Moriah Cemetery at I-435 and Holmes in Kansas City.

Today's average baseball fan would be hard-pressed to recognize the name of John Kling, let alone cite any of his accomplishments. Generations ago, he received a measure of recognition from sportswriters voting for induction into the Hall of Fame. Kling never garnered enough ballots to be a close call, but in 1937, 1938, 1939, 1942, 1945, and 1946, his vote totals were the highest received by any player not inducted. In the inaugural year of 1936, Kling got more votes than his Cub teammates, future Hall-of-Famers Johnny Evers, Frank Chance, and Mordecai "Three Finger" Brown. More recently, in 1999, Kling was selected for the Chicago Cubs All-Century team.

While Kling's exclusion from the Hall of Fame is hardly tragic, it seems illogical, if not unjust. Today, his playing performance certainly argues strongly for induction. There are several possible reasons that may contribute to his absence—some of them troubling.

First, the cliché "out of sight, out of mind" applies. Kling's return to Kansas City placed him under the radar of most baseball writers. His absence from major league cities may have contributed to amnesia on the part of the Cooperstown voters. And he's been out of sight and out of mind for a long, long time now.

Second, many ballplayers have had rough relations with owners. Kling's contract conflicts are not unique, but his decision to leave baseball in 1909 did not help his cause.

Third, Kling's social conscience could have tipped the scales against him. The move to desegregate seating meant little to the sportswriting fraternity of the age who seldom championed social causes.

Fourth, some baseball historians refer to Kling as baseball's first Jewish star. In Mathewson's *Pitching in a Pinch*, Kling is referred to as "the Jew" by teammate Johnny Evers. Yet in Evers' book *Touching Second*, Kling's religion is not mentioned.

Anti-Semitism in America was at its zenith during the 1930s and questions surrounding Kling's faith may have harmed his Cooperstown chances. There is no hard evidence that this was the case, and we can't read the hearts and minds of the voters. But it would be ironic if Kling was snubbed by the Hall of Fame for this reason, because he was not Jewish.

This has not been an easy question for researchers to answer. Kling himself cared little about questions concerning his religion. His wife wrote the Hall of Fame to say her husband was baptized Lutheran. Kling's granddaughters note their mother and aunt married Jewish men, but assert that their grandfather was not Jewish.

Such questions bother us today and rightly so. Lutheran or Jew, John Kling was a mensch. Baseball's history needs to rediscover his career and his accomplishments.

David Mobley and the Rock Hill Chiefs

Bob Gorman

As dawn broke on August 26, 1952, in the small Southern town of Rock Hill, South Carolina, the day promised to be a hot one in more ways than just the temperature. The Rock Hill Chiefs, independent member of the Class B Tri-State League (North Carolina, South Carolina, and Tennessee) were about to play a small but significant role in a much larger revolution that was sweeping the nation, a revolution that would change forever race relations throughout America.

The Chiefs, financially strapped and desperate to boost attendance, announced that they planned to start David 'Pepsi Cola' Mobley in the outfield for that evening's game. Usually such an announcement would go unnoticed. In Mobley's case, however, the signing of this twenty-six-year-old outfielder threatened to tear the Tri-State League asunder, for Mobley was an African American, destined to be the first to play organized baseball in South Carolina and the first officially to play for a team in either of the Carolinas.

When Jackie Robinson broke the color barrier in organized baseball in 1946 as a member of the Montreal Royals, the world of professional baseball did not rush to embrace integration. In fact, it wasn't until 1959, twelve years after Robinson's debut in Brooklyn, that the last major league team, the Boston Red Sox, finally integrated. If the signing of African American players was slow at the major league level, it was downright glacial at the minor league level, especially in the South.

White Southern racism and the resulting Jim Crow laws that enshrined the separation of the races, dic-

tated that the integration of minor league teams in the South would be slow and painful. The first African American minor leaguers to play in the South came as members of visiting Northern minor league teams. In 1949, for example, Jim Pendleton of the St. Paul Saints and Ray Dandridge of the Minneapolis Millers became the first blacks to play against the Louisville (Kentucky) Colonels of the American Association. In 1950, Willie Mays broke the color barrier in the Interstate League when his team, the Trenton Giants, played the Hagerstown Braves in Maryland. The next year witnessed the first African American members of deep-South teams: J.W. Wingate of the Lamesa (Texas) Lobos and Percy Miller, Jr., of the Danville (Virginia) Leafs made brief appearances. It wasn't until the 1952 and 1953 seasons that integration made any lasting progress, when several African American players spent entire seasons with Southern teams.[1]

This gradual move toward integration had less to do with altruism than with economic factors. The five years immediately following the Second World War were a boom period for baseball at all levels. In 1946, for example, over 32 million fans attended minor league games, an increase of 22 million from the year before. In 1949 there were fifty-nine professional leagues in 438 cities and towns throughout the United States. In the early 1950s, however, with the beginning of the Korean War and the advent of television and air-conditioning, the minor league system began to contract rapidly. By 1959, there were only twenty-one minor leagues, nearly two-thirds less than in 1949.

A number of team owners saw integration as one answer to their economic woes. As Jackie Robinson

Bob Gorman *is head of reference at the Winthrop University Library, in Rock Hill, South Carolina.*

had proven, black fans would turn out in droves to see African American players. Many white fans might, too, because of the "novelty" of blacks and whites playing together.

South Carolina, although one of the most racially intransigent of the Southern states, was not immune to these larger economic and societal trends. From 1946 to the mid-1950s, two minor leagues had teams in South Carolina. The Class B Tri-State League, at varying times, included teams in Anderson, Florence, Greenville, Greenwood, Rock Hill, Spartanburg, and Sumter. The Class A South Atlantic League had teams in Charleston, Columbia, and Greenville. Total attendance at games for these South Carolina teams fell from a high of 811,268 in 1947 to 430,916 in 1951.

The Tri-State League began operation in 1946 with teams from Anderson and Spartanburg, South Carolina; Asheville, Charlotte, and Shelby, North Carolina, and Knoxville, Tennessee. The Rock Hill Chiefs joined the league the following year and would remain members until the league's demise in 1955. Unlike some league members, Rock Hill was an independent, community-owned franchise unaffiliated with any major league team. The team was haunted by financial difficulties throughout its nine-year existence. The league itself, like many others of its kind, was plagued off and on by financial concerns, adding and dropping teams as conditions required.

Through the late 1940s, there was no thought of adding African American players to any team's roster. As integration spread slowly in the early 1950s and attendance declined, however, pressures began to be felt throughout the Southern leagues to add black players.

In 1951, the first crack appeared in the foundation of segregated baseball in the Carolinas. In August, the Danville Leafs of the Carolina League signed twenty-year-old outfielder Percy Miller, Jr., a three-sport star at the city's all-black high school. Miller's first opponent was the Durham (North Carolina) Bulls. Ace Parker, the Bulls manager, said, "I think it is all right to play Negroes. I played with them in professional football and once the game is underway you don't realize that you have them on your team." Miller batted only .184 in 39 at-bats and was released at the end of the season.[2]

Later that same month, the Granite Falls (North Carolina) Graniteers, in their first and only year as members of the Class D Western Carolina League, recruited three African American players, becoming the first minor league team in North Carolina to integrate. For "The Rocks," as they were affectionately known—soon to be owners of the worst record in professional baseball history (14-96)—it was an act of financial desperation. Russell Shuford, Christopher Rankin, and Eugene Abernathy played their first game for the Rocks on August 25. Two more African Americans were added the next day and all five would play the final week of the season. In one of those odd footnotes to history, however, the Rocks' official scorer had lost interest in the team and had stopped reporting the games to the Howe News Bureau in Atlanta. This meant that, as far as professional baseball was concerned, the Rocks and their players no longer existed. In the statistics-bound world of organized baseball, this first-time integration of an all-white team in the Carolinas never happened. It would be up to Rock Hill to make it "official" the following year.[3]

In early spring 1952, rumblings began to be heard in the Tri-State League that the time was ripe for integration. League owners and general managers began to wonder if recruiting black players might not be the answer to the problem of plummeting attendance. In early April, the Asheville (North Carolina) Tourists fired the opening salvo in what was to be a bitter league war over integration when they announced they were thinking of signing Rufus Hatten—an African American resident of the city who had gone to spring training in Vero Beach with the Dodgers, parent club of the Tourists—as a catcher. Tourists manager Bill Hart said he would play Hatten in several exhibition games before the official beginning of the season. Reaction to the announcement was swift and adamant: two unidentified teams (reported to be from South Carolina) threatened to drop out of the league if Hatten played. The threat was sufficient to cause the Tourists to abandon their plans to use Hatten.[4]

The following month, Phil Howser, general manager of the Charlotte (North Carolina) Hornets, announced that they were giving a try-out to Russell Turner, a twenty-one-year-old pitcher at the city's all-black Johnson C. Smith University. On May 3, Turner pitched batting practice and stepped into the cage himself. The Hornets, members of the Washington Senators organization, were in the best position to be the first Carolinas-based team to officially break the color barrier. Charlotte was the largest city in the league and the Senators were making moves to sign black players. In fact, the Senators had signed African American players for their Erie, Pennsylvania, and Danville, Virginia, minor league clubs the year before. In an interview with *The Sporting News*, general manager Howser indicated that attendance problems were a factor in his decision to scout Turner. It would, in the words of *The Sporting News*, "give stubborn turnstiles a shot of oil." Once again, probably due more to pressure from other league members than to the young player's abilities, plans to sign Turner never came to fruition.[5]

The long, hot summer of 1952 was a dismal one financially for the Tri-State League. Attendance continued to decline as it had since 1949 and many of the teams were in serious financial trouble. The Rock

Hill Chiefs were especially strapped for cash. Not only did they not have a parent major league club from whom to draw players and financial help, but Rock Hill was one of the smaller towns in the league and the team never drew huge numbers to its games. By the end of 1952 attendance had fallen to slightly over 52,000, a drop of nearly 20,000 from the previous year.[6]

The Chiefs ownership had a crucial decision to make. They could continue to drift along as they had in the past or they could make a bold move in an attempt to attract more fan interest. Seeing what was happening to other teams when they signed black players, the Chiefs opted for boldness. Early on August 26, the Chiefs announced that they had signed David Mobley, a twenty-six-year-old resident of nearby Lancaster, South Carolina, to play outfield for that evening's game. Mobley had secretly worked out with the Chiefs several times, and had even sat in the dugout during the previous night's game. Word of his signing set off a firestorm of protest that threatened to destroy the Tri-State League.

The 5-foot-8, 175-pound outfielder was a former .318 hitter for the Birmingham Black Barons of the Negro American League. An Army veteran and participant in the Battle of the Bulge, he had played with the mixed-race Pacific Coast All-Star Service team and with the 39th Signal Corps team in France. He had recently been playing with the semipro Lancaster Tigers. The previous fall he had played an exhibition game in Charlotte against Jackie Robinson, Willie Mays, Luke Easter, and the Jackie Robinson All Stars. He was a popular player well-known to area fans for his fine fielding and power hitting.[7]

Mobley had experience playing second and third base, catching, and pitching in addition to his outfield duties. Chiefs' manager Leon Culberson assessed Mobley as someone who "can run well, hit the ball good, and has a fair arm." He planned to start Mobley in left field and to have him lead off.[8]

Signing Mobley seemed not to be a problem with his white teammates. This acceptance was probably a simple recognition of the reality of the changing demographics of baseball. Said manager Culberson of his squad, "Our players realize that if they are to play in higher class baseball leagues they will probably be playing on clubs which have Negro players."[9] It helped that Mobley was a familiar figure to both black and white fans and his future teammates. Reaction from the Knoxville (Tennessee) Smokies, Rock Hill's opponent for that evening's game, was similar. Smokies' manager Fred Gerkin made it clear that he and his players "had absolutely no objection to Mobley playing."[10]

Reaction from the Tri-State League board of directors and from officials of the other three South Carolina teams was not so generous. League president Bobby Hipps was besieged with phone calls. A major-

ity of the league's board of directors expressed opposition to Rock Hill's move and the Spartanburg Peaches threatened to leave the league immediately if Mobley played. South Carolina's two other teams, the Anderson Rebels and the Greenville Spinners, also indicated they would bolt. Although Hipps later said he had no personal opposition to the Chiefs' use of Mobley and that "the constitution of the league has nothing against it," he did contact Chiefs' president, Earl Sherer, and asked the team not to play Mobley.[11]

Hipps claimed to have made no demands of the Chiefs. "I am the moderator of the Tri-State League," he said two days later. "When I suggested to the Rock Hill directors and President Earl Sherer to delay the insertion of Mobley into the lineup on Tuesday night, it was because I had been asked to do so." He went on to explain his actions as being due to fear that the league would be torn apart. "There is much to consider in playing a Negro in this league. Some towns favor it, others don't. It is of the utmost importance that we have harmony for the betterment of the entire organization."[12]

Whether "demand" or "request," the Chiefs' management initially caved in to the pressure. Mobley was in the clubhouse, but took off his uniform when he was informed he would not play. Many area residents came to the game expecting to see Mobley play and expressed anger when they were told he wouldn't. Some even left. Seeing that their plans to play Mobley had resulted in a considerable increase in the gate (781 eventually purchased tickets, an increase of 502 from the previous game), the Chiefs' directors hurriedly met and reversed themselves. "We want to get you in the game, people want to see you, they're hollering for you to come into the game," the player was told. Mobley responded that he was ready when they were. He quickly dressed and was sent in to play left field in the fifth inning.[13]

Crowd reaction was very positive. "Apparently the great majority of fans at the game favored letting him play," the local newspaper reported. Mobley received a big round of applause when he came onto the field. "I had my crowd," Mobley said later. According to press accounts, "a considerable part" of those attending were African Americans. Many whites, too, expressed their support.[14]

The young player showed grace and courage in the face of such pressure. He had one fielding opportunity, a grounder, in the five innings he played and came to bat twice, going one for two. In his first at-bat in the bottom of the sixth, the left-hander attempted a drag bunt, but met the ball too hard and was thrown out in a close play at first. He opened the eighth with a sharp single to center, but was eliminated in a double play. The Chiefs ended up losing to Knoxville, 5-4.

After the game, Mobley said he had not been bothered by the on-again, off-again events of the day. "I wasn't nervous," he told a reporter. "I just wanted a chance to get into the ball game." When asked how it felt to get his first hit, Mobley responded, "I sure was happy then. I really felt like playing. If I had got another [at] bat I believe I would have got another hit." Reflecting on the game years later, he recalled being bothered a little while he waited in the clubhouse, but "it all went away and I got to feeling good. When I did go in, I was ready."[15]

A large contingent of supporters waited for Mobley at game's end. "Everybody was pulling for me when the game was over with. I had my people there. It was so exciting I didn't know what to do. It was really something."[16]

Manager Culberson had every intention of starting Mobley in the following evening's game against the Greenville Spinners, whose players had voted to take the field against Rock Hill. Said Culberson, "He will be my leftfielder."[17] This was not to be.

Bobby Hipps called Earl Sherer several times the day after the Knoxville game, asking the Chiefs' president not to play Mobley again until the league met to discuss the issue. In spite of the positive crowd response and the increased attendance at the previous night's game, Sherer bowed to league pressure. Shortly before the Greenville game, the Chiefs released an official announcement stating that Mobley would not be playing. "In compliance with the second request of Robert E. Hipps, president of the Tri-State League, the Rock Hill Chiefs have decided to remove David Mobley from their lineup. President Hipps said he made his request not to use Mobley after hearing sentiments of the Tri-State Clubs." A number of black fans left the game when word spread that Mobley would not be playing.[18]

Hipps was being somewhat disingenuous when he asked Rock Hill to wait until the league met to discuss and vote on the matter of integration. He had no plans to call a special meeting of the board of directors and the next regularly scheduled meeting of the league was in October, long after the end of the season. As a result, Mobley remained on the team roster through spring training the following year, but would never play another regular season game with the Chiefs.

Some of the North Carolina clubs were angered over the pressure that was put on Rock Hill not to play Mobley. Phil Howser, general manager of the Charlotte Hornets, was particularly vocal in his support of the Chiefs. "If Greenville and Spartanburg don't approve of Negroes playing, they better get out of the league because we expect to have one next year in Charlotte," he said two days after the event. "This is America," he continued. "I see no reason why we can't play Negroes if they're good enough. Baseball is entertainment and we don't object to applauding Negro entertainers—

why be different about baseball."[19]

Howser, however, indirectly seemed to criticize the Chiefs for their handling of the affair. "There is no point of playing a Negro for the novelty. This is unfair to his race and to the fans. But if a good one is available and he can make the ball club, there is nothing in the league rules that can keep him off," he told one reporter.[20]

Bob Quincy, sports columnist for the Charlotte News, was even harsher in his criticism of the Chiefs' methods. In a column entitled, THE DAVE MOBLEY CAPER: CHIEFS UNLIMBERED A HATCHET—NOW LEAGUE BLEEDS, he concluded that "Rock Hill, if they thought a Negro would be beneficial to the club or the box office, made the mistake of waiting too late in the season to make the move. It actually took the appearance of nothing more than a carnival stunt, although it may have been a sincere move to bolster the roster." He also criticized the league's "clumsy handling of the situation," concluding that it "didn't help the league or racial relations."[21]

Quincy did give the Chiefs some credit for their handling of the affair. "But Rock Hill turned up the hole card in the long run," he wrote. "There has been a galloping rumor of long standing that South Carolina had blue laws which prevented the use of Negroes in white athletic contests. The Chiefs broke down that bruit with one hasty swing of their hatchet. But it has left the Tri-State in something of a bloody mess."[22]

Rock Hill finished the season in last place. Although it did not have the lowest attendance in the league—that honor would belong to the Knoxville Smokies and the Asheville Tourists—Rock Hill's suffered that dramatic 20,000 drop. In spite of this, Rock Hill had every intention of fielding a team in 1953. According to club president Earl Sherer, "All told we are in better shape now than we were at the end of the 1951 season. If we can get a working agreement with a big league club [this was not to be] and keep interest alive until next year, I believe we can keep professional baseball in Rock Hill."[23] Petty revenge, however, almost prevented them from doing so.

Greenville was the most financially troubled organization in the Tri-State League. In mid-December, the Spinners announced they might have to fold "unless a fairy godfather with a pocket of cash enters the scene."[24] If a club left the eight-member league, another team would have to be dropped in order to make a balanced schedule possible.

Adding to the financial difficulties was the tension lingering over Rock Hill's attempt to integrate the league. Spartanburg let it be known it was still opposed to African American players. Charlotte, in turn, informed the league that it planned to sign at least one black player for 1953. Undoubtedly, the other South Carolina teams blamed Rock Hill for raising this issue.

The Tri-State League by-laws had no written policy or procedure for removing clubs should the league contract. However, there was an understanding that teams would be dropped on the basis of seniority. Under this procedure, the Gastonia (North Carolina) Rockets, which had joined the league in 1952, would be dropped if Greenville folded.

In early January 1953, Tri-State League president Bobby Hipps called a special meeting in Greenville to address the fate of the Spinners. Hipps informed Chiefs' president Earl Sherer that Sherer would not have to make the 100-mile trip to Greenville since "the session would be devoted to the Greenville problem entirely."[25] Much to his later regret, Sherer followed Hipps' suggestion and did not attend.

Two days after the conclusion of the meeting, an "extremely reliable source" contacted Chiefs' officials to inform them that "a move is under way to oust the club from the Tri-State League if Greenville is unable to field a team in 1953." The team's directors were enraged by Hipps' deception. "It would be to Hipps' advantage to keep any such move quiet until the last minute," an anonymous club official complained to the local newspaper. Hipps, of course, denied that any such discussion took place. "Nothing of the kind is in the air. The men who run the Rock Hill club are my loyal friends." He did admit that the league directors would vote to eliminate a team if Greenville left and that "there is nothing in the constitution governing such procedure and that seniority apparently would not necessarily be the determining factor."[26]

Why was Rock Hill under the gun? It was partly because Gastonia had drawn well in its first year of existence. In fact, it had the second highest attendance in the league behind the Charlotte Hornets, attracting 42,000 more fans than the Chiefs. Spartanburg, in particular, seemed anxious to retain the Rockets because of the team's apparent "drawing power."[27]

But attendance was not the sole reason Rock Hill was being marked for removal. Although no one would say so openly, there was considerable anger at Rock Hill, especially among the South Carolina clubs, for the Chiefs' confronting the race issue. As one sports columnist wrote, "Despite President Hipps' protestations to the contrary it seems apparent to this department that there is something rotten in Denmark, or more correctly, in the Tri-State League province." Although the reporter saw "no reason to distrust Hipps" for what was happening, Hipps was reminded that, as he himself said, "the Rock Hill owners are his loyal friends. Rock Hill has always voted to keep Hipps in as president when certain other cities around the circuit were out to cut the Asheville man's throat."[28]

Chiefs' officials responded to this crisis by calling for a public demonstration of the community's support for the team. According to one insider, "we want to continue but the people of the community must signify their desire for the Chiefs to continue."[29] An open forum to discuss the fate of the Chiefs was scheduled for the evening of January 8. At the same time, the Chiefs announced they had hired a new business manager, Fred Hartman from Morristown, Tennessee, and a new player-manager, Jimmy Burns. The team also "obtained a promise of badly needed player reinforcements from the Boston Red Sox and already has signed one Red Sox chattel to a Rock Hill contract."[30]

Over sixty people attended the Thursday evening meeting. The team said it needed $20,000 to operate in 1953. Those at the meeting pledged $2,000 toward that goal with club directors promising an additional $10,000. It was decided to launch a "citizens campaign" in which local residents would be asked to provide the remaining $8,000 needed. Time was of the essence. Hipps had called another special meeting for the following Sunday, so drive leaders gave themselves just two days to raise the $8,000. By doing so, and doing it quickly, they hoped to demonstrate in a very incontrovertible and concrete way that the Rock Hill community enthusiastically supported the Chiefs.[31]

The so-called "Miracle Drive" more than met its goal. Over $10,000 was pledged by local citizens and businesses and area textile mills. Team representatives Sherer, John T. Roddey, and Darwin Broome headed to the Greenville meeting in a very positive state of mind. Not only could they demonstrate community support for the Chiefs, they also had the open support of the influential Charlotte Hornets.

The January 11 meeting left the Chiefs' fate in limbo. Although Greenville announced formally that it was folding, the league dithered over whether to try to find a replacement or reduce the league to six teams. League officials called for a third special meeting to be held in Spartanburg on Sunday, January 19. Rock Hill officials left Greenville feeling optimistic. "The Club representatives handled themselves very well and inspired confidence that the Chiefs will be sounder financially and stronger afield than last year," reported one observer.[32]

The week between meetings turned out to be the turning point for the Chiefs. Not only did the fund drive exceed its $20,000 goal, but the club received unofficial word that the Knoxville Smokies were most likely to be dropped. There were three reasons for this apparent shift in feeling. First, according to one reporter, "Rock Hill's feat of putting up the necessary cash in so short a time has won the city considerable respect around the league."[33] Second, because Knoxville was the most distant of the league members, "it would be the logical team to sit out the 1953 season."[34] Finally, the New York Giants announced that they would no longer be affiliated with the Knoxville club, leaving the Smokies in a very precarious financial situation.[35]

No decision was made at the third special meeting, on January 24. The league hoped to continue with eight members by finding backers to revive the Greenville Spinners and to support the Knoxville Smokies. The issue became moot on January 30 when the Knoxville city council announced it was closing down the Smokies' stadium to build a new sports complex on the site. Since Knoxville would suspend play for the year it would take to build a new stadium, the league dropped its plans to find new backers for Greenville and decided to reduce membership to six clubs.[36] The Rock Hill Chiefs had overcome attempts to expel them. The team would remain a member of the Tri-State League until the league folded at the end of the 1955 season.

As for David Mobley, his baseball career did not end on the evening of August 26, 1952. Although he remained on the Chiefs' roster, he returned home to Lancaster where he resumed playing for the semipro Tigers. He was to cross paths with the Chiefs again when his Tigers played Rock Hill in an exhibition game on April 3, 1953. He lined into a triple play as the Chiefs won the contest, 3-1.[37] On April 7, Mobley was officially cut from the Chiefs and sent to Knoxville to play for the Smokies of the Class D Mountain States League (not the team of the same name that played in the Tri-State League).[38]

Mobley was not the only African American player in the Mountain States League. Brothers Jim and Leander Tugerson were Mobley's teammates, and the Maryville-Alcoa (Tennessee) Twins also had three African American players. With the eleven Cuban players and Cuban manager on the Morristown (Tennessee) Red Sox roster, the Mountain States League, as one reporter put it, was "truly a Pan-American league."[39]

Mobley was the starting left fielder for the Smokies during the early part of the season. In one game he hit a single, a triple, and a homer, putting an end to the razzing coming from the opposition bench. After a couple of months, however, he decided to return to Lancaster, where he resumed his very successful semipro career, playing well into his forties.[40]

In retrospect, was Rock Hill's signing of David Mobley a "carnival stunt" done simply for the "novelty?" Or was it "a sincere move" and "a noble experiment?" In truth, it was probably both. Clearly, the team acquired Mobley in a late-season attempt to improve attendance. And his appearance proved that calculation to be correct, at least in the short run. But the team was also willing to weather the storm it must have known was coming. Spartanburg, at least, was dead serious about leaving the league if Mobley continued to play, and the other South Carolina teams probably would have followed suit in a show of solidarity. Such an event would have destroyed the Tri-State League.

But even though he got to play only five innings, Mobley demonstrated the maturity and talent to be successful in the Tri-State League. When asked his assessment of Mobley's skills, Knoxville manager Fred Gerken commented on his hitting ability and speed. And manager Culberson publicly stated his desire to start Mobley in the next game. If the Chiefs were using Mobley as a "novelty," they also recognized that he could contribute to the team over the long run.

Rock Hill must be given credit for attempting what other teams only talked about. For all its blustering about acquiring "qualified" black players, the Charlotte Hornets had not done so. The Chiefs certainly demonstrated some courage by forcing the issue. And the event was more than just symbolic. The Chiefs' acquisition of a black player, no matter how aborted, drew national attention to the continuing problem of successfully integrating Southern teams. Both *The Sporting News* and the Pittsburgh *Courier*, a leading African American newspaper, wrote about the Mobley affair.[41] Because of the Chiefs' actions, integration did proceed in the league the following year when the Hornets signed two black Latin players. For all its clumsiness in the matter, Rock Hill had indeed opened the door to the future.

David Mobley is a true American hero. Through his determination and courage, and his simple desire to play the game he loved, he, along with the other early African American players, forced America to live up to the best of her ideals. It is because of the efforts of individuals like David Mobley—the Jackie Robinson of South Carolina—that baseball became in every sense the *National* Pastime.

Notes:

1. For a thorough discussion of the integration of Southern teams, see Bruce Adelson, *Brushing Back Jim Crow: the Integration of Minor-League Baseball in the American South* (Charlottesville: University Press of Virginia, 1999).

2. Jim L. Sumner, *Separating the Men from the Boys: the First Half-Century of the Carolina League* (Winston-Salem: John F. Blair, Publisher, 1994) 45.

3. Wilt Browning, *The Rocks: the True Story of the Worst Team in Baseball History* (Asheboro: Down Home Press, 1992) 108-11.

4. Red Miller, "Tourists Delayed But Will Arrive in City Tonight," *Asheville Citizen* 11 April 1952: 25; "Tourists Marion in Exhibition Tonight," *Asheville Citizen* 12 April 1952: 9.

5. Eddie Allen, "Golden Bull Hurler May Join Stingers," *Charlotte Observer* 4 May 1952: 21-B; Bob Quincy, "Hornets on Market for Negro Player," *Sporting News* 14 May 1952: 41.

6. Connie Morton, "Connie's Corner," *Herald* [Rock Hill] 25 August 1952: 8.

7. David Mobley, personal interview, 21 April 2000.

8. Connie Morton, "Rock Hill Chiefs Sign Lancaster Negro; Will Play in Outfield Tonight at Stadium," *Herald* [Rock Hill] 26 August 1952: 1.

9. Morton, "Chiefs Sign Lancaster Negro" 1.

10. "Mobley Plays as Chiefs Ignore Hipps' Request," *Herald* [Rock Hill] 27 August 1952: 9.

11. Connie Morton, "Negro Player Stirs Big Tri-State Loop Rumpus," *Herald* [Rock Hill] 28 August 1952: 1; Bob Quincy, "The Dave Mobley Caper: Chiefs Unlimbered a Hatchet - Now League Bleeds," *Charlotte News* 28 August 1952: 12-B.

12. Quincy, "Mobley Caper" 12-B.

13. Mobley, interview.

14. Connie Morton, "Chiefs Bow; Play Greenville in Pair Tonight," *Herald* [Rock Hill] 27 August 1952: 9; Mobley, interview.

15. "Mobley Plays" 9; Mobley, interview.

16. Mobley, interview.

17. "Mobley Plays" 9.

18. Morton, "Negro Player" 1.

19. Morton, "Negro Player" 1.

20. Quincy, "Mobley Caper" 12-B.

21. Quincy, "Mobley Caper" 12-B.

22. Quincy, "Mobley Caper" 13-B.

23. Connie Morton, "Connie's Corner," *Herald* [Rock Hill] 27 September 1952: 7.

24. Bob Quincy, "Howard Explains the Educational Values of Traveling Often," *Charlotte News* 15 December 1952: 4-B.

25. George McClelland, "Rock Hill Chiefs May Be Forced Out of League If Greenville Leaves Tri-State, Report Says," *Herald* [Rock Hill] 6 January 1953: 1.

26. McClelland, "Forced Out" 1.

27. McClelland, "Forced Out" 1.

28. George McClelland, "Sports...By George," *Herald* [Rock Hill] 6 January 1953: 8.

29. "Fate of Chiefs Rests on Open Meet Tonight," *Herald* [Rock Hill] 7 January 1953: 1.

30. "Fate of Chiefs" 1.

31. "RH Citizens Open Two-Day Drive to Retain Ball Club," *Herald* [Rock Hill] 9 January 1953: 1.

32. George McClelland, "RH Chiefs' Status Still Unchanged After Loop Meet," *Herald* [Rock Hill] 12 January 1953: 1.

33. George McClelland, "Sports...By George," *Herald* [Rock Hill] 16 January 1953: 8.

34. Irwin Cobb, "Hipps Sees 6-Club Tri-State Loop for '53," *Spartanburg Herald* 18 January 1953: B1.

35. "Giants Pull Out of Knoxville; Greenville Works to Save Club," *Spartanburg Herald* 21 January 1953: 8.

36. "Tri-State Down to Six Clubs," *Herald* [Rock Hill] 31 January 1953: 7.

37. "Chiefs Hold Nine Inning Intra-Squad Game," *Herald* [Rock Hill] 28 March 1953: 7; "Chiefs Aim for Fourth in Row Against Fliers," *Herald* [Rock Hill] 4 April 1953: 7.

38. "Chiefs Travel to Reidsville for Exhibition with Luckies," *Herald* [Rock Hill] 7 April 1953: 9.

39. "Mt. States Teams Set to Open," *Knoxville News-Sentinal* 25 April 1953: 4.

40. Mobley, interview.

41. Bob Quincy, "First Tri-State Negro Player Released in Harmony Move," *Sporting News* 3 September 1952: 35; Alex Rivera, "Dixie Fans Cheer Player as Owners Force Withdrawal," *Pittsburgh Courier* 6 September 1952: 14.

Pitcher hurt warming up

PHILADELPHIA, Oct. 2 (AP)—Bill Posedel, pitcher for the Dodgers, received a broken jaw today while warming up during a game with the Phillies. He was in the bullpen with catcher Gilly Campbell. After he had delivered a pitch something in the game attracted his attention. As he turned to look, Campbell's return throw struck him in the jaw. He was taken to Temple University Hospital.

—Charlie Bevis

A Home Run King Without a Headstone

David Stevens

Chicago's own predecessor to Ruth, Maris, and McGwire is in a pauper's grave two miles from Wrigley Field

In 1999, while sports fans worldwide focused on the final days of the thrilling Sammy Sosa–Mark McGwire home run race, it was discovered that the longtime Chicago Cubs star who held the single-season home run record for the thirty-five years prior to Babe Ruth is in an unmarked, pauper's grave in renowned Rosehill Cemetery on Chicago's North side.

Ned Williamson's major league home run record (27, set in 1884) endured longer than any but Roger Maris's 61. Williamson lived only nine more years after setting the record, dying at age thirty-six. Cubs owner Albert Spalding's mistreatment of Williamson contributed to the popular shortstop's demise, and was a rallying point in the most dramatic revolt by athletes in history—the Brotherhood Rebellion that led to most of the best National League players bolting their clubs to form the Players' League.

Williamson rests in the same cemetery as Aaron Montgomery Ward, founder of Chicago-based Montgomery Ward's, which signed Sammy Sosa as an endorser before going out of business at the end of 2000. Ironically, Aaron Ward's distant cousin, shortstop–attorney John Montgomery Ward, led that players' revolt as president of sports' first union. John Ward was a close friend of Williamson's.

David Stevens *wrote* Baseball's Radical for All Seasons: A Biography of John Montgomery Ward. *He is pretending to write a biography of Cap Anson.*

Ned Williamson

Some baseball historians consider Williamson's record a fluke, since it was aided by some very friendly confines. After Williamson set an all-time record for doubles (49) in 1883, the ground rules for the short right field fence (196 feet) at Chicago's Lake Front Park were changed, making balls hit over it home runs in 1884, instead of doubles, as in the park's first two years. Wisely, the righthanded Williamson altered his swing to take full advantage of the new ground rule. In 1885, the Cubs (then known as the White Stockings) moved to West Side Park, and the temporary home run boom ended.

Ned (also called Ed) Williamson was a superb all-around athlete, starring on five Chicago pennant winners (including two world champions), and leading the league in fielding five times.

But Williamson was best-known for his kind heart, in an era when players beat up umpires, and even drank on the field. In the 1880s, there were some blacks in the minor leagues, and Williamson empathized with them, citing spikes-high slides by racist white opponents as injuring blacks. He zeroed in on the hypocrisy of blacks in the majors being mistreated team mascots: "haughty Caucasians say it's OK to have darkies carry water, but not in the lineup." John Montgomery Ward fought to bring blacks to the majors, and through the players' union to make baseball a cleaner game for fans. Williamson was one of the first to join the union, founded in 1885.

The plot heard around the world—In 1888, three years after baseball was unionized, sporting goods magnate Spalding set out to spread baseball throughout the world by taking the White Stockings and an all-star team managed by Ward on an Australian Tour that became global. Columbia law graduate Ward and the articulate Williamson buried their heads in books, while their unmarried teammates partied.

In an exhibition game in Paris, Williamson fell in terrible pain attempting a steal on a rocky makeshift field beneath the Eiffel Tower. The contest came to a dead stop. According to longtime White Stockings manager, the great first baseman Cap Anson, he "tore his knee cap on the sharp sand and gravel…he was still confined to his room in London when we sailed for home." The injury was improperly treated by a local physician. Williamson was forced to pay his own medical bills. Spalding refused to pay the union member anything, except $150—his fare home.

By the time Williamson finally returned to the U.S., everything in baseball was about to turn upside down. While union president Ward was incommunicado on the Pacific, the owners had passed a plan that slashed salaries to a $2,500 maximum, and even required rookies to sweep ballparks. The owners refused to meet with the union until after the 1889 season.

Midway throught 1889, Williamson ventured a comeback. While he limped, his comrades roared. In secret, they voted to launch their own league, with their own savings. Four days after the 1889 World Series, Ward announced the formation of the Players' League. The mistreatment of Williamason was a graphic example of the owners' callousness, and was a rallying point for the baseball Brotherhood.

That offseason, the players, bolstered by additional investors, built new stadiums. The Players' League outdrew the other leagues in 1890, and played a cleaner, more exciting game, but the National League owners' all-out war quickly wiped out the rebel effort. Ward racked up his league's demise to: "Treachery, Stupidity, and Greed."

Williamson hit only .195 in the Players' League. He wired Spalding, pleading to return to Chicago and the National League. But Williamson never played again and was broken in spirit. He opened a Chicago saloon, encouraging his tendency to drink too much. Friends said the hard-working Williamson put too much of himself into his business. Anson lauded him as "good natured and good hearted."

A bloated, almost unrecognizable Ed Williamson died of kidney failure three years later, on March 3, 1894—the thirty-fourth birthday of John Ward. He had blown up from his rookie weight of about 170 to almost 300 pounds. Death came to him at the Hot Springs, Arkansas resort where he had rehabbed his knee to prepare for the PL. Today he lies in Rosehill's pauper's row, along Peterson Avenue near Ravenswood Avenue, on the other side of the cemetery from the mausoleum of his retailing Chicago contemporaries Aaron Montgomery Ward and Richard Sears. More recently, Jack Brickhouse, longtime Cubs announcer was laid to rest in Rosehill.

In 1887, Williamson won $200 and a diamond locket for the second longest baseball throw to that time: 401 feet. Ed's double-play partner, second baseman Fred Pfeffer, recalled that Williamson made the greatest play he ever saw. He leaped straight up, making a barehand stab fully extended. Then before Williamson hit the ground, he threw out a runner at home. In a poll of twelve baseball greats, taken the year Williamson died, he was the most frequent choice for the best player of all time. In 1900, Anson wrote, "Ed was in my opinion, the greatest all around player the country ever saw."

The Beginning and End of Nicollet Park

Stew Thornley

For sixty seasons, the Minneapolis Millers made their home at a place described by former Minneapolis *Tribune* writer Dave Mona as "soggy, foul, rotten, and thoroughly wonderful Nicollet Park." One of the most revered minor league ballparks, Nicollet Park was home to a pennant winner in its first season and its last.

Alpha
Friday, June 19, 1896

In May, 1896 the Minneapolis Millers of the Western League were given thirty days' notice to find a new home. The property at First Avenue North and Sixth Street, which included Athletic Park, had been sold and the Millers, tenants since 1889, evicted.

The final game at Athletic Park was played May 23. The Millers then left on an eastern road trip, not knowing where their new home would be when they returned.

Four sites were under consideration. A location along Kenwood Boulevard, across Hennepin Avenue from Loring Park, was the favorite, but the city council refused to vacate certain streets in the Kenwood area. In late May, after the streetcar company announced it could better service a park near Lake Street, a decision was made to locate the field at 31st Street and Nicollet Avenue, within a block bounded on the north by Lake Street. The ground was quickly graded; bleachers, grandstands, and fences hastily erected, and within three weeks the field was ready for baseball.

All that remained for the wooden structure was a name. Three Minneapolis newspapers invited readers to submit suggestions. From that list a panel of writers selected the name Wright Field, in honor of Harry Wright, one of the game's founding fathers. The new moniker did not receive a warm reception, though, and for the next year the stadium was referred to in the papers as the "new ball park." It wasn't until 1897 that the name Nicollet Park was first used.

Whatever the name, the new grounds opened Friday, June 19, 1896 (on the fiftieth anniversary of what is regarded as the first official baseball game ever played—at the Elysian Fields in Hoboken, New Jersey). The Millers opened the park with a come-from-behind, 13-6 win over the Milwaukee Brewers. Varney Anderson held the Brewers to eight hits, while Charley Frank hit the game's only home run, a two-run shot over the rightfield fence in the sixth inning.

In their new home, the Millers went on to win their first Western League pennant in 1896. Nicollet Park remained the home for Minneapolis teams in the Western League, American League, Western Association, American Association, and Northern League through 1955.

Omega
Wednesday night, September 28, 1955

Although the playing area at Nicollet Park seemed spacious when it opened in 1896—especially in contrast to tiny Athletic Park—soon enough the ballpark at the corner of 31st Street and Nicollet Avenue acquired its own reputation as a bandbox.

Stew Thornley *is the author of* On to Nicollet: The Glory and Fame of the Minneapolis Millers, *which won a SABR-Macmillan Baseball Research Award in 1988. He is also the author of a more recent book on the Polo Grounds. In researching baseball, Stew has attended games across the United States, including Puerto Rico, as well as in Japan and Cuba.*

Millers	ab	r	h	po	a	e
Connors 2b	4	2	1	0	2	1
Lally lf	4	1	0	2	0	0
Wilmot cf	5	1	1	1	1	2
Werden 1b	6	3	2	12	0	0
Frank rf	5	3	3	2	0	0
Schriver c	5	3	1	5	0	0
Kuehne 3b	5	0	3	2	2	1
Ball ss	4	0	2	3	6	2
Anderson p	4	0	1	0	1	0
	42	13	14	27	12	6

Brewers	ab	r	h	po	a	e
Nicol cf	6	2	0	0	1	1
Weaver lf	4	2	2	2	1	1
Hartman 3b	5	1	2	2	4	3
Twitchell 1b	4	1	0	15	0	0
Baker rf	4	0	1	1	0	0
Merzenz ss	4	0	1	0	2	2
Taylor 2b	4	0	0	2	3	1
Speer c	4	0	1	5	0	0
Clausen p	4	0	1	0	2	1
	39	6	8	27	13	9

Minneapolis	100	003	540	3	14	6
Milwaukee	203	000	100	6	8	9

Earned runs-Minneapolis 5, Milwaukee 1. S-Lally, Wilmot. HR-Frank. SB-Connors, Lally 2, Kuehne, Anderson. DP-Hartman-Taylor-Twitchell. BB-By Clausen 4. SO-By Clausen 4, by Anderson 1. HBP-By Anderson (Weaver). First base on errors-Minneapolis 8, Milwaukee 4. Time-Two hours. A-3,500.

Sluggers, particularly lefthanded swingers, took advantage of the short distance, only 279 feet, down the rightfield line. In 1933, the Millers' Joe Hauser set a professional single-season record with 69 home runs, 50 of them hit at Nicollet Park.

In 1955, the final season for Nicollet Park, the Millers set a league record with 241 home runs and won the regular-season American Association pennant. In the Association playoffs, the Millers beat the Denver Bears and Omaha Cardinals in four-game sweeps to advance to the Junior World Series, against the Rochester Red Wings.

The Red Wings and Millers split the first six games of the series, bringing it all down to the seventh game, in what would also be the end for Nicollet Park. While the Millers had relied on a potent offense throughout the year, they were just as dependent on their ace pitcher, Al Worthington, who had won 19 games during the regular season. He was even more valuable in the playoffs. Worthington had appeared in 10 of the Millers' first 14 playoff games, winning five without a loss. He had been the winning pitcher in relief the night before the finale and had a 3-0 win-loss record in the Junior Series up to that point. Minneapolis manager Bill Rigney made it clear he wouldn't hesitate to call on Worthington in the seventh game if he needed relief help. In the meantime, Rigney had a more pressing decision—deciding on a starting pitcher. The tough series with Rochester had depleted the pitching ranks to the point that Rigney resorted to a strange method for determining the Game 7 starter. According to Tom Briere, a reporter for the Minneapolis *Tribune* and the official scorer at Nicollet Park, Rigney rolled a ball into the middle of the locker room before the final game and asked, "Who wants it?" The ball was snapped up by

Bud Byerly, normally a reliever, who said, "I thought I should be the guy because I was the most rested."

"One thing about Byerly," reported Rigney, "was that he wouldn't walk anyone on the bases."

Rigney was right in that prediction, although Byerly had other problems. The first batter of the game, Howie Phillips of the Red Wings, connected on a 2-1 pitch for a home run, a fitting start to Nicollet Park's final game. Singles by Jackie Brandt and Allie Clark, sandwiched around a groundout by Joe Cunningham, produced another run. An error and hit batsman helped Rochester load the bases with two out and force Byerly from the mound. He had lasted only two-thirds of an inning before giving way to Floyd Melliere, who retired Ebba St. Claire on a grounder to end the threat and then quieted the Red Wings in the ensuing innings.

However, Rochester had a 2-0 lead that it held through the early innings behind the pitching of Cot Deal, who had already won two games in the series. Deal retired the first two batters in the fourth before Monte Irvin beat out an infield single and went to third on a double by Rance Pless. Bob Lennon, who had tied with George Wilson for the team lead with 31 home runs during the regular season, sent an 0-2 fastball over the fence in right to put the Millers ahead, 3-2. Carl Sawatski followed Lennon's blast with one of his own, a line-drive home run to make the score 4-2. Irvin increased the lead to 5-2 with a long home run in the sixth.

The Red Wings finally got to Melliere in the seventh, scoring two runs on a walk, double, and throwing error. With the Millers' lead cut to a run, Rigney waited no longer. He signaled to the bullpen for a weary Worthington, who trudged in and closed out the in-

Nicollet's Last Game
Wednesday night, September 28, 1955

Rochester Red Wings (International League) vs. Minneapolis Millers (American Association)
Game 7—1955 Junior World Series
Wednesday night, September 28, 1955

Red Wings	ab	r	h	rbi	po	a	e
Phillips 2b	5	2	3	2	2	2	0
Brandt cf	5	1	2	0	3	0	0
Cunningham 1b	4	0	0	0	9	1	0
Clark lf	2	0	2	1	1	0	0
Burgess rf	2	0	0	0	2	0	0
Benson ss	4	0	0	0	0	1	0
Van Noy rf-lf	4	0	0	0	2	0	0
Jok 3b	2	1	0	0	0	3	0
St. Claire c	3	0	0	0	4	1	0
Deal p	3	0	0	0	1	0	0
Markell p	0	0	0	0	0	0	0
Wooldridge p	0	0	0	0	0	0	0
a-White	1	0	1	0	0	0	0
	35	4	8	3	24	8	0

Millers	ab	r	h	rbi	po	a	e
Ortiz 2b	4	0	0	0	1	2	0
Bollweg 1b	5	1	3	2	9	4	2
Wilson rf	4	1	0	0	1	1	0
Irvin lf	4	2	2	1	1	0	0
Pless 3b	4	2	2	0	0	1	0
Lennon cf	4	1	3	5	6	0	0
Sawatski c	3	1	2	1	4	0	0
Bressoud ss	4	0	0	0	1	0	0
Byerly p	0	0	0	0	0	0	0
Melliere p	2	0	0	0	3	3	0
Worthington p	2	1	1	0	1	2	0
	36	9	13	9	27	13	2

```
Rochester      200 000 200-   4  8  0
Minneapolis    000 401 40x-   9 13  2
```

LOB-Rochester 7, Minneapolis 6. 2B-Pless 2, Phillips, Lennon. HR-Phillips, Lennon, Sawatski, Irvin, Bollweg. S-Ortiz.

Pitching Summary	IP	H	R	ER	BB	SO
Deal (Loser)	6	8	5	5	0	3
Markell	.2	3	4	4	1	0
Wooldridge	1.1	2	0	0	1	0
Byerly	.2	3	2	2	0	0
Melliere (Winner)	6	2	2	1	2	1
Worthington	2.1	3	0	0	0	3

HBP-By Byerly (Jok). U-Guzzetta (IL), Crawford (AA), Linsalata (IL), Taylor (AA). A-9,927. T-2:20.

ning. The Millers gave Worthington a cushion with four runs in the last of the seventh—two on a home run by Don Bollweg, the last ever hit at Nicollet, and the final two on a double by Lennon.

Worthington retired the Red Wings in order in the eighth and struck out the first two batters in the ninth before giving up a pair of singles. The next batter was Jackie Brandt, who tried to keep the rally going by bunting for a base hit on Worthington's first pitch. However, Worthington charged off the mound, pounced on the bunt, and threw Brandt out to end the game, the Junior World Series, and Nicollet Park.

Worthington later said he had a feeling that the pitch to Brandt would be the final one. "I do remember thinking on the mound, 'You are throwing the last pitch in the ballpark.'" he recalled. "It was somewhat of a sad feeling."

First inning—Rochester: Howie Phillips hit a 2-1 pitch over the rightfield fence for a home run. Jackie Brandt singled to left and took second on Joe Cunningham's ground out to Bollweg. Allie Clark's single to left scored Brandt. Vern Benson reached base on Bollweg's error as Clark stopped at second. The runners held as Jay Van Noy flied to Lennon. Stan Jok was hit by a pitch to load the bases. Floyd Melliere relieved Bud Byerly and retired Ebba St. Claire on a grounder to Ortiz. Rochester 2, Minneapolis 0

Minneapolis: Lou Ortiz grounded to Phillips. Don Bollweg singled to right and went to second when George Wilson grounded out to Cunningham. Monte Irvin struck out.

Second inning—Rochester: Cot Deal tapped back to Melliere. Phillips flied to center. Brandt grounded to Ortiz.

Minneapolis: Rance Pless flied to Brandt. Bob Lennon flied to Clark. Carl Sawatski flied to Brandt.

Third inning—Rochester: Cunningham flied to Lennon. Clark singled to right but was thrown out, Wilson to Bressoud, trying for a double. Benson grounded to Bollweg, Melliere covering.

Minneapolis: Tom Burgess went in to play right field and Van Noy moved to left. Ed Bressoud grounded to Benson. Melliere and Ortiz grounded to Jok.

Fourth inning—Rochester: Van Noy grounded to Bollweg, Melliere covering. Jok grounded to Melliere. St. Claire walked. Deal flied to center.

Minneapolis: Bollweg grounded to Cunningham, Deal covering. Wilson grounded to Phillips. Irvin beat out an infield hit down the third-base line and stopped at third on Pless's double to left. Lennon hit a high 0-2 fast ball over the rightfield fence to give Minneapolis a 3-2 lead. Sawatski followed with a line drive into the rightfield screen to make it 4-2. Bressoud struck out. Minneapolis 4, Rochester 2

Fifth inning—Rochester: Phillips grounded to Pless. Brandt fanned. Cunningham grounded to Bollweg, Melliere covering.

Minneapolis: Melliere struck out. Ortiz flied to Van Noy. Bollweg popped to Cunningham.

Sixth inning—Rochester: Burgess flied to Irvin. Benson popped to Ortiz. Van Noy flied to Lennon.

Minneapolis: Wilson flied to Burgess. Irvin hit a 400-foot home run over the wall in deep right-center. Pless flied to Burgess. Lennon beat out an infield hit in front of the plate and took second on Sawatski's single to right. Bressoud popped to Cunningham. Minneapolis 5, Rochester 2

Seventh inning—Rochester: Jok walked. St. Claire flied to Wilson. Deal grounded to Melliere as Jok moved to second. Phillips doubled to left, scoring Jok. Irvin's throw to second found the bag uncovered as Phillips took third on the throw and scored when

Bollweg finally cornered the ball and then threw wildly to third. Al Worthington relieved and gave up a single to left to Brandt. Cunningham tapped back to Worthington. Minneapolis 5, Rochester 4

Minneapolis: Duke Markell took the mound in place of Deal. Worthington beat out an infield hit to third. Ortiz sacrificed, St. Claire to Phillips. Bollweg homered to right on a 3-2 pitch. Wilson walked. Irvin popped to Phillips. Pless doubled to left, Wilson stopping at third. Floyd Wooldridge relieved Markell. Lennon doubled to right to bring home Wilson and Pless. Sawatski walked. Bressoud struck out. Minneapolis 9, Rochester 4

Eighth inning—Rochester: Burgess struck out. Benson flied to Lennon. Van Noy grounded to Bollweg, Worthington covering.

Minneapolis: Worthington flied to Brandt. Ortiz grounded to Phillips. Bollweg singled to right. Wilson flied to Van Noy.

Ninth inning—Rochester: Jok and St. Claire struck out. Charlie White batted for Wooldridge and singled to left. Phillips moved White to second with a single to center. Worthington fielded Brandt's bunt and threw him out at first to end the game. In the last game played at Nicollet Field, Minneapolis won the contest, 9-4, and captured the Junior World Series, 4 games to 3.

Sources:

"Nicollet Park: A Colorful Page in Baseball History" by Dave Mona, Minneapolis *Tribune,* November 6, 1966.

Alpha—"Wright Field," Minneapolis *Tribune,* June 17, 1896; "A Glorious Tale: Minneapolis Opens the New Park with a Victory," Minneapolis *Tribune,* June 20, 1896, p. 7; "They Tempted Fate: Millers Toy with the Friday and Thirteen Superstitions," Minneapolis *Journal,* June 20, 1896, p. 12.

Omega—Tom Briere's scorebook. Correspondence with Al Worthington, 1984. Conversation with Tom Briere, 1998. September 29, 1995 Minneapolis *Tribune:* "Millers Win Junior World Series Title: 9,927 See Last Game at Nicollet Park" by Leonard Inskip, p. 1; "Miller Home Runs Produce 9-4 Win, First Junior Crown" by Tom Briere, p. S1. September 29, 1955 Minneapolis *Star:* "Melliere Was Real Hero of Millers' Final Victory" by Bob Beebe, "Nicollet's Finest Year Season of Comebacks" by Halsey Hall, and "Old Nicollet Goes Out with Perfect Finish" by Charles Johnson, p. 40; "Nicollet's Last and Finest Hour," p. 60.

Spalding's Tourists in Bristol

Patrick Carroll

On March 15, 1889, the first competitive game was played at the newly completed Gloucester County Cricket Ground at Ashley Down, Bishopston, in the historic English seaport city of Bristol. The contest was not a cricket match but rather an exhibition game between two teams of American professional baseball players. The press coverage given the event—including stories headlined "THE AMERICAN BASE BALL PLAYERS IN BRISTOL," which appeared in two separate journals—indicates that the bemused incomprehension with which many modern Britons react to the American national pastime hasn't altered much in 111 years.

The visit came at the climax of a world tour that had begun in November, 1888 and had taken baseball to Australia, New Zealand, Ceylon, Egypt, and continental Europe. The tour was the brainchild of Albert Goodwill Spalding and its purposes were a typical mixture of that Gilded Age archetype's passionate missionary zeal for the game, go-getting business "push," and his often Machiavellian politicking.

The choice of Bristol for the tourists' first game in Britain was no coincidence. Both Spalding and Gloucestershire recognized the opportunity for some mutually beneficial commercial backscratching. A company had been formed to build the new cricket ground, had bought twenty-six acres of farmland for £6,500, and would spend another £2,000 to prepare the site for first-class cricket. Dr. W. G. Grace was the club's representative on the company board, and he and his

fellow-directors saw in the Americans' visit a fine chance for some preseason marketing. Grace at the time was forty years old, and still easily the premier batsman in first-class cricket, although his effectiveness as a bowler of the top rank was on the decline. Grace and Spalding, then thirty-eight, would have been a well-matched pair. Both were physically imposing men—Grace particularly so, at 6-foot-2, with a long House of David beard—and had out-sized personalities to match. Spalding realized the great publicity value of associating the prestigious W. G. with his tourists.

As might have been predicted of an English March, the weather was uncooperative. The Clifton *Chronicle* noted: "They originally intended to play their first match in England...on the Gloucester County Ground in honour of Dr. W. G. Grace, the champion cricketer, but the great floods forced the postponement at the last moment." Similarly, the Bristol *Observer* commented, "It was rather an honour that they should have consented to make their first English appearance in the County of the Graces, but the weather, which here flooded a quarter of the city... in the English Channel gave the base ballers such an unmerciful pitching and tossing as they crossed from France, that they admitted they landed at Victoria [the London railway terminus for boat trains] fairly done up, and could on Saturday last scarcely have done justice to a game which requires in the fullest sense the exercise of all the physical faculties and plenty of mental keenness."

In the face of these circumstances, the tourists played their first games in and near London. On March 15, six days later than the originally planned arrival in

Patrick Carroll *is a freelance writer living in Cornwall, England. A past chair of SABR's UK/Europe History Committee, he has been a New York Mets fan since the club's inception and has the scars to prove it. His son, Liam, plays slick middle infield for the Great Britain national baseball team.*

Bristol, the *Western Daily Press* ran this rather prickly and defensive paragraph: "The base ball players yesterday raised their siege of London, and today advance upon the provinces, beginning at Ashley Down. We in the provinces are not going to take our opinions about base ball from London, any more than we take our opinions about cricket. The public assembled at Ashley Down today will be as competent to form an opinion upon the game as the critics at Lord's, or as the crowds at the Oval…But it seems worth noting that the base ball players seem to have interested London rather than converted it from a belief in cricket."

The Bristol *Times & Mirror* next day struck a less curmudgeonly note in its very full report, which commenced: "The band of Americans who have been touring around the world giving exhibitions of their national game of base ball arrived in Bristol yesterday morning from London. They were met at the Joint Railway station by several gentlemen, with whom they drove to the Grand Hotel. Subsequently the teams and a few others interested in athletic sports in the city were entertained at luncheon by the directors of the County Ground Company. The Duke of Beaufort [a long-standing friend and patron of the Grace family], to whom all the visitors had been introduced, presided."

After listing various individuals in the party of about fifty present, including all the players and several local dignitaries, the report noted toasts of the Queen and the President, before mentioning that "Mr. E. G. CLARKE, in proposing 'American Base Ball Clubs' asked local athletes not to hastily form an opinion on the merits of the game they were about to witness, for like cricket, it had many fine points, which require some knowledge of the game to appreciate. Mr. SPALDING, in acknowledging the compliment, referred to the kindness with which they had been received during their tour in every part of the world where they met Englishmen. He appealed to Bristolians not to prejudge the game, and said until they had seen it played two or three times it was impossible to form anything approaching a correct idea of its merits. He wished they had been able to fill their original engagement, for they would have considered it a great honour to have made their first appearance in this country in the home of the best-known Englishman in the world—W.G. Grace (applause). Mr. [Cap] ANSON [whom Mr. Spalding described as the 'W.G. of America'] called upon the Americans present to give three cheers for Dr. W. G. Grace." Everyone then headed for the County Ground.

The *Times & Mirror* report then continued, under the subhead HOW THE GAME IS PLAYED, with a diagram of a baseball diamond and a 400-word digest of the rules, beginning, inevitably, "The game, which is a natural development of rounders…" The game report, under the further subhead CHICAGO VS. ALL-AMERICA, es-

timated the crowd at just 3,000, attracted "by the novelty of the sport and the beautiful state of the weather," and noted that the ground, "despite the recent severe rains was in excellent condition." This may also be credited in some degree to Grace, who throughout the construction period had visited the site almost daily, apparently making life hell for the builders and groundsmen.

The teams were given as follows:

ALL AMERICA		CHICAGO
T. L.[sic] Brown	Pitcher	J. Ryan
W. Earle	Catcher	A. C. Anson
G.[sic] Crane	Long[sic] Stop	T. P. Daly
F. H. Carroll	1st Base	M. Baldwin
J. Manning	2nd Base	F. N. Pfeffer
G. A. Wood	3rd Base	T. Burns
T.[sic] Healy	Left Field	M. Sullivan
E. Hanlon	Centre Field	J. K. Tener
J. G. Fogarty	Right Field	R. Pettitt

This line-up contains a few curiosities. The *Times & Mirror* wrote: "It will be observed by those who have read the accounts of the matches already played in this country, that several important alterations were made in the posts assigned to the various players. The most celebrated pitcher of each side was given a rest, and Daly, the great catcher of the Chicago team stood at short slip [sic], his usual position being occupied by Anson." I take the rested pitchers to have been Chicago's Mark Baldwin (154-165, 3.36 ERA, lifetime) and the All Americans' John (not. T.) Healy (78-136, 3.85 ERA, lifetime). The All Americans' starting pitcher here was presumably the speedy Liverpool-born outfielder Tom Brown (whose middle initial was T., not L.), and whose major league pitching career consisted of twelve games (2-2, 5.29). Jimmy Ryan, the Chicago starter, was also primarily an outfielder who pitched during his eighteen-year major league career in 24 games (6-1 3.63). This chopping and changing of positions may have been a result of fatigue at the end of a long tour. Despite the fill-ins and the 10-3 score (Chicago won) observers complained the pitchers enjoyed such a marked superiority over the batsmen as to render the game tedious.

On the All American team, the players were by no means the elite group their name implied. They may have been the best Spalding could get for the money he was willing to pay. Of course one All American player—a Banquo's ghost at the Grand Hotel luncheon and a salient absentee from Ashley Down—was John Montgomery Ward. This popular and charismatic star had been asked by Spalding to captain the All Americas. Ward was the moving force behind and within the Brotherhood of Professional Base Ball Players, and more than one historian has speculated that Spalding took him on tour to get him out of the United States while his fellow magnates ratified the infamous Brush Plan, which formulated a draconian new standard contract designed to severely curtail players' rights and conditions. Ward stuck with the tour to Britain, then headed home to see what measures could be taken to counteract Spalding's and the other club owners' machinations. All of this cut-and-thrust ultimately culminated in the Players' League revolt of 1890.

The day after the game, the *Western Daily Press* continued in the waspish vein of its previous day's note. Under the head "CRICKET'S COMPETITOR" the article began: "Probably out of the thousands of people who went to Ashley Down yesterday to watch the match between the Chicago and All American base ball players there would not be very many who were sufficiently 'enthused', as the Americans would say, to witness a return match if one had been arranged. It is necessary, indeed, to guard against excessive depreciation of a game which is clearly more interesting to play than it is to watch. It is very likely extremely fascinating to the striker to try to hit balls delivered with great skill by the pitcher, but the spectator must require to have his sympathies quickened by partisanship in order to be roused from the depressing effects which the repeated failures to hit produce in his mind."

The piece (it would be inaccurate to call it a report) continues with the same tone of frank prejudice and lofty patronizing which only ignorance can perfectly produce. I have heard American sportscasters (notably Harry Caray on one particularly toe-curling occasion which happened to coincide with my fiftieth birthday) treat cricket with the same brand of fatuous facetiousness that is always the mark of the truly ill-informed.

The *Times & Mirror*, while more restrained and less obnoxious in tone, did have the same faults and virtues to find in the American game. It remarked: "The Americans deserve all the praise they have received for their marvellous fielding. Certainly cricketers could learn much from them in throwing, though doubtless with a little practice our county men would make just as brilliant deep-field catches." The paper's reporter did, however, join in the general discontent at the apparent superiority of pitcher over batter. The English found the regular failure of the hitters monotonous, and the crowd of 3,000-4,000 thinned out considerably by the end of the seven-inning game.

Those who did leave the game early missed what must have been an entertaining post-game diversion wherein, according to the Bristol *Observer*, "a few of the chief members of the Gloucester team [had] a chance to bat against [the Americans'] peculiar delivery." The cricketers, with one or two exceptions, were conspicuously unsuccessful in dealing with the American pitchers. W. G. Grace was not one of the exceptions. The *Western Daily Press* man noted that "Dr. Grace,

who would probably be able to hit most full pitches with only a broomstick, was not able to stop many of the balls delivered to him." Easily the most effective of the cricketers was W. G.'s elder brother, Dr. E. M. Grace. E. M. was known as "The Coroner," although I am unable to say if this sobriquet referred to his medical or his sporting activities. He was not anything like his brother's equal as an all-around cricketer but was renowned for the prodigious length of his hitting. He was what cricketers call a "slogger" and such was the force and velocity of his strokes—many what in the English game are called "cross-bat" drives—that at one period he was banned from playing at a number of village cricket grounds as a severe danger to both players and property.

The final verdict of the more or less sympathetic *Times & Mirror* reporter was that baseball was altogether unlikely to supplant cricket in the affections of the English, but would be more entertaining if the teams played fewer innings and were the batsmen "armed with a larger club, or with an instrument more in the shape of the cricket bat." In other words, if it was more like cricket, people who liked cricket would like it better. The *Western Daily Press* ended its coverage in the same patronizing tone that had infused its entire article: "The experience gained yesterday confirms the impressions which descriptions of the game produced, that is that base ball is an admirable game—for Americans." I don't know if Al Spalding, who generally speaking had the scruples of a stoat and, to quote the great A. J. Leibling's friend, Colonel Stingo, "the soul of Jimmy Hope the bank robber," lifted and reversed this phrase directly from the Bristol writer, or whether it was a general usage, but he wrote in his 1911 autobiography: "Cricket is splendid game—for Britons."

Of course, ignorant disdain has for much more than a century been the attitude of most Americans toward cricket and most Englishmen toward baseball. It is telling to note that two recent, voluminous, and apparently thorough biographies of W. G. Grace, while mentioning the building of the new Gloucestershire County Ground, make not the slightest mention of its inaugural competition, and their respective indexes contain no entries for either baseball or Spalding. Alas, the combination of airy ignorance, blinkered chauvinism, and complacent prejudice that has left the two great (mainly) English-speaking nations unable to appreciate each other's traditional bat, ball, and running games, which themselves share a common ancestry, leaves those who have a genuine love and appreciation of both sports to sit in the stands, either at Ashley Down or Shea, pondering questions like: "Why didn't Al Spalding and Harry Wright scout E. M. Grace when they toured England back in '74? He would've been a helluva prospect."

Did Ike Play Pro Ball?

Evelyn Krache Morris

Dwight Eisenhower was the archetypal American success story: a boy from rural Kansas who made it into West Point and began his journey to five-star general and president of the United States. But a rumor has dogged this exemplary career: Eisenhower allegedly played baseball for money. Instead of being just another facet of the Eisenhower legend, this rumor, if true, could have given the story a very different ending.

Upon entering West Point, Eisenhower signed a card stating that, among other things, he had never played sports for money. The recently-formed NCAA took a dim view of prospective college athletes who had lost their amateur status. If Eisenhower had played for money and the NCAA had discovered it, his college eligibility might have ended. More important, Eisenhower the cadet had pledged to abide by the West Point honor code. If had not told the truth about his amateur status, he could have been tossed out of West Point, and his military career would have ended before it began.

Eisenhower graduated from West Point in 1915, and the rest is, as they say, history. The rumor about his playing professionally surfaced in June 1945. Mel Ott, then managing the Giants, asked Eisenhower if it was true. Eisenhower was vague about the details, as he was every other time the question was posed. According to the New York *Times*, Eisenhower told Ott and Braves manager Bob Coleman "the one secret of my life." As a student at college, he told them, he once

Evelyn Krache Morris *is an analyst with DeMarche Associates in Kansas City, a part-time grad student in American History, and a devout Mets fan. She thanks Lloyd Johnson for his help on this article.*

played professional ball under the assumed name of [manager "Affie"] Wilson. It was in the Kansas State League, he said, but when they asked him what position he played, he replied, "That's my secret." Confusing the issue further, Eisenhower told the Associated Press later that month: "I was a center fielder…But I wasn't a very good center fielder and didn't do too well at it."

The issue dogged Eisenhower for the rest of his life. He eventually directed his staff to avoid answering questions about his baseball career. A 1961 note from his secretary, Ann Whitman, to Col. Robert Schulz stated: "DDE did play professional baseball one season to make money, he did make one trip under an assumed name (did not say whether Wilson or not). But, he says not to answer this because it gets 'too complicated.'"

The letter indicated that Eisenhower played professionally very briefly. Perhaps he played for money in unrecorded local semipro games. Players sometimes received a share of the gate receipts—as much as $5–$10 for a well-attended game. Even this token payment would have compromised Eisenhower's amateur status, but no box scores were published, so there is no way to tell if Eisenhower played or not.

Sports were clearly important to the future president during his youth. Dwight Eisenhower grew up in the small town of Abilene, Kansas, and like many small-town boys, dreamed of getting out. Also like many boys, he thought he could to this by becoming a professional baseball player. Dwight played both football and baseball during high school and focused on sports. "During Dwight's high-school years his interests were, in order of importance, sports, work, studies, and girls." (Ambrose, p. 33) When he went to West Point in June 1911, he looked forward to continuing his athletic career, including baseball.

He did play both baseball and football at West Point, but he had only limited opportunity to play professional baseball. He graduated from Abilene High School in 1909, remained in Abilene during 1910, and left for West Point in June 1911. He returned home for his last extended visit during the summer of 1913. These are the only years during which Eisenhower could have played professionally.

Abilene was a member of the Central Kansas League, which attracted players from as far as Fort Worth, Texas, and actively recruited from other leagues. Baseball in Abilene was already big business; an article ran in the Abilene *Daily Chronicle* exhorting citizens to attend games to "help baseball which is helping Abilene." The town even "broadcast" some road games. A player would call in the action to a local office, where the play-by-play would be shouted through a bullhorn to the crowd waiting on the street. When Eisenhower graduated from high school in 1909, the Central Kansas League was an established part of an Abilene summer.

But Eisenhower's summer also included work. He had made a deal with his older brother Edgar ("Big Ike"). "Little Ike" agreed that both would work at the local creamery during the summer of 1909. Edgar would matriculate at the University of Michigan in September, while Dwight would work through the winter to finance Edgar's education. After Edgar completed a year, it would be Dwight's turn and Edgar would work while Dwight attended school.

There may not have been a roster spot available for Dwight even if he had been available. He was young— just out of high school—and if he can be believed, a mediocre center fielder. Besides, he already had a job. The Abilene team had older men on it, men for whom baseball was a living, not a hobby.

Edgar was due to return from Michigan in 1910, but for some reason, the brothers' deal fell through. Edgar stayed in Michigan; Dwight remained at the creamery, rising to night manager by the end of 1909, which meant that he worked 6 PM to 6 AM in 1910.

This did not allow much time for baseball. Based on the published accounts and box scores in the Abilene *Daily Chronicle*, there is no evidence that he played under either his own name or his manager's. The real Affie Wilson played first base. There is no record of "Wilson" playing center field.

Eisenhower left for West Point in the first week of June, 1911. He was leaving a town with no professional baseball team at all: the Central Kansas League had folded after a bank cashier absconded with the revenues from the 1910 season. Some CKL players moved over to the Kansas State League. This league was more competitive than the CKL, and since its season didn't start until May 22, it is unlikely that Eisenhower played for Abilene's entry. Interestingly, the announcement in the *Daily Chronicle* of Eisenhower's West Point appointment mentioned his intelligence and amiability but not his athletic achievement. If he had played on the hometown team, the local paper would probably have mentioned it.

While at West Point, Eisenhower came to prefer football to baseball. In November 1912, he did serious damage to his knee during a college football game. He was devastated to learn from the doctor that he would never play football again. In fact, the tendon and cartilage damage was so severe that it nearly ended his West Point career altogether.

Eisenhower made one final extended trip home for ten weeks during the summer of 1913. The Central Kansas League was still defunct. A center fielder who "wasn't very good," and who also had a badly damaged knee would probably not have played in the highly competitive Kansas State League.

There is no record in any local paper of Eisenhower—under any name—playing for a professional team. He was probably not a good enough player to compete in the two circuts available to him. His injury makes it hard to imagine that he could have played during 1913 when timing and maturity might have allowed him to.

If Eisenhower played baseball for money, it was most likely in local semipro games, which still would have put him in violation of both the NCAA and the West Point honor code. It is also possible that Eisenhower, a returning war hero, was having a little fun with major league managers and, intentionally or not, exaggerated his own baseball accomplishments. One thing seems almost certain, though: Dwight Eisenhower did not play true professional baseball.

Sources:

The Abilene *Chronicle*

Ambrose, Stephen E. *Eisenhower.* Vol. 1. New York: Simon and Schuster, 1983.

Kindred, Dave. "He was a Coach without Peer," *The Sporting News.* June 6, 1994, p. 8.

Koettting, Thomas B. "One Strike on Ike: Secret of Center Field Could Have Changed History," The Wichita *Eagle.* May 3, 1992, p 1A

Sullivan, Neal J. *The Minors.* New York: St. Martin's Press, 1990.

Note from Ann Whitman to Col. Robert Schulz, August 3, 1961. Overland Park, KS 66209.

Boston's Dealt Out of a Trolley Series

Jack Walsh

"Phew, man, that was the golrammest baseball stretch ah have seen. I've seen a lot more baseball than anybody in this room, believe me."

—Leroy "Satchel" Paige, October 3, 1948, after the Boston Red Sox and Cleveland Indians ended the season in a dead heat.

Don't worry Satch, we believe you.

The 1948 American League pennant race was nip, tuck, and tuck. All through the summer campaign, Boston, Cleveland, and New York took turns nipping and tucking. Heading into the final week, the three teams were deadlocked at 91-56.

On Sunday, October 3, the Red Sox hammered the Yankees, 10-5, while Detroit's "Prince Hal" Newhouser tamed the Indians, 5-1, before 74,181 screaming Cleveland fans. This forced a one-game playoff for the American League pennant. Earlier in the week the Red Sox had won the coin flip and home team advantage. It would be winner take all at Fenway Park, and if the Sox won, Boston's blissfuls could bank on a daily trolley hop between Kenmore Square and Commonwealth Avenue for a "Boston Only" matchup with the Braves.

"I've learned one thing for sure this season," Ted Williams said after beating the Yankees, "You can't ever tell about this game of baseball; anything can happen."

Jack Walsh *is a tormented fan of the Boston Red Sox. Along with Marshall Cook, he wrote* Pack Your Bags: Baseball Trade Secrets. *He lives in Townsend, Massachusetts.*

The Envelope (Ball), Please—Teddy was right. Playoff day was full of surprises. If sports radio call-in shows had been around, Ma Bell would have rung up huge profits. "Name that starter" frenzy began immediately after Sunday's game and continued until game time. Pick up the morning Boston *Globe*, and it was a pair of righties on the mound: Bob Lemon versus Ellis Kinder. One Cleveland *News* writer, Ed McAuley, hit the jackpot. He predicted that Gene Bearden would get the nod for Cleveland. None of the Boston press even came close to naming Boston's starter. Manager Joe McCarthy gave the ball to Denny Galehouse. Indian skipper Lou Boudreau, and 33,957 stunned Boston fans, thought he was bluffing.

He wasn't.

Galehouse—Do you believe in fate? Were it not for two seemingly chance 1947 trade, and one almost-trade that wasn't made, Boston fans might have jumped on the trolley between Fenway Park and the Allston Wigwam (Braves Field).

On June 20, 1947, the St. Louis Browns sold Denny Galehouse to the Boston Red Sox for an undisclosed sum. The Browns drew a paltry 526,435 fans in 1946 and were always looking for money.

Denny appeared briefly for Cleveland in 1934 and 1935. He tossed over 100 innings for them in 1936, 1937, and 1938. On December 15, 1938, he was traded to the Red Sox along with Tommy Irwin for Ben Chapman. Tommy never made the Sox ball club, but Ben went on to give the Indians two good years. In 1939 Chapman batted .290 and knocked in 82 runs. The next year he hit .286.

In his two years with the Red Sox, Galehouse went 15-16 with an ERA of 4.83. The Red Sox sold him and his lefty pitching partner "Old Folks" Fritz Ostermueller to St. Louis in 1940. Like most Boston pitchers, Galehouse's record improved when he left Boston. In his six years with St. Louis he went 50-58 but had a fine ERA of 3.43. His best year was 1943 when he went 11-11 with an ERA of 2.77. Over his career, Galehouse was the consummate .500 journeyman. He put in fifteen years, ending his major league career at 109-118.

In Galehouse's first start after being traded, Fenway was swarming with lady fans taking advantage of a fifty-cent admission. On Ladies Day, Denny dazzled the gals and the Tigers. He bested Virgil Trucks, 8-2, holding Detroit to six hits. He continued to shine throughout the 1947 season. Galehouse was 1-3 when he traded uniforms, but was 11-7 with a 3.32 ERA for Boston. He led the American League in control, giving up only 2.48 walks per game.

On the day of the playoff in 1948, fans couldn't understand why McCarthy gambled with the 8-7 "soon to be infamous" righthanded pitcher. Granted, Cleveland did have a slew of righthanded hitters in the meat of their lineup (Boudreau, Ken Keltner, and Joe Gordon.) And yes, Denny was no stranger to pressure. In 1944 with the St. Louis Browns, he pitched two World Series games against the crosstown Cardinals. He won the first game of the Series, 2-1, losing his shutout with two out in the ninth.

But that had been four years ago, and despite a fast start in Boston and a decent record with the Red Sox, by October 3, 1948, he was stone cold. His last start had been sixteen days earlier, when he was shellacked in the fourth inning by his former Browns teammates. The last time he faced the Indians he had been yanked in the second inning.

In the playoff Denny never made it past the fourth inning. Ellis Kinder replaced him but didn't fare any better, and the Indians were American League champs.

Bearden—One writer calls Galehouse's start "inexplicable." Boston fans called it a curse. Whatever it was, Gene Bearden sealed Boston's playoff fate. For that, and for wrecking Boston's World Series chances, the Red Sox can thank the damn Yankees, Casey Stengel, and Bill Veeck.

Six months before the Browns sold Galehouse to the Red Sox, New York shuffled Bearden to Cleveland, with pitcher Alan Gettel and outfielder Hal Peck, for infielder Ray Mack and catcher Sherman Lollar.

Bill Veeck, the Indians owner, wanted two pitchers. The Yanks gave him Gettel, who had been 6-7 with the Yanks. The other pitcher would be a minor league prospect. New York boss Larry MacPhail gave Veeck his choice of one of six minor leaguers.

When in doubt, call in the "Old Professor." Casey Stengel was managing the Yankee farm club at Oakland and gave Beardon a glowing recommendation. "He's your man," Casey said. "Don't hesitate."

Veeck didn't.

"The Yankees didn't know it." Bearden remembers, "but it was the best break I ever got in my life."

Well, not exactly. Bearden was lucky to be alive. On July 6, 1943, the Japanese torpedoed his ship, the USN light cruiser *Helena.* Bearden, a young 2nd class Machinist Mate, was seriously wounded trying to save his mates. After two years in rehab, he took to the mound an aluminum head plate and aluminum spike in his knee.

Gene Bearden ran the Red Sox right off the rails. Working on one day's rest (he had blanked the Tigers 8-0 on Saturday), he held the Sox to five hits with a flurry of knucklers, en route to his 20th win of the season.

"Gene Bearden's flood of knuckle ball pitches," Boston sportswriter Jerry Nason wrote, "swarms upon the plate like a covey of geese coming into a marsh."

Bearden's knucklers and sliders cooked Boston's goose. His only mistake was the one and only fastball he served up to Bobby Doerr. Doerr smashed it over the left-field wall.

Boudreau—Offensively, Lou Boudreau, the thirty-one-year-old player-manager, took charge of the game early. In the first inning, he hit a solo homer that set the stage for Cleveland's victory.

Boston tied the score in the bottom of the first, but Indians' third baseman Ken Keltner finished Galehouse off with a three-run blast in the fourth. By game's end, Lou reached base five times, scoring three runs, going 4-for-4 with two singles, two homers, and an intentional walk.

Yet Lou Boudreau might not have been in the lineup if Bill Veeck had had his way. The previous October, the Indians had kept Boudreau instead of trading him to the Browns for Vern Stephens.

Bill Veeck had bought the Indians in June, 1946. He wanted Al Lopez as his skipper. He liked Boudreau as a player but he couldn't split Lou down the middle. So, he preempted media focus on the 1947 Yankee-Dodger World Series by attempting to peddle Boudreau.

This blockbuster trial balloon exploded in his face.

Get rid of their sparkplug? Never. Cleveland fans immediately flooded the post office with hate mail.

The Cleveland *News* entered the fray by running a front-page mock election to measure fans' blood pressure. The turnout was brisk, the pressure high, with Boudreau garnering 90 percent of the 100,000 votes. Instead of giving Boudreau the boot, Veeck gave him a two-year contract. He remained in Cleveland to put up Hall of Fame batting and fielding records. In his thirteen years with the Indians, he batted .296 and led the league in doubles (45) in three different years. In eight of the thirteen years, he led all shortstops in fielding average. And in 1948 he murdered the Red Sox.

Post Mortem—Gene Bearden starred in the World Series, but his greatness was short-lived, and ironically Stengel was partly responsible for his fall. Casey replaced Bucky Harris as Yankees manager in 1949. Familiar with Gene's knuckler, he knew that it broke low, veering outside the strike zone. He told his players to wait Bearden out. "Until Casey spread the word, John Thorn and John Holway write, "Gene had been winning games by throwing balls."

Beardon became ineffective. He ended his seven-year career with a 45-38 record. An amazing 44 percent of those wins were recorded in 1948.

Following the Red Sox' 8-3 loss to Cleveland, sportswriter Grantland Rice, referring to the National League champion Braves, wrote, "Boston still retains half the script and half the plot."

When Cleveland went on to win the World Series in six games, Boston was left with no script, no plot, and no world champion. Were it not for those three deals in 1947—two completed and one blocked by fan outrage—the Boston Red Sox and Boston Braves might have shared pennant glory.

Bibliography:

Boston *Globe*, October 2-8, 1948.

Boston *Herald*, June 24, 1947 and October 2-8, 1948.

Cook, Marshall J. and Walsh, Jack. 1998. *Pack Your Bags: Baseball's Trade Secrets*. Indianapolis: Masters Press.

Creamer, Robert. 1984. *Stengel: His Life and Times*, New York: Simon and Schuster.

Enright, Jim. Editor. 1975. *Trade Him!* Chicago: Follett Publishing Company.

Seidel, Michael. 1991 *Ted Williams: A Baseball Life*. Chicago: Contemporary Books.

Stout, Glenn. 1989. "Pitching Puzzle." In *Boston Magazine*, (October) 85-91.

Thorn, John and Holway, John B. 1987. *The Pitcher*. New York: Prentice Hall Press.

Transcendental Graphics

Gene Bearden

It seemed like a good idea at the time

In 1888 Al Reach, the former major leaguer turned sporting goods magnate, came up with a well-intentioned invention that might unwittingly have altered the competitive balance between batter and pitcher more dramatically than any other single innovation in baseball history. Al's brainstorm was a seamless baseball, "as smooth and even as a rubber ball." Commented the Toronto Globe: *"it is the cat-gut stitches that hurt the hands, and the new ball will no doubt become very popular with the players." Especially with all those spiring hitters who could never quite master the breaking stuff.*

—David McDonald

Dick Higham, Star of Baseball's Early Years

Larry R. Gerlach and Harold V. Higham

Richard "Dick" Higham is one of the forgotten pioneers of professional baseball's formative years. He is one of only a few dozen men who played the full term of baseball's first professional league, the National Association (1871-1875), and the early years of the National League (1876-1880). While the average career of a professional player was six years, Higham played for a decade. He ranked among the foremost players of the day, but his subsequent banishment as an umpire by the National League in 1882 [see TNP 2000] has obscured his accomplishments as a player.[1]

Family background—Dick Higham was born on July 24, 1851 in Ipswich, County Suffolk, England to Mary and James Higham, who were innkeepers. He was two when the family emigrated to New York City in 1853. James's brother George and his wife Sarah and son Frederick emigrated to New York at about the same time. The brothers set up a tailoring business that continued through the Civil War.

James, an avid cricket player, was a member of the American All-Star teams that lost only once while playing the Canadian All-Stars from 1856 to 1860 as part of a continuing International Series between the two countries.[2] A principal officer in the New York Cricket Club, he staunchly opposed the efforts of the rival St. George's club to charge admission to matches to defray the cost of paying professional players.[3] In 1865,

James opened a restaurant in "the English style" called The Office, at 13 East Houston Street. It became a gathering place for many enterainment and sports notables of the time. When James died suddenly in July 1872, following his wife's death the previous year, the New York *Times* on July 10 made particular note of his passing:

> **Mr. James Higham,** the well-known cricketeer, and keeper of a popular English restaurant in this City for many years, died yesterday, in the forty-fifth year of his age. Mr. Higham was at one time, and for many years, one of the leading players in the New-York Cricket Club, and did much to foster the game in its infancy. The deceased was a man of many fine points, and his sudden death will be regretted by a large circle of friends.

Just shy of his twenty-first birthday, Dick Higham was on his own.

From semipro to professional—Like many sons of English immigrants—Al Reach and the Wright brothers among them—who grew up in and around New York City in the 1850s and 1860s, Dick Higham moved easily between the cricket pitch and the ball diamond. He occasionally played cricket into the early 1870s for the New York Club, whose home grounds were at the Elysian Fields, site of the Knickerbockers' first interclub contest, but his principal sport was baseball.[4]

In 1869, young Dick reached the upper echelons of local baseball as catcher for the amateur Empire club

Larry Gerlach *is a professor of history at the University of Utah.* **Harold V. Higham** *is an attorney-at-law. 2001 is the 125th Anniversary of the inaugural year of the National League, and the 150th Anniversary of Dick Higham's birth.*

in the National Association of Base Ball Players, a consortium of professional and amateur teams. He quickly demonstrated an aggressive style, once claiming an "out" after catching a foul ball on the first bounce off the reporter's table, but lost his claim when the umpire ruled that the table was on, but not of, the playing field.[5] By season's end he had advanced to the Unions of Morrisania (now the Bronx), a second-tier semipro club that played both amateur and professional teams and whose players shared gate receipts.

Higham returned to Morrisania for the 1870 season. Playing mostly second base but also catching some, the eighteen-year-old emerged as an excellent batter, starting the season as the team's cleanup hitter but soon moving to the key leadoff position. He was chosen to participate in a highly publicized benefit game on August 6 between two picked nines made up of professional and amateur players. Conspicuous among his veteran teammates and opponents, young Higham played second base and got two hits for the New York team in a 14-6 loss to the Brooklyn squad.[6]

On October 18, Higham debuted with the salaried Mutual Club, one of the top four professional teams in the country. Playing third base and batting eighth, he got three hits and scored a run in a 12-12 tie against the Athletics of Philadelphia called after ten innings on account of darkness. During a 23-7 drubbing by the Cincinnati Red Stockings on November 2, the utility infielder "reluctantly" moved to catcher after Charley Mills injured a finger in the first inning. Appearing "very nervous" in the "post of danger behind the bat," Higham was jolted by two foul tips, one in the face and one in the chest, and seemed "overjoyed" to switch positions with shortstop John Hatfield in the sixth inning.[7] Sent behind the bat again on November 5 against the Atlantics, Higham's lack of experience produced "a miserable fiasco." He reportedly was "afraid to stand close behind the bat and when he stood back, balls flew by him with most astonishing regularity." His replacement, Hatfield, also proved "a miserable failure" necessitating pitcher Rynie Wolters to finish the game behind the plate.[8] The abortive catching experiment aside, Higham finished the season on a respectable note, hitting a combined .302 against professional teams with the Unions and Mutuals.[9]

The National Association—Higham again opened the 1871 season at second base with Morrisania as the Mutuals fielded only veteran players for the inaugural season of the National Association of Professional Base Ball Players, the first professional circuit.[10] But Mutuals manager Bob "Death to Flying Things" Ferguson had decided to groom young Higham as the club's future catcher, a key position inasmuch as the backstop directed infield play. Higham caught several exhibition games for the Mutuals against amateur clubs in May, and on June 1, almost two months shy of his twentieth birthday, made his "big league" debut in a 7-3 win over Rockford's Forest City club, "catching in first-rate style" and allowing only one passed ball.[11] Higham remained with the club as team's "tenth man," substituting mostly at second base and continuing to catch in exhibition games. An August 10 performance behind the plate against the amateur Atlantic club drew special commendation as he "caught all through the game with much judgment and ability."[12] He moved into the starting lineup as the regular second baseman on August 1 against the White Stockings in Chicago, when Charlie Smith suffered a "mental breakdown" and left the club.[13]

If Higham's talent was evident, so was his temper. Following a 37-16 trouncing at Troy on July 3, several Haymakers and Mutuals got into "quite a disturbance" during which Trojans first baseman William "Clipper" Flynn "struck" Higham. On July 13, Troy won the rematch in Brooklyn, 9-7, and as the teams were leaving the field, Higham, who did not play, punched Flynn in the face, supposedly "without the slightest provocation." As a bleeding Flynn ran toward the team's carriage, a melee involving players, fans, and club officials ensued. A show of armed force by Brooklyn police, forewarned about the possibility of trouble, halted the brawl.[14]

Higham appeared in only 21 National Association games, but posted the second highest batting (.362) and slugging (.415) averages on the team while playing second base (12), the outfield (8), and catcher (1).[15] At season's end, premier New York baseball writer Henry Chadwick wrote of Higham: "He is very young, but has been playing base ball and cricket for the last ten years [and] is a very good infielder and heavy batsman." The *Clipper* thought "Higham makes a very fair second baseman and a good change catcher," but criticized him for his "fondness for growling and fault-finding," although he had noticeably "moderated the rancor of his tongue."[16]

At age nineteen, Dick Higham debuted professionally with a club that in many ways personified the negative perceptions that would plague his baseball career. The Mutuals were a very talented team, noted especially for heavy hitting, but the team's performance was maddeningly erratic. Some members were undisciplined and disputatious, prone to individual over team play, and given to questionable personal habits and associations with unsavory characters. In particular, the Mutuals had been haunted by the specter of gambling ever since three members were expelled from the Association in 1865 for throwing a game. While the prevalence of gambling posed a potential threat to the integrity of professional ball, the gambling charges hurled at the Mutuals and other clubs were surely exaggerated. That gambling was conducted openly before and during games throughout the 1870s and into the 1880s indicates that the various clubs tacitly condoned wagering, probably to draw spectators. Widespread betting on baseball was not surprising given the popularity of gambling in nineteenth-century America.[17]

In 1872 Dick Higham discovered the advantages of "free agency." Hired on a season-to-season basis without any ongoing contractual commitments to a particular team, players annually were free to sign with teams to better their financial or playing situations. Higham did both by joining the inaugural edition of Nick Young's Lord Baltimores, known as the "Canaries" for their yellow pants and black-and-yellow stripped silk shirts and hats. The second-year player, the lone nonveteran on the club, performed admirably. Acquired to spell veteran receiver and team captain Bill Craver, Higham divided his time mostly between catcher (25) and the outfield (24 games), but also demonstrated his versatility by playing first, second, and third. He was the best hitter on a powerful hitting club, leading the team in batting average (.343) and runs scored (72) while clubbing the first two home runs of his professional career. He also committed 55 errors for a poor .796 fielding percentage, although he performed noticeably better behind the plate than in the field. Noting that Higham was "prone to growl, and is not always amenable to discipline," Chadwick felt that in his first full professional season he had gained a "considerable reputation" as a catcher having "played very finely in some matches" and that his batting was "one of his strong points, his cricketing experience giving him an advantage in this respect."[18]

Higham returned in 1873 to the Mutuals. A series of dismal performances renewed suspicions of gambling, perhaps heightened by the team's financial backers' decision to abandon fielding a salaried team in favor of an experimental system wherein four players—Dave Eggler, John Hatfield, Nat Hicks, and Bobby Mathews—received salaries while the others shared a portion of the gate receipts.

The team floundered, but Higham flourished. A valuable jack-of-all-trades, he divided his time equally among the outfield (19 games), second base (18), and catcher (17). Batting second behind Eggler, he hit .314, the third-best average on the team, and was second in runs scored and RBIs. Chadwick's postseason commentary praised Higham's "excellent play behind the bat," declaring that "he won several games for the Mutuals by his catching." However, he also reiterated that "Dick is rather careless in his habits, impulsive in temper, and in some respects not a model player; but we think he can be relied upon for honest service. He comes of good, honest cricketing stock, and has a worthy man's reputation to sustain."[19]

Manager of the Mutuals—In 1874 Higham was the Mutuals' principal catcher (48 games), but saw considerable duty in the outfield (33) and spot duty at first and second. A preseason report claiming that the club "contains some of the best ball material in the country," but sorely needs "a vigorous, exacting captain" to impose discipline and maximize performance proved accurate.[20] With the team posting a modest 13-12 (.520) record twenty-five games into the season, Higham replaced veteran shortstop Tom Carey as manager on June 27 and posted a 7-3 win over Hartford.

Higham's aggressive leadership by example sparked the Mutuals to three straight victories. On July 2 he scored what proved to be the winning run in the tenth inning in spectacular fashion as the "Mutes" defeated Philadelphia, 12-9. Following a single to center by Joe Start, Higham attempted to score from second and slammed into the Pearls catcher, folding him up "like a jack knife" and causing the ball to roll away as three runs crossed the plate.[21] Indeed, under Higham's direction the weak-hitting club went 29-11 (.725), reaching first place on September 28 before fading badly to finish 7-1/2 games behind Boston. The "united effort" that brought the team to first place was undermined when players "got into discord one with the other."[22] Whatever the case, the second-place finish was the club's best in the National Association.

Dick Higham could take pride in the team's performance, but not his own. Perhaps because of managerial distractions, his batting average dropped below .300 for first time (.261). He did, however, hit his third homer, lead the team in doubles (14), and post the league's best fielding average for catchers (.852). As usual, Chadwick praised Higham's skill while criticizing his attitude: "Higham's play as catcher in the Mutual nine reached quite a high mark. There is however, ample room for a new school of trained catchers—players who can be taught to 'play for the side' at all times and on all occasions, and who, moreover, will refrain from growling at umpires."[23]

Rumors of crooked play were frequently directed toward National Association players, and Higham was the target of such intimations for the first time in 1874. On July 9, the Mutes led Philadelphia, 5-0, after five innings, but in the sixth a "bad muff" by Higham and an error and a wild throw by Hatfield enabled the Pearls to tie the score. The next inning Philadelphia scored the final run in a 6-5 victory without a hit, prompting the New York *Herald* on July 15 to assert: "A few more games like the one in the Union grounds last week and good-bye to the national game." Following the White Stockings' 5-4 defeat of the Mutuals in Chicago on August 5, the Chicago *Tribune* declared the game had been "disgraced by palpable and unblushing fraud" and implicated Higham in the fix. The Mutes had handily defeated Chicago in all five previous meetings and led,

4-2, after five innings when Bobby Mathews suddenly announced he could not pitch due to a strained groin muscle. Chicago, heavily favored by gamblers, promptly tied the game in the sixth as Hatfield offered up "perfectly fair and easy" pitches that could be "batted with perfect ease," while Higham "neglected" a batted ball and uncorked "a terrific overthrow" leading to two runs. Then, with one out in the ninth and a runner on third, Higham "started on a slow steal from first, in fact so slow as to seem deliberate, and was put out easily" before the runner could score from third.

A local doctor subsequently declared that Mathews had been "ailing for the past two days," but the *Tribune* continued to charge the game was "a steal" and pointed to Carey, Hatfield, Higham, and Mathews as suspects. In a thinly veiled reference to Higham as manager, the paper noted that prior to the questionable contest "a prominent member of the nine, holding a responsible position, was on a 'spree'" with Mike McDonald, a Chicago political boss tied to gambling interests, who subsequently invested heavily in pools on the game. And a correspondent identified only as "Chelsea" alleged that "three outsiders make it a business to travel with the Mutual Club" and identified Hatfield, Higham, and Candy Nelson as having "an interest" with one or more of them.[24] As typically was the case, the allegations were neither investigated nor proved.

Captain of the White Stockings—Instead of heading to Hartford in 1875 as was rumored, Higham signed with the Chicago White Stockings for the sizable salary of $2,200. To some, his signing was "incomprehensible" given the suspicions of crooked play in Chicago during the past season.[25] Actually, it was not surprising. Given the prevalence of wagering, it was equally easy for the press, which was generally disdainful of professional players, to allege gambling as the cause of the erratic performances so frequent in the 1870s as it was for players to actually collude with gamblers. (Most of the allegations of crooked play stemmed from fielding miscues, common when players lacked gloves.) While game-fixing was a reality, clubs, whether because of the difficulty of obtaining conclusive evidence or the consuming pursuit of victory, routinely declined to banish players suspected of dishonesty and eagerly signed the good ones whether their reputations were tainted or not.

Whatever the truth about Higham in 1874, the impressive late-season performance of the Mutuals outweighed questions about his integrity, and even the cynical *Tribune* admitted that he was regarded as "a good catcher and a hard worker."[26] Chicago had re-entered the league in 1874 for the first time since the Great Fire of 1871, and the team's directors, chief among them William Hulbert, who purchased a controlling interest in the club in June 1875, were

determined to capture league supremacy. They aggressively sought Higham as captain and leadoff hitter, hoping his prowess with the bat, defensive skills behind the plate, and aggressive play would lead the team to the pennant.[27]

Featuring six new regulars and new uniforms, the White Stockings started fast, boasting a 10-2 record on June 1. Unfortunately, dissension quickly appeared. On April 24 the Chicago *Tribune* warned fans "not expect anything wonderful of the Chicago club" because "the nine is pretty well split up into factions and cliques. There seems to be a Higham's party and a [Scott] Hasting's party, and, if such is the case, the club's prospect is poor indeed."[28]

The warning was prophetic. The White Stockings faded fast. Manager Jimmy Wood was not a disciplinarian, and internal bickering soon became rampant. Higham bore the brunt of the blame for the team's demise. Able to catch in only 24 games due to sore hands, he played right field (14) and second base (13). Whatever the position, he was error-prone. On June 12 he committed six errors in a 24-7 loss to the Red Stockings, and two days later made five miscues in an 11-4 loss to the same club. He also batted an uncharacteristically low .236 in 42 games with only 12 RBIs.

Inevitably, Higham's poor performance in the field and at the bat led to suspicions of game-fixing. Rumors that some Chicagos were in collusion with gamblers increased after losses to the Philadelphia Pearls on June 22 and 24. Things came to a head after a 4-2 loss on June 26. The Chicago *Times* flatly declared that "the contest was a dishonest one from first to last, and that a certain member of the White Stockings purposely played a poor game in order to enrich his friends who backed the visiting nine to win, taking odds of almost two to one." The paper declared that all the Whites played to "their general average" except Higham: "The loss of the game must be attributed to Higham. He caught well enough behind the bat, but the Philadelphias stole bases on him with impunity, and whenever he did try to catch them he threw so wildly that he helped them along toward home plate. He was really the cause of losing the game, but the *Times* does not feel at liberty to make positive charges without further proof."[29]

Interpreting plummeting attendance as evidence that the public had "lost faith in the intent of the nine to win every time they could," the club's directors met on June 28 to take measures to restore confidence in the team. Their first acts were to suspend Dick Higham for an indefinite period and to "depose" him as team captain. They also offered a $500 reward for evidence that any player had taken money to throw a game, announcing that they "will not insist on absolute proof, such as the law would require, but will pay the reward named for evidence that will convince any fair man of the guilt of the accused party."[30]

When no evidence of crooked play was immediately forthcoming, the Chicago *Times* changed its tune and argued that Higham was "fairly entitled to exoneration" and reinstatement. The paper argued that he must be judged innocent for lack of incriminating evidence, and charged that the directors made an "invidious distinction" in unfairly singling him out for disciplinary action. Higham may not have been the only White Stocking rumored guilty of foul play against Philadelphia, but he was a convenient and likely target for the directors, given previous suspicions of throwing games. Thus the Chicago *Tribune*, admitting that Higham "is one of the best players in the country when he wants to be," maintained that the directors did "a wise thing" in suspending him: "It may be Higham's fault, or his misfortune, that he is suspected of purposely losing games, but in either case he is better out of the nine until he can regain confidence as an honest player." As the *Tribune* noted, "the principal cause of suspicion attaching to Higham is the character of the men he is uniformly to be found with. It is not always safe to judge a man by the company he keeps, but it is no credit to any man to be seen continually, and almost exclusively, with thieves and bunko ropers."[31]

When no evidence against Higham materialized, the directors declared the charges "without foundation" and reinstated him, apparently on condition that he would not be back next season.[32] He returned to the lineup on July 3, but his erratic play continued. This comment after a loss to Boston on July 17 was typical: "Higham had too many errors, though he played pluckily and did some brilliant work."[33]

The end to a dismal sojourn in Chicago came on August 17 in an 8-4 loss to the Philadelphia Athletics. The White Stockings led, 4-1, after seven innings, but gave up five runs in the eighth thanks to the "miserable throwing and general bad playing" of Higham, who committed four errors in the inning. The crowd was "loud in their denunciation" of the second baseman, and the newspapers resumed allegations of crooked play. Reiterating that Higham "certainly can play better when he wants to," the press asserted that he performed "as if he was utterly dazed" in letting "balls go by him without attempting to stop them" and that his "horrible bungling work" made it "quite evident that he did not want to save the Chicagos from defeat." The *Inter-Ocean*, which had earlier criticized the directors for suspending Higham, now declared that the player had some explaining to do:

> Probably Higham can explain what he was doing with a Chicago character at Pratt's billiard hall waiting for the pool selling, and when he found there was none what point he gave his companion when they both went to Foley's and

there bought pools on the Athletics. Many persons, who claim to know, boldly assert that Higham was in partnership in the investments. He may have an excuse, but the fact that he does not play here next season and his former reputation lead observers to think that he is playing now to fleece the public, and of this he has been accused heretofore. He must either admit that he sold yesterday's game or acknowledge that he cannot play ball. In either case the Chicago management can easily do without him.[34]

The directors "laid off" Higham for the August 18 game against the Athletics and released him on August 19. Whether Higham resigned or was terminated is not clear, but the Chicago *Tribune* was explicit about the rationale: "There have lately been many apparently well-grounded suspicions that he has sold games and has been guilty of dishonest conduct in many of the contests of the season. His fate should serve as a warning, and convince base-ball players that selling out games is a practice that cannot easily be concealed, and that eventually it is certain to be discovered." The *Inter-Ocean* agreed, hoping that "with the unreliable material out of the nine" the team would play better and "in harmony hereafter."[35]

Higham returned to New York City hoping, as the Brooklyn *Eagle* announced on August 23, to "resume his place in the Mutual nine." The next day he umpired the Mutuals' 3-2 loss to Hartford, and took the field for the Mutes three games later against Boston on September 1. Defeated by the Red Stockings in eiÄ‡t consecutive games, the Mutuals decided to "do a little experimenting" by inserting Higham behind the bat in place of Nat Hicks. The *Eagle* thought it "not a good change by any means," but Higham made only one error, batted cleanup and stroked two hits in a 13-7 loss.[36]

The woefully weak-hitting Mutuals desperately needed Higham's bat, and he did not disappoint. He hit .391 in 15 games, posting a smashing .469 slugging average. But suspicions of crookedness continued. When the St. Louis Brown Stockings rallied to tie in the Mutuals 7-7 in their season finale on October 29, the "wretched play of Higham behind the bat" was considered a factor in a game thought to have been influenced by gamblers.[37] And in postseason reviews, Dick Higham was identified as one of the "black sheep" whose crooked play was "undermining the game."[38]

Redemption—Professional baseball and Dick Higham both enjoyed a renewal in 1876. The National League's inaugural season marked the accepted beginning of "major league" baseball, and Higham's debut with the Hartford Dark Blues marked his redemption as a player. Signed as a substitute, he quickly became the starting right fielder and backup catcher.[39] On May 13 Higham had the dubious honor of hitting into the first triple play in major league history during a 28-3 shellacking of the Mutuals, but he subsequently earned the distinction of recording the league's first notable batting streak by hitting safely in 24 consecutive games from August 12 through the end of the season.[40]

The only newcomer on a Hartford team that finished second to Boston in 1875, Higham enjoyed one of his finest seasons, leading the team in hits (102), batting average (.327), and slugging percentage (.407) and finishing in a three-way tie for the league lead in doubles (21). Despite a late-season swoon caused by "internal dissensions" and unspecified allegations of "crooked work," the Dark Blues, thanks largely to Higham, finished the league's initial season in second place, six games behind, ironically, the Chicago White Stockings.[41]

In 1877, due to poor attendance by the home town fans, the Dark Blues moved to Brooklyn, but without Dick Higham. George Keck, manager of Cincinnati, was reported to have engaged Dick Higham, "...one of the best players in the country..." for his team. However, Keck had also offered a position to Jack Manning, late of the Bostons. It was first reported that Manning's terms were unacceptable and Higham was projected to fill out the team. In fact, when the National League teams were announced for 1877, Higham was listed with Cincinnati and Manning for Boston. However, Manning apparently capitulated and agreed to terms with the Western Red Stockings. The National League rosters having been set, Dick Higham was signed as captain of the "League Alliance" Syracuse Stars for 1877.[42]

The Stars were a solid club, playing .500 ball against National League teams (17-16) and winning the Eastern division title. Higham was involved in a pivotal play in the most memorable game of the season—a fifteen-inning scoreless tie with the National League's St. Louis Brown Stockings on May 1. In the eighth inning, Davey Force of the Browns, beaten at home by center fielder Pete Hotaling's throw, collided with Higham, who dropped the ball. Although the collision appeared to be unintentional, the umpire correctly called Force "out" to maintain the tie. Higham, who had one of the team's two base hits in what was then the longest deadlock in professional baseball history, performed brilliantly behind the plate and in the tenth inning "covered himself with glory" by "gobbling" a foul fly with his left hand.[43]

Overall, however, Higham had a disappointing season. He hit .257 in 97 games, the lowest batting average of his professional career. His fielding was also subpar as he ranked thirteenth among outfielders (.794), eleventh among those playing in double-digit games. And his demeanor detracted from his play. Following a su-

perbly played 2-0 Stars victory over the National League's Hartfords, the press commended the Syracuse players for their "gentlemanly deportment" save for Higham, a "constitutional growler," although it was allowed that he had been "quite moderate in his grumbling."[44]

The Stars disbanded after the season, but Higham rebounded in 1878 with the National League's newest entry, the Providence Grays, managed by former Baltimore and Hartford teammate Tom York. Ben Douglas, the club's business manager, thought enough of Higham to advance him funds from his own pocket in the winter of 1877 to ensure his services for the Grays—an act that counters earlier allegations of crooked umpiring by Higham.[45] Playing in all 62 games, he enjoyed a career-best season at the bat. From his customary leadoff spot, he hit .320, eighth best in the league, and led the league in doubles (22) and runs scored (60), tied for second in runs produced (88), and ranked fifth in total bases (117). He joined with York (.309) and league batting champion Paul Hines (.358) to form the first all-.300 hitting outfield in National League history. Playing exclusively in right field, except for catching part of one game, Higham's fielding continued to deteriorate. His .808 fielding percentage ranked ninth on the team, ahead only of the catchers and eighteenth among the league's twenty-five outfielders. Still, he played a major role in helping the Grays to a third-place finish, eight back of powerful Boston.

Despite an impressive showing at the bat, Higham in 1879 once again found himself out of the National League. Whether George Wright, the new Providence manager, declined Higham's services or he again opted for a better salary in an inferior circuit is unknown. Whatever the case, Higham signed with the new Capital City Club of Albany in the National Association for $1,200. The Capital Citys, one of two Association clubs in Albany, was a bust from the beginning. Optimism, fueled by the highest payroll in the circuit, quickly turned to pessimism as the team lost every home game amid growing rumors of dissension and crooked play.[46] Compounding the on-field problems was the allegation that while signing players, manager Candy Cummings and an unidentified key player had secretly negotiated with investors in Rochester to acquire the team in case the Albany venture proved unsuccessful. It was later reported that the team's best players, including Dick Higham, "acted honorably with the directors throughout and refused to enter into [the] little scheme."[47]

On May 9 the team was transferred to Rochester as a member of the International League and renamed the "Hop Bitters" after a patent medicine manufacturer. Named team captain in recognition of his knowledge of the game, Higham became a favorite with the young fans. But it was another disappointing year on the field

Source: *Baseball's First Stars*, Ivor-Campbell, Tiemann, and Rucker, eds., SABR, 1996.

Richard "Dick" Higham

Batted Left, Threw Right   Hgt: 5' 8-1/2"   Weight: 171 lbs.

Year	Team	Lg	G	AB	R	H	2B	3B	HR	RBI	SB	BA	POS	PO	A	E	FA
1870	Mrris Uns/Mutes	PR	27	139	42	52	(64 Total Bases)					.302	2B-C	82	70		
1871	New York Mutuals	NA	21	94	21	34	3	1	0	9	3	.362	2B-C	49	30	26	.752
1872	Lord Baltimores	NA	50	245	72	84	10	1	2	38	3	.343	C-O-2	181	33	55	.796
1873	New York Mutuals	NA	49	245	57	77	5	4	0	34	1	.314	O-2-C	150	42	50	.793
1874	New York Mutuals*	NA	65	333	58	87	14	3	1	37	5	.261	C-RF	263	47	70	.816
1875	Chicago**/Mutuals	NA	57	272	56	74	10	3	0	22	6	.272	C-2-O	219	74	71	.805
1876	Hartford Dark Blues	NL	67	312	59	102	**21**	2	0	35	–	.327	RF-C	99	35	26	.838
1877	Syracuse Stars**	LA	97	413	58	106	3	2	0	–	–	.257	C-OF	322	60	99	.794
1878	Providence Grays	NL	62	281	**60**	90	**22**	1	1	29	–	.320	RF	77	28	25	.808
1879	Capital Cty/Flwr City	NA	27	125	26	36	4	1	0	–	–	.288	RF	24	5	12	.707
1880	Troy Trojans	NL	1	5	1	1	0	0	0	0	–	.200	RF-C	1	0	0	1.000
Major League Totals			372	1787	384	549	85	15	4	204	(18)	.307		1039	289	323	.804

*Player/Manager   **Captain

Numbers in bold italics led league

as he batted a combined .288 in 27 games with Albany and Rochester and recorded by far the lowest fielding percentage of his career (.707).[48] The Hop Bitters, too, fell on hard times and after fifteen games was dissolved and reconstituted in early July as an independent, barnstorming club.[49]

Retirement—Dick Higham retired after the Albany-Rochester debacle. He was twenty-eight, just shy of the average retirement age (29.6) for players at the time and had played ten professional seasons, four more than the average career.[50] He was still a solid hitter, but his batting was not strong enough to overcome his weaknesses in the field. Now a resident of Troy, Higham played in one more National League game in 1880, perhaps as a favor for his old manager, Bob Ferguson. He started behind the plate for the Troy Trojans against Boston on May 25, but switched to the outfield after allowing two passed balls. He garnered one hit in five at-bats and committed two errors.[51]

By 1888 he had moved to Kansas City, Missouri, where he was employed as a bookkeeper at the Turf & Field Restaurant. On September 6, he married Clara Learned in St. Paul's Church, Kansas City, Kansas. Their first son, Harold, was born on December 18, 1889. By 1896, the family moved to Chicago, Clara's hometown, where Higham became bookkeeper at John Curly's restaurant. A second son, George, was born that year. Sometime in 1900 Richard and Clara separated. She and the boys moved first to Milwaukee and then to New York while Richard remained in Chicago. They never divorced.

Richard "Dick" Higham entered St. Luke's Hospital on February 16, 1905, suffering from Bright's disease—otherwise, nephritis, an inflammation of the kidneys. He subsequently contracted pneumonia and died on March 18, 1905 at age fifty-three. Two days later he was buried in Mount Hope Cemetery.

Postscript—Dick Higham was one of the notable players of professional baseball's formative decade. His career, which began in the amateur era and spanned the 1870s, illustrated many of the common characteristics of the times—"growling," "hippodroming," erratic performances, and frequently switching teams and leagues. Participating in the inaugural seasons of both the professional National Association and the National League, he played with and against the great names of early "major league" baseball, including Cap Anson, Ross Barnes, Candy Cummings, Davey Force, Bobby Mathews, Al Spalding, Joe Start, and George Wright.

Higham was known as an excellent batter, posting a career batting average of .307, besting .300 five times in seven "major league" seasons.[52] Unusually versatile, he played mostly catcher, second base, and right field, but also appeared in at least one game at every position except pitcher. Several appointments as team captain or manager spoke to his leadership abilities and expert knowledge of the game. The accusations and allegations of his formative years were not part of his later playing career.

Dick Higham the player has been lost in baseball's memory because of his subsequent notoriety as an umpire, but his accomplishments as one of organized baseball's first stars must not be forgotten.

Notes:

1. See Larry R. Gerlach and Harold V. Higham, "Dick Higham: An Umpire at the Bar of History," *The National Pastime: A Review of Baseball History*, Vol. 20 (Cleveland: Society for American Baseball Research, 2000), p. 20-32.

2. John I. Marder, *The International Series* (London: Kaye & Ward, Ltd., 1968), pp. 49-67.

3. George B. Kirsch, *The Creation of American Team Sports, 1838-72* (Urbana: University of Illinois Press, 1989), p. 32.

4. The New York *Clipper*, August 6, 1870; New York *Times*, September 8, 1870, and July 13, 1871.

5. Preston D. Orem, "Baseball (1845-1881) From the Newspaper Accounts" (Altadena, CA: typescript, 1961), p. 90.

6. Played at the Union Grounds in the Williamsburg section of Brooklyn, it was the second of two benefit games played to raise money for the wife and four young children of William J. Piccot, baseball reporter for the New York Tribune, who died unexpectedly on July 18 at age 33. The first game, played on July 26 at the Capitoline Grounds in the Brownsville section of Brooklyn's Bedford-Stuyvesant district, pitted the Atlantics against a "Picked Nine" from the Alpha, Eckford, Harmonic, and Star clubs. The August 6 game pitted the players from the Atlantics, Eckfords, and Stars (Brooklyn) against a composite team of Actives, Mutuals, and Unions (New York). The contests and donations raised $740 for the family. New York *Clipper*, July 30, August 6 and 13, 1870; New York *Tribune*, July 19, 25, 27 and August 8, 1870; New York *Times*, July 22, 24, 27 and August 7, 1870.

7. Cincinnati *Daily Enquirer* and Cincinnati *Gazette*, November 3, 1870.

8. New York *Times*, November 6, 1870; Orem, "Baseball," p. 122.

9. Unless otherwise indicated, Higham's seasonal professional batting and fielding statistics are those calculated by Robert L. Tiemann and appearing in Frederick Ivor-Campbell, et. al., eds., *Baseball's First Stars* (Cleveland: Society for American Baseball Research, 1996), p. 77.

10. See William J. Ryczek, *Blackguards and Red Stockings: A History of Baseball's National Association, 1871-1875* (Jefferson, NC: McFarland, 1992).

11. New York *Times*, May 16, 23, and 24; June 2, 1871.

12. New York *Times*, July 21 and 22, August 11, 1871.

13. New York *Clipper*, August 12, September 2, and November 11, 1871.

14. New York *Tribune* and New York *Times*, July 14, 1871.

15. David Nemec, *The Great Encyclopedia of 19th-Century Major League Baseball* (New York: Donald I. Fine Books, 1997) contains a seasonal computation of player statistics for each team.

16. New York *Clipper*, n.d., 1871, Henry Chadwick Scrapbooks, I, pp. 63, Albert Spalding Collection, New York Public Library; New York *Clipper*, November 11, 1871

17. For baseball, see Daniel Ginsburg, *The Fix Is In: A History of Baseball Gambling and Game Fixing Scandals* (Jefferson, NC: McFarland, 1995); for gambling in America, see Henry Chafetz, *Play the Devil: A History of Gambling in the United States from 1492-1955* (New York: C. N. Potter, 1960).

18. Unidentified newspaper article, Chadwick Scrapbooks, I, p. 93.

19. New York *Clipper*, February 21, 1874.

20. Unidentified newspaper article, April ?, 1874, Albert Spalding Scrapbooks, I, n.p.

21. New York *Herald*, July 3, 1874.

22. Brooklyn *Eagle*, October 20, 1874. The New York *Mercury* on October 18 was more specific, declaring that the Mutuals were highly skilled players who considered "integrity of character, habits of daily life, [and] daily associates" as "secondary matters" and gave "little thought" to "playing for the side," a key component of winning.

23. New York *Clipper*, December 19, 1874.

24. Chicago *Tribune*, August 6-9, 1874; Chicago *Times*, August 6-9, 1874. For an account of McDonald's influence and connections, see the Chicago *Times*, August 2, 1874. Amid the controversy, the Mutuals, including Higham, joined by several White Stockings, on August 7 lost a two-inning cricket match 87-86 against the Chicago Cricket Club. Chicago *Tribune* and Chicago *Times*, August 8, 1874. See also Orem, "Baseball," p. 194-196.

25. "But there is one thing about this Chicago club which is wholly incomprehensible to us. Last year, when the Mutuals were in Chicago, the local papers of that place called them a lot of thieves and blacklegs, declaring that Higham, and one or two others, had a certain game played with the White Stockings, and asserted that Higham would sell a game at any time. It must be acknowledged that there was something very suspicious about his action while in Chicago, but yet the managers of the White Stocking club turn round and engage him for this season at a salary of $2,200 a year! However, this is none of our funeral, and if Chicago will dance she must pay for the music." St. Louis *Republican*, June 1, 1875, reprinted article from the New York *Sportsman*.

26. Chicago *Tribune*, April 24, 1875.

27. Hulbert and Nick Young, the White Sox business manager, pursued Higham just prior to the end of the 1874 season. On October 26 Hulburt ordered Young to go to New York and try to sign Higham for $2,000 with a ceiling of $2,500. Higham agreed to a contract in early November. Chicago Cubs Records: Impressed Letters of William A. Hulbert, October 24 to November 11, 1874, Chicago Historical Society.

28. Commentary on the Higham-Hastings cliques also appeared in other newspapers, e.g., the Hartford *Courant*, May 18, 1875 and the St. Louis *Republican*, June 1, 1875.

29. In the game Higham had one passed ball and four "overthrows." The White Sox 5-2 loss to the Pearls on June 24 was also thought to be "out of tune." Newspaper reports alleged that "a parcel of bunko men, low gamblers, and general disreputables" had raised a large pool in favor of Chicago and negotiated with a key Philadelphia player, probably third baseman Mike McGeary, to throw the game. During the game, a Chicago player presumably got wind of the deal and wanted in on the action. When refused, he arranged with some teammates to double-cross the gamblers and throw the game to Philadelphia. The Pearls won the game with three runs in the final inning. Chicago *Times*, June 25 and 27, 1875; Chicago *Tribune*, June 25-28, 1875; *Inter-Ocean*, June 23, 25 and 28, 1875. Ginsburg, *The Fix Is In*, p. 27, claims that Higham was the player who discovered the fix and was involved in the double-cross. We have found no evidence to support that contention.

30. Chicago *Tribune*, June 29, 1875. National Association rules prohibited players and umpires from being "directly or indirectly interested" in wagering on games in which they were participants. In 1874 a new rule stipulated the permanent expulsion of any player who bet on a game involving his team and a year's suspension of players betting on other games. That season the Philadelphia Pearls expelled John Radcliff for betting $350 against his own team. See Ginsburg, *The Fix Is In*, pp. 25-26.

31. Chicago *Tribune*, *Inter-Ocean*, and Chicago *Times*, June 29 and 30, 1875. Following Hartford's June 29 game in Chicago, the Hartford *Courant* on June 30 reported: "Higham was not allowed to play as management have lost confidence in him, charging him with being interested in selling games, etc. of late."

32. Chicago *Tribune*, July 4, 1875; *Inter-Ocean*, July 1 and 3, 1875.

33. Boston *Herald*, July 18, 1875.

34. *Inter-Ocean*, Chicago *Times* and Chicago *Tribune*, August 18, 1875.

35. *Chicago Tribune*, August 20, 1875. On August 21 the Chicago *Times* referred to Higham's "withdrawal," while the *Inter-Ocean* used the term "released." Hulbert wrote the following statement dated August 19, 1875: "To whom it may concern. This is to certify that Richard Higham has been honorably released from his contract with the Chicago Base Ball Association for the season of 1875 and that his contract has been duly canceled." Chicago White Sox Correspondence, May 28, 1875—October 28, 1876, p. 72, Chicago Historical Society. Hulbert's letter may have meant Higham had been found innocent or may have been intended to allow him to join another team since players deemed guilty of fixing games were permanently expelled from the league.

36. New York *Times*, August 25, September 2, 1875; Brooklyn *Eagle*, September 2, 1875. Higham apparently did not accompany the Mutuals on a road trip to New England for four games against Hartford and Boston in late August.

37. Orem, "Baseball," p. 239-240.

38. For example, the Chicago *Tribune*, February 5, 1876, scoffed: "The Mutual Club, our pets, had too many Jack Nelsons and Dick Highams in it." In a scathing denunciation of crooked playing, the St. Louis *Globe Democrat* named the Philadelphia Pearls and the Mutuals as "the black sheep in the flock" and listed Higham among those players who should be "at once emphatically informed that their services are not desired." And the Brooklyn Eagle placed him as the catcher on their "all star" team of "rogues." Others on the "fixer-team" were pitcher—George Zettlein, Pearls; first base—Bill Craver, Centennials; second base—Mike McGeary, Pearls; short stop—John Radcliff, Centennials; third base—Davey Force, Athletics; left field—Fred Treacy, Pearls; center field—George Bechtel, Athletics; right field—Joe Blong, Brown Stockings; substitutes—Dickey Pearce and Frank Fleet, Brown Stockings. Ginsburg, *The Fix Is In*, pp. 29-30.

39. Boston *Herald*, April 9, 1876. Higham was not on the roster as of January 24, 1876. Unidentified newspaper article, 1876, Chadwick Scrapbooks, I, p. 135.

40. In the fifth inning of the Mutuals game, Higham hit a line-drive to second baseman Bill Craver, who threw to first baseman Joe Start to double-off Jack Remsen and then took Start's return throw to retire Jack Burdock at second. Frank Williams first noted Higham's hitting streak in "The Records Committee Newsletter," Society for American Baseball Research (December 1997), p. 1. The streak began against Alonzo "Lon" Knight of the Philadelphia Athletics; on October 21 Higham got three singles against George "Foghorn" Bradley of the Boston Red Caps, but saw his skein end as it was last game of the season.

41. The team finished strong in October after jettisoning Tommy Bond, the principal source of disharmony. New York *Clipper*, October 28, 1876.

42. Chicago *Tribune*, February 18 and March 4, 1877. For the Alliance, see Harold Seymour, *Baseball: The Early Years* (New York: Oxford University Press, 1960), pp. 98-103, and David Pietrusza, *Major Leagues: The Formation, Sometimes Absorption and Mostly Inevitable Demise of 18 Professional Baseball Organizations, 1871 to Present* (Jefferson, NC: McFarland, 1991), pp. 49-52.

43. St. Louis *Globe-Democrat*, May 2, 1877. See also Lloyd Johnson, "Longest 1877 Duel of Zeroes Put Syracuse on Map," *Baseball Research Journal*, 13 (Cooperstown, NY: Society for American Baseball Research, 1984), p. 44. The Stars, who won an invitational tournament in Chicago in September, finished with a 68-45-3 record and outscored their opponents 620 to 447. Ron Gersbacher, Liverpool, NY, has compiled a complete listing, with some commentary, of the Stars season.

44. Brooklyn *Eagle*, June 8, 1877. A report on the game in an unidentified Hartford paper also commented on Higham's "constitutional infirmity." Chadwick Scrapbooks, I, p. 141.

45. David Arcidiacono, *Middletown's Season in the Sun: The Story of Connecticut's First Professional Baseball Team* (n.p, n.p, 2000), p. 116. Douglas was owner of the Mansfield club in 1872 when allegations of dishonest umpiring and drunkness were levied in the press against Higham. If the allegations were true, and not a put-on, it is unlikely that Douglas would have sought out Higham or that Higham would have appeared before the Providence board of directors in a vain attempt to save Douglas's job in 1878. Ibid., pp. 95-96, 117.

46. The Albany *Daily Evening Times* not only accused some players of drinking excessively and failing to practice, but also charged: "Their playing was entirely different from what it was represented to be; the most insignificant club walked away with them. The number of errors committed, and those too, by the men who were receiving the highest salaries, led to but one conclusion, that something was rotten in Denmark." Quoted in Pietrusza, *Major Leagues*, pp. 56-57.

47. Albany *Journal*, May 9, 1879; Rochester *Democrat and Chronicle*, May 10 and 12, 1879; Rochester *Union and Advertiser*, May 10, 1979.

48. The press wrote of his playful banter with youngsters, "Higham won the hearts of the boys yesterday." Rochester *Democrat and Chronicle*, May 14-15, 1879.

49. Tim Wolter, "The Rochester Hop Bitters," *The National Pastime: A Review of Baseball History*, No. 17 (Cleveland, OH: Society for American Baseball Research, 1997), pp. 38- 40.

50. Statistical computations by Harold Higham of players who spent more than one year in the National Association and National League from 1870 to 1880.

51. Boston *Herald*, May 26, 1880. The Trojans' regular second baseman, Ferguson, and catcher, Bill Holbert, did not play in the game.

52. Excluding the token, one-game appearance in 1880.

The 1919 Orioles

Thomas A. Pendleton

Anyone who knows even a little about minor league history knows about Jack Dunn's Baltimore Oriole dynasty that won seven straight International League pennants from 1919 through 1925. Every one of the seven teams won more than a hundred games—aided, admittedly, by the expansion to a 168-game season in 1921. For the entire run the Orioles played .687 ball, and for the middle of the streak—the 1919 and 1925 teams were clearly the weakest—they averaged .701. Perhaps the most striking evidence of the domination of the Oriole dynasty is the fact that of 49 seasons' series with their opponents, Dunn's teams won 46, lost one, and tied two. Since the loss and one of the ties came in 1925, they were 41-0-1 for their first six years.

How was this remarkable record achieved? The largest factor was hitting. This judgment is counter to received wisdom on the matter. Bill James, for example, says in his *Historical Baseball Abstract* that "the rest of the team wasn't up to the level of the pitching." True, several Baltimore pitchers compiled impressive won-and-lost records, and, as a group, they were far more successful in the majors than the Oriole hitters—Lefty Grove himself won 300 games. But, as James has often noted, pitchers' won-and-lost is in large part a function of their team's performance, and, whatever major league success can tell us about talent, it obviously has nothing to say about minor league performance.

Thomas A. Pendleton *is a professor of English at Iona College in New Rochelle, New York, the co-editor of* The Shakespeare Newsletter, *and the last surviving fan of Jack Dunn's Baltimore Orioles.*

Baltimore's pitching was usually quite strong, and sometimes exceptionally strong. But Orioles hurlers seem to have led the league in ERA only two or three times over the seven years. (Spalding and Reach guides don't report team ERAs. The best that can be done is to add up individual innings and earned runs; in an average year, we can account for about 95 percent of the team's total innings pitched [total putouts divided by three]. On this basis, it seems clear that the Baltimore staff led the league in ERA twice ('21 and '23), with a third year too close to call ('24). In the other four years the Orioles pitchers were second once, third twice, and sixth [!] once.)

Opponents' runs allowed gives the same picture. Again, the guides do not report the figure, and one can only calculate proportionally from individual innings pitched and runs allowed to estimate total runs allowed. Here it seems that the Orioles allowed the fewest runs twice, and clearly didn't in four other years, with the seventh year again too close to call.

Runs allowed is the basic measure of defense, and defense, of course, includes fielding as well as pitching. Orioles' fielding seems to have been good, perhaps verging at times on very good. They never finished lower than third in fielding percentage, twice leading the league and twice finishing second. A number of individual players were by reputation very good fielders. The second base combination of Max Bishop and Joe Boley had outstanding reputations; Merwin Jacobson was considered an excellent center fielder; and at least a couple of the catchers, Ben Egan and Wickey McAvoy, seem to have been strong defensively. A pitching staff backed by a good defense that leads the league in fewest runs, or in earned runs, only two or three times clearly can't have been the most significant factor in seven consecutive years of success.

A look at the offensive stats for the Baltimore dynasty immediately confirms that hitting was the great strength. The most significant statistics are these;

Year	G	R	H	TB	HR	BA
1919	149	859*	1524*	2032*	37*	.299*
1920	155	992*	1765*	2362	59	.318*
1921	167	1140*	1831*	2654*	102*	.313*
1922	169	991	1734*	2505*	112*	.301
1923	166	1069*	1747*	2617*	141*	.310*
1924	167	1061*	1692	2625*	166*	.300
1925	166	980	1682	2662*	188*	.301

All the starred figures led the league. With one exception, the other nine totals were second best, and usually a close second. The Orioles were runners-up in runs scored twice—991 to 993 in 1922, and 980 to 990 in 1925; twice in hits—in 1924, 1,692 to 1,707, and in 1925, 1682 to 1,690; once in total bases—2,362 to 2,378 in 1920; and three times in batting average—.301 to .302 in 1922, .300 to .310 in 1924, and .301 to .305 in 1925. The one third-place finish was the Orioles' 59 homers in 1920, behind the 101 of the Akron Numatics (yes, that's what they called themselves), who in their only year in the International League led in homers, total bases, doubles, and slugging percentage. I suspect funny fences.

Baltimore's totals constitute an awesome level of offense. For the entire seven years, the team batted .308, including pitchers, reserve infielders, third-string catchers, and on a couple of occasions, Jack Dunn himself. The home run totals toward the end of the string are equally impressive. The 1925 team's 188 is more than any major league team accumulated until the 1947 Giants hit 221. Admittedly, prorating to 154 games would reduce the total to 171, the same number hit by the 1930 Chicago Cubs, which was at the time the major league record; and clearly behind the 1936 Yankees, who broke that record with 182. Oddly, however, both the 1930 Cubs and the 1936 Yanks had more at-bats than the 1925 Orioles. Why so, I can't explain.

Most important, however, is runs scored, however scored. For the entire seven-year run, the Orioles averaged 6.23 runs per game. What that figure means can be made clear by observing that the 1927 Yankees averaged 6.29. Jack Dunn developed an offense that for seven consecutive years scored runs just the least bit less than the '27 Yankees. And this is to slightly understate the matter. Excluding 1919, the year before the lively (or cleaner or more frequently changed or more uniform or more unspat-upon) ball was introduced, the Orioles scored 6.30 runs per game, or a hair's breadth *more* than the '27 Yankees.

Adaptability—In creating, and even more in maintaining, this remarkable offensive machine, Jack Dunn displayed a superb judgment of talent, great perseverance, probably a fair amount of luck, and, perhaps more than anything else, an ability to adapt to the game as it changed.

One dimension of this ability is obvious from the yearly statistics. Dunn's Orioles transformed themselves from a high-average, speedy, "little ball" club to a fearsome collection of home run hitters; and of course, they did it without ever dropping a pennant. Oriole Stadium, which Dunn took over from the defunct Federal League Terrapins, had reasonable dimensions—about 310 down each line and about 450 in dead center. But the fences were low, the ball carried well, and in later years, Oriole sluggers posted astounding totals. Buzz Arlett had 52 homers in 1932, George Puccinelli hit 53 in 1935, Howie Moss had 53 in 1946, and Joe Hauser set the all-time league record of 63 in—when else?—1930.

Dunn had no home run hitter of that magnitude. In fact, individual totals were always comparatively modest. Jack Bentley led the team from 1919 through 1922 with 11, 20, 24, and 22 homers respectively, and led the league only in 1921. In 1923, Max Bishop hit 22; in 1924, Dick Porter had 23, Joe Cobb 22, and Fritz Maisel 20; and in the final year, Clayton Sheedy hit 26 and Johnny Roser 25. No other Oriole had as many as 20 in a season.

It sounds almost like a math puzzle that of the 1925 team's 188 homers, the top two hitters combined for only 51. Ruth (60) and Gehrig (47) had 107 of the '27 Yankees' 158; Hack Wilson (56) and Gabby Hartnett (37) 93 of the '30 Cubs' 171; and even Gehrig (49) and DiMaggio (29) 78 of the '36 Yankees' 182. The secret for Jack Dunn was volume, and once it became clear—by 1921 or so—that the homer was a highly effective weapon, he accumulated a large number of hitters who could, did, and were encouraged to shoot for the friendly fences. This, by the way, included the number nine spot in the order. In 1925, the pitching staff produced at least 15 home runs.

Finding a lot of good hitters was always Dunn's highest priority, and the basis on which the dynasty was founded in 1919. At that time a good hitter meant not a home run slugger, but a high-average hitter, ideally a line-drive hitter with some extra-base power, the ability to bunt, and, for frosting on the cake, the speed to steal bases.

Dunn found his hitters in 1919, but the very fact that he went looking for them testifies to his insight into the changing nature of the game. The war year of 1918 had been (and remained until 1994) the worst in the history of organized baseball. Attendance dropped sharply even from the downward trend initiated by the challenge of the Federal League in 1914, and Secretary of

War Newton Baker's "Work or fight" order in June, 1918, had sent great numbers of ballplayers into the armed forces or war-related industries. The major league season, already abbreviated, ended abruptly on Labor Day, and the World Series was the most poorly attended before or since. In the minors, things were even worse; subject to the same pressures as the majors, 11 of 21 minor leagues failed to complete their schedules in 1917, and nine of 10 in 1918, the International League being the only exception.

Even after the Armistice in November. 1918, most of baseball was pessimistic about the upcoming season. The majors kept their war-time 140 game schedule and reduced rosters to 23 men, and in the minors, only 15 leagues resumed play. Jack Dunn, however, saw opportunity. It was a buyer's market for players, with hosts of returning servicemen and war workers, war-time major league replacements, and free agents from defunct leagues—all available for an aggressive believer in the game's future. Jack Dunn proceeded to do what he did best: he found a lot of good hitters.

I'll return to that shortly, but there's a second strategy Dunn pursued, also in response to baseball's changing conditions: once you've found your good hitters, hold on to them as long as you can.

Building the dynasty—In 1918, the foundering minors, exasperated by the majors' unwillingness to help

Jack Dunn

them, and long aggrieved by the majors' one-sided use of player options and the draft, withdrew from the National Agreement and put an end to the majors' right to draft minor leaguers. Not surprisingly, the foremost opponent of the draft was Jack Dunn himself, and, in spite of great pressure from Kenesaw Mountain Landis, appointed Commissioner of Baseball in late 1920, Dunn managed to preserve his and his league's exemption from the draft until the end of the 1924 season. Thus, he could and did refuse to part with the star players he had developed unless he was paid what he considered a fair price (which the baseball establishment considered outrageous) and unless he still had sufficient strength to keep his string of pennants going. He dropped one of his 1919 regulars after the season, but he was able to keep the other seven for an average of better than five years.

Dunn had what is called a "competitive" team in 1918—third place, 14 games out—and three of his regulars returned the next year. But since one of them batted seventh and another eighth, obviously the great offensive strength of the 1919 club was overwhelmingly the result of the new players he found.

The 1919 batting order, and in large part the line-up for the next five years, went as follows:

1. Fritz Maisel, third base. Maisel, a stocky righthanded hitter, had played short for Dunn's 1911 through 1913 teams, and had gone on to a largely unsuccessful seven years with the Yankees and the Browns, although in 1912, he led the league with 74 stolen bases and set a Yankee team record that stood until Ricky Henderson broke it in 1987. Maisel was one of two players who performed for all seven of Dunn's winners. At twenty-nine, he was a good deal older than most, and in the later years of the dynasty he was often referred to as the captain or even assistant manager. He did, in fact, become the team's manager after Dunn's death in the winter of 1928. Maisel hit over .300 every year of the streak except 1923, when illness held him to 99 games and a .275 average. For his size, about five-foot-seven and 160 pounds, he had surprising power. He hit 20 homers in 1924 and 18 in 1925. From the fielding statistics, he seems to have been just average to good, always finishing about the middle of the fielding averages and always making his share of errors. In 1919, he hit .336, led the league in runs scored (135) and doubles (44), and finished second in total bases (258) and stolen bases (63).

2. Otis Lawry, left field. Like Maisel, Lawry was short and extremely fast. Unlike him, he was slight (133 pounds), batted left-handed, and had almost no power. He had begun his career with Connie Mack's dreadful Athletics in 1916 and 1917. At one point, he was supposed to succeed the aged Napoleon Lajoie at second base. But Lawry hit not at all for Mack, who shipped him to his friend Dunn. He hit .396 in 25 games late in

1917 and, as the Orioles' regular second baseman in 1918, .317 with a league-leading 35 stolen bases and a tie for the most hits with a modest 149. The acquisition of Maisel pushed Max Bishop, the previous year's third baseman to second—a stroke of genius or luck—and Lawry to the outfield. There's nothing in the fielding records that seems useful in judging his defense. He was very fast, which is a great plus, but since his positions were second and left, his arm was probably not strong. Lawry remained the regular left fielder until 1924, when he was traded to Jersey City. He hit over .300 for the first four Oriole winners, and .299 (with a league-leading 41 SB) in 1923. In 1919, at the age of 25, Lawry won the batting title with a mark of .364, was second to Maisel in runs scored with 132, and third behind him with 56 stolen bases.

3. Merwin Jacobson, center field. Tall, slender (about 6 feet and 165 lbs), a left-handed batter and thrower, Jacobson had performed in the International League as the regular center fielder for Rochester in 1916 and for the Toronto pennant winners in 1917. He was out of baseball in 1918, probably in war work, but Dunn liked what he had seen, and Jacobson became the center fielder for the first six of the Orioles' champions. He seems to have been a great favorite in Baltimore, as well he should have been. He was fast and, since he was always among the leaders in putouts—for a team that almost invariably recorded the most pitchers' strikeouts—he seems to have been excellent defensively. As a batter, he was even better, hitting .351, .404, and .340 for the first three years of the dynasty. In 1922 he was seriously beaned and dropped to .306 in 128 games. Then he hit .328 and .306 in his last two years in Baltimore. Jacobson's .404 and 235 hits in 1920 were the highest twentieth-century marks for the league, although Jack Bentley broke both records the next year. Jacobson was a line-drive rather than a long-ball hitter, his best home run totals being 12 in 1921 and 18 in 1924. Perhaps his relative lack of power and his age (31) prompted Dunn to let him go in 1925. For the first of the Baltimore winners, however, Jacobson was clearly the best hitter in the league: along with batting .351, he led in hits with 203 and total bases with 277; was third behind Maisel and Lawry with 115 runs, and fourth behind them with 37 stolen bases. There were no official RBI totals for Jacobson's first three—and best three—years, but it would be surprising if he wasn't well over 100 for each, and extremely unlikely that he wasn't the league leader for 1919.

4. John Honig, right field. Honig had last played in 1917 in the South Atlantic League, hitting .349 in 48 games before it folded. Honig is something of a mystery man since he played for only the 1919 team, then spent three years on Baltimore's ineligible list, and returned to the International League to play semi-regularly for Newark in 1923. Dunn apparently wanted a strong righthanded hitter at cleanup to break the string of lefties—Lawry, Jacobson, and Bentley. In 1919, Honig filled the bill nicely with a .320 average and, for 1919, fair power (228 total bases). We don't know why Dunn dropped Honig, but he found other good righthanded hitters to replace him in right field and in the batting order—Bill Holden in '20 and '21, Irish Jimmy Walsh in '22 and '23, and Twitchy Dick Porter and Tilly Walker later, although in the last years, the batting order and the defense changed a good deal.

5. Jack Bentley, first base. Bentley was a beefy six-footer who began his career in 1913 as an eighteen-year-old lefthanded pitcher for Washington. He did fairly well in very limited action, but was eventually sent to the minors, first to Minneapolis and then to Baltimore. He pitched pretty well, though not often, for Jack Dunn, who began Bentley's conversion to an everyday player. In 1917 in 92 games at first and in the outfield, he hit .342. Bentley was not, however, Baltimore property in 1918. He was drafted, first by the Red Sox and then by the Army, where he spent the season, seeing considerable combat. Dunn had to re-acquire him for the 1919 season, during which Bentley (still only twenty-four) played first in just 92 games—perhaps because of injury, perhaps because of a late discharge. He hit .324 with 11 homers, the second-best total in the league. Then came the explosion. Bentley batted .371 with 231 hits and 20 homers in 1920; then .412 with 246 hits, 397 total bases, 47 doubles, and 24 homers—all league-leading figures, and the first two league records for the twentieth century. Finally, in 1922, .351 with 219 hits and 22 homers. At the same time, he operated as a spot starter—not as a reliever, as is sometimes claimed—and was about as close to being unbeatable as possible, with won and lost records of 16-3, 12-1, and 13-2. It was his dual achievements as pitcher and slugger, far more than his good, but hardly startling home run totals, that won him the nickname "the Babe Ruth of the Minors."

Bentley seems to have been anxious to return to the majors, and after the '22 season, he was sold to the Giants for what was considered the exorbitant price of $65,000. To the surprise of most, John McGraw used Bentley as a pitcher and occasional pinch hitter. McGraw may well have been right. The fielding statistics credit Bentley with remarkably few assists, which suggests a first baseman with almost no range. In any case, he did fairly well as a pitcher for the Giants' pennant winners of 1923 and 1924, with records of 13-8 and 16-5.

6. Joe Boley, shortstop. Another of Dunn's finds and, with Maisel, the only other player on all seven Orioles winners. Boley, a slender six-footer, had had only 33 games (.244) with Harrisburg of the New York-Penn League in 1917, before serving in the military for the entire 1918 season. Only twenty-two in 1919, the right-handed hitting Boley finished with a .301 mark and fielded excellently. He continued to do so for the entire streak, hitting over .300 six times; his high was .343 in 1922, and even in his off year he hit .291. He was usually at or near the top in putouts, assists, and fielding percentage. Within a few years, he was considered the best shortstop in the minors (and priced accordingly by Dunn). Boley was finally sold to the Athletics after the 1926 season, at the age of thirty, and was a solid contributor, though not a star, on Connie Mack's last three great teams in 1929, '30 and '31.

7. Max Bishop, second base. A rookie third baseman for the 1918 team, Bishop was the youngest of the 1919 regulars at just nineteen, and for the first five years of the Orioles' streak, usually the weakest hitter. Youth and injuries held him to averages of .260 or less three times, although he posted two big years—.319 in 1921, and .333 in 1923, with a surprising 22 homers to tie for the league lead. His 1923 performance led to his sale to the Athletics at the relatively young age (for an Oriole) of twenty-four, and he had the longest major league career of any of Baltimore's position players. I suspect that Dunn was willing to part with Bishop because he had Dick Porter ready to take over second. (He did, and won the batting title in 1924 with a .364 average.) Bishop was an outstanding defensive second baseman both for Baltimore—he usually led in fielding percentage—and in the majors. In the big leagues, Bishop, only five-foot eight and 155 pounds, never demonstrated the power he had shown with the Orioles; instead, he became a leadoff man so adept at coaxing walks that he won the nickname "Camera Eye."

8. Ben Egan, catcher. One of the three regulars returning from the 1918 team, and, at thirty-five, much the oldest starter. Egan was in his third tour of duty with the Orioles, having first played there in 1910-11, and then returning in 1914, only to be sent to the Red Sox as part of the Babe Ruth–Ernie Shore deal, when Federal League rivalry forced Dunn to break up his league-leading team. Egan was a righthanded hitter, a rangy six-foot-two, and since he was continually employed although he seldom hit well, it would seem that his strength was his defense. He was the first-string catcher for the first three of Dunn's champs, and hit .331 in 1920 and .270 in 1921. The guides give his 1919 average as .341, but, in one of their little mysteries, report that he had 63 hits in 238 at bats—which works out to .265. (Actually, the math is such that a .341 average is impossible for either 63 hits or 238 ABs.) Whatever he hit, Egan caught 71 games.

As seems to be the case for the first four years of the streak, Dunn used his second-string catcher as his backup at first, too. In 1919, although there's no breakdown for games at different positions, Wade Leffler apparently spelled both Egan and Bentley, as he certainly did for the next two years. Leffler hit .282 in

1919; then .336 and .316. When Bill "Lena" Styles took over the job for the next two years (hitting .315 and .316 with excellent power), Leffler moved to the Eastern League, where he won back-to-back batting titles in 1923 and '24, in the latter year nosing out a kid named Gehrig—.370 to .369.

Two final comments on the team that founded the dynasty. First, it was built on speed. In 1919, the three burners at the top of the order finished one, two, three in runs scored (Maisel 135, Lawry 132, Jacobson 115), and two, three, four in stolen bases (Maisel 63, Lawry 56, Jacobson 37—Ed Miller of Toronto led with 83). In 1920, they again finished one, two, three in runs (Jacobson 161, Lawry 155, Maisel 145), totaling an amazing 461 runs in 461 games, a run a game apiece. In 1921, they came close to repeating that record: Jacobson scored 163, second to Maurice Archdeacon of Rochester (who would play center for the 1925 Orioles); Maisel was third with 154; and Lawry, who missed 33 games, tied for seventh with 130—447 runs for 454 games. In '22 Jacobson was beaned, in '23 Maisel became ill, and in '24 Lawry was traded, so, as a trio they had no more such years, although individually they had some impressive seasons. For example, in '25, Maisel, at the age of thirty-five, led the league with 145 runs scored.

The three speedsters' stolen-base totals for 1919 (156) was much their best. With his team average up to .318 in 1920 and .313 in 1921, Dunn quickly learned that basestealing had become a riskier tactic. But the speed was always there, and Dunn used it effectively, if less often. In 1923, Lawry led the league with 41 steals and Jacobson tied for runner-up with 36; they were caught stealing only eight and seven times respectively. And the year before, Maisel was even more efficient, with 30 steals in 33 tries. In fact, for the four years, 1922-25, for which totals were kept, the Orioles as a team stole successfully in 67, 72, 83, and 80 percent of their attempts. This is about half a century before the sabremetricians demonstrated that to be effective a steal must succeed two times out of three. Jack Dunn seems to have known already.

Dominance—Finally, it should be noted that the 1919 team that began the streak only *seems* to have been weaker offensively than its successors. Its team batting average, runs scored, hits, total bases, and home runs were all exceeded by each of the other six winners, but taken in context, the 1919 club had much the most dominant offense.

The key difference, of course, is that 1919 was the last year before the lively (or whatever) ball arrived. The 1919 Orioles posted totals that would have been good for a strong team in the early '20s, but they did it against the dead ball, although, compared to what the other International League teams did in 1919, it might have seemed that the lively ball got to Baltimore a year early.

The 1919 Orioles hit "only" .299, but the rest of the league hit .263, and even the runner-up team hit just .276. Even more indicative of their dominance is what in retrospect seems their modest 859 runs. But their opponents averaged only 603, and the second-place team scored just 656, over 200 less than Baltimore. What this means on a per-game basis is that the Orioles scored 5.77 runs per game, and the other seven teams just 4.07. That's about a run and three-quarters more than the opposition *per game*. I don't know of another team—major league or minor—that outscored its rivals by that margin.

Actually, given this huge offensive edge, it might seem surprising that the 1919 Orioles didn't do better than their 100-49 (.671) record. The answer is easy: defensively, they were no better than mediocre. Again, by working from individual pitchers' innings and runs allowed, and projecting a proportionate figure for the entire season, the '19 Orioles allowed 622 runs or 4.17 per game. Subtracting those 622 projected runs and the Orioles' 149 games from the league totals produces an average of 4.30 runs allowed per game for the rest of the league. Defensively, the 1919 team was just about as average as possible. The pitching actually looks a little worse than that. The team ERA works out to about 3.16, which sounds good until you realize that this was a pitchers' year, in which the Orioles' 3.16 was sixth in the league. The first of Dunn's pennants was clearly won at the plate.

The Orioles got better defensively, especially on the mound. In 1920, Dunn added Johnny Ogden and Lefty Grove, and Jack Bentley returned to pitching. In 1921, he added Tommy Thomas. But even though the opposition closed some of the offensive gap in years to come, the Orioles always maintained a large edge over their league—first as line-drive hitters leading in average by a comfortable margin, and then, increasingly, as long-ball sluggers, setting a new International League record for home runs every season from 1921 through 1925. They were always much better offensively than their competition, and they always won. Not a coincidence.

Sources:

I have relied primarily on the *Spalding* and *Reach* guides from 1919 to 1926 (both print the same stats); James Bready's *The Home Team* and Fred C. Leib's *The Baltimore Orioles* supplied a few biographical details.

Jimmy Dygert's Forgotten Feat

Lyle Spatz

Dygert, p. Phila. Amer.

While searching through *The Sporting News*'s 1934 Record Book one afternoon, looking for I forget what, I made an interesting discovery. It was a small paragraph on the bottom of page 40 entitled "Shut-Out Feat Overlooked," whose first sentence read, "Walter Johnson isn't the only American League pitcher with a record of three shut-outs in four days."

Well, like most baseball fans, I was familiar with Johnson having done this, but I had never heard of anyone else managing it. Yet twenty-six years after Johnson did it, someone had discovered that Philadelphia A's pitcher Jimmy Dygert accomplished the same feat at the tail end of 1907, one season *before* the Big Train. Dygert's victims were Cleveland on October 1 and 3, and Washington on October 4. And while Johnson did it for the seventh-place Senators in pressure-free games against last-place New York, Dygert's three shutouts came as the second-place A's were struggling to overtake the first-place Detroit Tigers.

As the 1907 American League season entered its final ten days, Chicago and Cleveland were still alive, but realistically the race had come down to two teams: Philadelphia and Detroit. On the morning of September 25, the two were tied for first place, each with a won-lost percentage of .600—the A's at 81-54, and the Tigers at 84-56. Each team won its next two games, and as they prepared to begin a three-game series at Philadelphia's Columbia Park on the 27th, the A's were first at 83-54 (.6058) and the Tigers second at 86-56 (.6056).

Detroit's Bill Donovan, on his way to a spectacular 25-4 season, beat Eddie Plank, 5-4, in the series opener, and the Tigers took a lead they would never relinquish.

Lyle Spatz *is the chairman of SABR's Baseball Records committee. He is the author of two books on New York Yankee history and the co-author of the recently published,* The Midsummer Classic, *the complete history of major league baseball's All-Star Game.*

Saturday's game was rained out, and with Sunday baseball forbidden in Philadelphia, a doubleheader was scheduled for Monday the 30th.

Although Columbia Park's capacity was about 15,000, a crowd of more than 24,000, the largest of the season, was in the park, with the overflow standing in foul territory and behind ropes in the outfield. Dygert, a 3-1 winner over Chicago on the 26th, started for the A's, but was ineffective. Appearing rattled, he committed two second-inning errors that allowed a run, after which manager Connie Mack replaced him with Rube Waddell. The A's built a 7-1 lead after five, but the Tigers rallied to tie it at 8-8 in the ninth on Ty Cobb's two-run homer. Each team scored in the tenth, but it stayed 9-9 until darkness caused the umpires to call it after seventeen innings.

The actions of the overflow crowd were influential in deciding the outcome of this game, as they often were in this era. Unruly fans had interfered with play several times, which led both sides to register vigorous, if futile, protests. Cobb, who was in his first full season of stardom, would later call this game the most thrilling he ever played in.

Of course there was no second game, and so on the morning of October 1, Detroit's record was 87-56 (.608), while Philadelphia's was 83-55 (.601). Both teams had seven games to play, and the fact that the A's had played five fewer games than the Tigers was not a consideration. As was the custom of the time, they would not make up these games, nor would they make up any remaining games should they be rained out. Detroit's final seven games would consist of four at Washington and three at St. Louis. The A's would play three at home against Cleveland and four at Washington.

Despite his shaky outing the day before, Mack chose Dygert, whose record stood at 17-9, to start the October 1 series opener against the Naps. Dygert responded with his third shutout of the season, blanking Cleveland, 4-0. He allowed just four hits, and Philadelphia's first-inning run off Cleveland pitcher Heinie Berger was all the support he needed. Dygert had held the Naps to just two safeties, by Rabbit Nill and manager Nap Lajoie, through the first eight innings. Cleveland added singles by Harry Bemis and Bill Hinchman in the ninth, and had the bases loaded with two out before Dygert ended it by getting Joe Birmingham to ground out to second baseman Danny Murphy.

As the 8,000-plus fans departed, the scoreboard showed Detroit trailing Washington 3-1, but the Tigers would rally to win, 5-3, to maintain their .007 lead. The following day the Tigers won two at Washington, 9-5 and 10-2, while the A's Eddie Plank lost to Cleveland and Jake Thielman, 4-3. Detroit was now 90-56, while Philadelphia was 84-56—a three game lead with just five games remaining.

With both Rube Waddell and Chief Bender hurting, Mack went to Dygert again for the home-season finale, although Dygert had spent the previous day sick in bed. This was an absolute must-win game for Philadelphia, and Dygert, with his spitball working to perfection, came through with another shutout. He allowed three hits, walked one, and struck out nine in disposing of the Naps in one hour and 20 minutes. The A's put two two-run innings together against Walter Clarkson to come away with the 4-0 victory.

However, the Tigers won again at Washington, further reducing Philadelphia's pennant chances. The A's would have to win all four games at Washington (two doubleheaders) while Detroit lost two of three at St. Louis. Or they could win three of four with the Senators, if the Tigers lost all three to the Browns.

Plank pitched the opener of the October 4 doubleheader against the Senators, losing, 2-1, in ten innings (coincidentally to Walter Johnson, then a rookie). Philadelphia's situation was now desperate. They had to win their three remaining games and hope that the Tigers would lose their three.

For the first of these games, game two of the doubleheader in Washington, Mack again gave the ball to Dygert. For the second consecutive day, and third in the last four, the twenty-three-year-old righthander rewarded his manager with a shutout. He captured his twentieth victory of the season as the A's blasted Tom Hughes and the Senators, 8-0. Washington managed five hits off Dygert, who fanned seven and didn't walk a man. The next day, October 5, the A's swept both games from Washington, but the Tigers pounded St. Louis, 10-2, to clinch the pennant.

Perhaps it's because of Philadelphia's failure to win the pennant that Dygert's feat was so long overlooked. Nevertheless, it was a truly remarkable accomplishment. Within the space of four days, with the American League pennant riding on every game, he had pitched three shutouts, allowing just 12 hits and three walks, while striking out 24 batters over the 27 innings. When Johnson pitched his three shutouts against New York on September 4, 5, and 7, 1908, his log for the three games was 12 hits allowed, one walk, and 12 strikeouts.

Dygert's streak of three consecutive shutouts, as well as his 27 consecutive scoreless innings, ended in his first appearance of 1908. Although he won the April 18 game at Boston, 4-2, the Red Sox did reach him for a first-inning run. He finished 11-15 that year, but won just 13 games over the next two seasons, his final ones as a big leaguer.

Dygert did have one last hurrah as a minor leaguer. Pitching for the Baltimore Orioles of the Eastern League in 1912, he compiled a record of 25-12, while leading the league with 218 strikeouts. Two years and 11 wins later, at age 29, his career was over.

Del Drake

Thomas D. Drake

For over a century, Findlay and Hancock County, Ohio, have had a rich athletic heritage. From Dummy Hoy in the 1880s to John Kidd and Doug Martin in the 1990s, professional athletes from Hancock County in baseball, football, basketball, golf, auto racing, shooting, motorcycle racing, and horse racing have competed successfully with America's best.

One of the earliest of these athletes was my grandfather, Delos Daniel Drake. He was a man's man in a man's world—an exceptional baseball player at an early age, an expert marksman, an avid hunter and fisherman, a bronco bustin' cowboy in the offseason, a man who loved a good cigar and a good story. He had a colorful vocabulary. He never heard a cuss word he didn't use—frequently. He was handsome. I think the picture of him in the 1911 Detroit team photograph where the team members are dressed in suits shows him to be one of the most handsome men I've ever seen. He was revered by his three sons, two of whom are living and will no doubt be critiquing every word I say about their beloved Dad. He was a devoted husband to my grandmother, who was in poor health the last thirty years of her life.

About a year or so before Ty Cobb died in 1961, he invited Grandpa to Georgia to go quail hunting. Grandpa had to say no, because he did not feel he could leave my Grandmother for an extended period of time. Cobb played major league baseball for twenty-four seasons and had hundreds of teammates over his

career. What does it say about Del Drake, who played only one season with Cobb—1911—that the Georgia Peach invited him to his home to hunt nearly fifty years later? I don't know how much of the stuff written about Cobb today is true. What I do know is that my Grandfather must have made quite an impression on him.

Just who was this Del Drake? If he were here today, what would he reveal to you about himself? How would he describe his career in baseball? Would he present it as one of high accomplishment during which he played with or against the giants of his day—teammates Ty Cobb, Wahoo Sam Crawford, and Eddie Plank; rivals Walter Johnson, Cy Young, Big Ed Walsh, and Shoeless Joe Jackson, to name just a few? Or would Del describe his career like a lost love—so bright and promising in his teens, but, in the end, marked by disappointment and unfulfillment—full of broken promises, missed opportunities, poor timing, what-ifs, and shoulda-beens?

From my earliest memories until shortly before he died on October 3, 1965—the final day of the baseball season that year—I saw my Grandfather nearly every day. I knew him well—not as well as my Dad and uncles did, but better than most kids know their grandparents. If Del were here today, I guarantee you one thing: he would tell it like it was.

He was born in Girard, Ohio, on December 3, 1886, the son of a dentist and the grandson of a physician. The entire family of three generations moved to Findlay around 1890. To understand Del Drake's career in baseball, you must understand the two dominant themes in his life. The first was his relationship with his father. Del's father, William H. Drake, was born in 1863. Several early 1900s newspaper accounts

---

Thomas D. Drake *practices law in Findlay, Ohio. He is a 1974 graduate of Notre Dame, a longtime SABR member, and in spite of their treatment of his grandfather, is an avid fan of the Detroit Tigers.*

state that he had been a professional baseball player in the 1880s in Chicago on a team owned by Hall of Famer Cap Anson, the star of the day. William Drake owned the Findlay semipro team in the 1890s. He supported and encouraged Del's development in baseball—so much so that when young Del was offered a contract by the Detroit Tigers in 1902, at the age of fifteen, there was no objection when he quit Findlay High School to devote more time to his athletic pursuits.

Let's look at some of the early highlights in his baseball career. In 1902, Del's name starts showing up in the newspaper. He was playing ball with and against players several years older than he. We have a picture taken in 1902 of the Findlay Elks and the Toledo Elks baseball teams. You can tell from the photo that most of the other players are in their twenties. One newspaper story indicates that in 1902 Del batted .476 for Findlay. Findlay High School had no team in those days, so Del played for college teams around northwest Ohio. One newspaper account describes his hitting five straight doubles in a game for Findlay College.

In 1903 Del, his father, and the rest of the town team were arrested for playing ball on Sunday in Arcadia, where they used Reeves Park to avoid Findlay's ordinance against Sunday ball. Findlay's Arcadia games drew crowds so large that local ministers prevailed upon the mayor to have the ballplayers arrested. My cousin has the original bail bond that my great-grandfather and great-great-grandfather posted for the release of the team from jail.

We know so much about Del's early days because his beloved mother kept track of his every move. When Del went off to play in other towns, she would subscribe to the local newspaper and carefully paste the box scores and news accounts of her only son onto the pages of what eventually ran to three dental catalogues, which we still have.

After 1906, the newspaper articles written about Del suggest his great desire to get to the big leagues. This is not surprising, because that year a senseless tragedy had befallen the man he loved the most—his father. William Drake was in the prime of his life—forty-three years old, a successful dentist in robust health. In March, he presented himself for initiation into the Modern Woodmen of America. The initiation rite required his arms and legs to be tied to a seat similar to a pommel horse, which was secured to the inside of a large metal wheel. This wheel was rolled around the lodge room while my Grandfather was astride the seat. Somehow, William Drake's back was broken, he became blind, and he never worked another day the rest of his life. The tragedy that befell William undoubtedly caused financial hardship and increased Del's desire to make it to the big leagues and stay there. Maybe this was the bond that Del and Cobb shared, for Cobb as

you may know also lost his father under tragic circumstances. In 1905—one month before Ty came to Detroit to play for the Tigers, his father was shot to death by his mother, who claimed that she had mistaken Cobb's father for a burglar.

Stymied—The other dominant theme in the career of Del Drake was the injustice of the Reserve Clause, the standard provision in every minor league and major league contract until the 1970s, which prevented free agency and bound a player to the team that owned his contract.

From 1904 through 1908, when not nursing injuries, Del made a favorable impression on the writers covering his teams. He hit .429 for the Findlay squad in 1904; made the All Star team of the Protective Association with Massilon and Niles, Ohio, in 1905; was an All Star again with Newark, Ohio of the Ohio and Pennsylvania League in 1906; batted .308 with Mansfield of that circuit in 1907, and split the 1908 season between Newark of the Eastern League, and Johnstown of the Tri-State League. He went to spring training with Detroit from 1908 through 1910, but each year, Detroit sent him down for the season.

Several of the newspaper articles saved by my great-grandmother mention Del's anger at Detroit for refusing to either bring him up or trade him to another organization. We have several letters from the owners of the Tigers and the New York Giants, and from other baseball officials in response to his requests to be released or traded.

He had some great years in his early twenties. Playing center field for the Wilkes-Barre Red Barons in 1909 and 1910, for example, he batted .340 and .345, and led the league in hits. Despite his strong play in the minors, there were factors that may have contributed to Del's inability to stick with the Tigers. For a few years, he went to Arizona to work as a cowboy after the season. We have several pictures of him in full cowboy regalia topped by a ten-gallon hat, pointing his Colt .45 as if in a gunfight. One year, he broke his ankle when he fell off a horse. He also once contracted yellow fever during spring training, and he broke a leg and a thumb playing ball at other times. He also came along at a time when the Tigers had two future Hall of Famers in the outfield and were the best team in the American League, winning the pennant, 1907-09.

Still, he must have wondered what it would take to make the club. In 1910, he hit ten home runs and batted over .400 in spring training at San Antonio. The Tigers sent him down.

The Red Barons won the New York State League title both years he was there. And Wilkes-Barre brought him together with my grandmother. Del was a natural lefthanded thrower and hitter who had learned at an early age that he couldn't elude a ball thrown at his head while batting lefty. Out of self-preservation, he taught himself to bat righthanded. Nonetheless, one day in 1910, he was beaned and taken to the hospital in Wilkes-Barre with a broken nose. One of the nurses tending to him later became Mrs. Del Drake.

In 1911, Del finally made the Tigers. He first appeared in a game against Cleveland on April 30. The Tigers trailed, 4-1, going into the bottom of the ninth, and strung together several hits to win the game, 5-4. Del had a pinch-hit single as part of the rally.

The Tigers started out in 1911 much as the 1984 Tigers did, winning nineteen of their first twenty-one ballgames and thirty of their first thirty-five. However, their pitching wore down as the season progressed, and they finished in second place, 13-1/2 games behind Connie Mack's Philadelphia Athletics. Del hit .279 in 95 games, with one home run, nine triples, and 20 stolen bases. He had two hits in one game off Walter Johnson, and he also started a triple play by fielding a line drive at first base.

At Detroit, he made his mark in a couple of other ways. According to Bill James, Del and outfielder Davy Jones were involved in the first documented case of regular-season platooning. Also, until Mark Carreon came to play for Detroit in 1992, Del was the only Tiger position player who threw left-handed and batted righthanded.

After the season, though, the Tigers never brought him back up. He played in the highest minors for Providence and Kansas City in 1912 and 1913, then jumped to the St. Louis team of the new Federal League for 1914 and 1915.

When the Federal League folded, Del returned to the minors for two more seasons. In 1917, at thirty, and with his second child on the way, he was given his release by Scranton and he called it a career. He returned to Findlay, where he continued to play baseball for local teams in the Industrial Leagues into his early forties. In the late 1930s, he coached his sons Del, Jr. and Bob on the Findlay College baseball team. His 1939 team beat Toledo, Kent State, and Bowling Green,

Del Drake with the Detroit Tigers in 1911

and posted a winning percentage of .823, the highest in Ohio that year.

Del Drake never made it to Cooperstown, but he was a Hall of Famer in my book. I want you to know that I saw him not long ago. On September 27, 1999, I took my Dad to the last game ever played at Tiger Stadium. This was only fair, since he took me to my first game there. Brother Fritz came, too, as did Greg Meyers, who had taken me to my only World Series game there in 1984. After the game was over, they opened up the gates in center field, and one by one, more than 70 former Tigers came out and took their old positions on the field. For a moment, I closed my eyes and there was Del—young and strong and swift—running out to left field. It was the greatest sight I ever saw.

Return with us now to those thrilling days of yesteryear. From out of the past comes the thunderous kee-rack of the great bat, Hondo. The Washington Senators ride again.

Hondo

John Holway

Mark McGwire may have smashed Roger Maris' mark, but he hasn't come close to Hondo's 600-footers.

Hondo, of course, was Frank Howard, the hulking blond bomber of the old Washington Senators, who blasted cloud-scrapers in almost every park he played in in the 1960s.

McGwire's longest to date sailed 545 feet. The big league record, by Mickey Mantle, is a reputed 565 feet in Washington's Griffith Stadium in 1953. Howard's longest: over the roof of Yankee Stadium, on September 29 1970. Estimated distance: 580 feet, plus.

The umpire called it foul by four inches.

"I thought it was fair," Howard says laconically. "So did everyone else."

"Frank was the McGwire and Griffey of his day," declares Ron Menchine, "the Voice of the Senators" when Hondo was in his heyday thirty years ago. "I think if Frank were playing today, he would maybe have broken Maris' record already. If he faced the pitching that these guys are facing now, it wouldn't be impossible for him to hit 75 to 80 a season."

The upper deck in Washington's RFK Stadium once blossomed with white-painted seats, each marking a Howard blast. "How far would those upper deckers have gone in Camden Yards," Phil Wood of Baltimore's WTEM once asked Frank.

"Upper deck," he replied. (No one has reached that target since the park was built.)

Ted Williams took over as Senators manager in 1969. Hondo? Who was this guy? "Very shortly after that, I

found out. I thought, 'Boy, he hits the ball farther and harder than anybody I've ever seen.'" Older guys had told Ted about some of Babe Ruth's mighty clouts. "Well, Frank Howard did that for me."

Yet almost no one remembers Hondo today, or his Yankee Stadium bombshell. He ended with 382 for a fourteen-year career. He had his best home run years— 44, 48, and 44—in 1968-70, the height of the era of pitching dominance. If Hondo had played today, who knows how many homers he would have clouted—or how far they would have flown?

If Frank had worn an "NY" on his cap instead of a "W," he would surely be remembered today in the same breath with Mickey Mantle. And his Yankee Stadium blow would be as famous as Mantle's drive that hit the facade just below the right field roof. The roof is gone now, and the mystique of the House That Ruth Built—no fair ball ever went out of the park—remains intact. But several eye-witnesses insist that that's another one of baseball's myths.

Big Frank doesn't talk much about it. Like the original Hondo, John Wayne, he doesn't say much about anything beyond "yep," "nope," or "Howdy, Ma'am."

I caught up with him at Camden Yards, where he was slapping fungoes as bench coach of the Tampa Bay Devil Rays. What about the Yankee Stadium blast?

"That's been debated for years," he says. "It was a foggy night," and nobody saw exactly where the ball landed, but he thinks it "probably" cleared the roof. Frank thinks the ball may have left the park fair, then curved away from fair territory. "Clete Boyer, the Yankee third baseman, thought it was fair."

His Senator teammates insist that Howard's drive did

John Holway's Complete Book of the Negro Leagues *is due out in May.*

go out, and went out fair. "Do I *remember* it?" exclaims Senators pitcher Jim Hannan, who is surprised that anyone else does. "The unbelievable thing was that it went out above the top of the foul pole."

With three decks, Yankee Stadium had the highest foul pole in baseball, but even it didn't reach the old roof, 118 feet above the field. The leftfield pole was 301 feet from home, and the roof was about 50 feet beyond that.

"Over the foul pole?" gulps ex-Senator Dick Bosman. "It went over the *lights*!"

"It had a lot of juice to it," Hannan agrees. "It was still on its way up, like you hit a golf ball. We lost sight of it in that gray-green facade. We waited to see if it came bouncing around in the stands." But no kids scrambled to chase it, and if the ball did land inside the park, it hasn't been found to this day.

Hannan, now a businessman in Annandale, Virginia, says the third-base ump signaled foul and held his hands four inches apart, "Who's got eyes *that* good?" Jim demands. "You couldn't tell. Couldn't even see it."

Who was the umpire? Box scores then didn't give the names of the umps as they do now. We do know that Nick Avants, a rookie in only his third major league game, was behind the plate, because Senators manager Ted Williams had come out to argue with him earlier.

"It was absolutely the hardest hit ball I've ever seen!" Avants declares from his home in Little Rock. "It got to the top of the Stadium before he could take three steps out of the batters' box. You couldn't tell from where I was whether it was fair or foul, or went right over the roof or right under the roof. But it was ungodly. I was glad I didn't have to call it; I don't know what I would have done. I had a lot of respect for him, because he didn't argue the call. There was no big row."

Howard never would show the umpires up, Hannan says, so he waited until he had trotted back to the dugout before exploding. "Jim," he yelled to Hannan, "they're taking bread and butter out of my mouth! That ball was fair."

"Don't yell at me," his teammate replied, "I'm on your side!"

Could it be that the umpire was, consciously or unconsciously, protecting the legend of Yankee Stadium? If Mantle had hit it, would it have been called fair?

"I think the umpire legitimately thought it was foul," says Hannan. "But a guy hits it that far, and it's that close, you give it to him."

The newspapers the next morning are no help. The two Washington reporters, Merrill Whittlesy of the *Star* and George Minot of the *Post*, mentioned "a long foul" by Howard but gave no other details. Minot says today that he doesn't remember it.

Three New York writers—Leonard Koppett of the *Times*, Joe Trimble of the *Daily News*, and Leonard Cohen of the *Post*—didn't mention the blow at all.

Koppett, now living in California, is defensive when asked. He can't remember either, and repeats the mantra that "no fair ball has ever been hit out of Yankee Stadium." If Mantle had hit it, it is hard to imagine that anyone would have forgotten it.

There were no computers thirty years ago to estimate distances. Francis Mirabelle, a ballistics expert at the Army's Aberdeen Proving Grounds in Maryland, says a batted ball (or an artillery shell) attains its maximum height at 60 percent of its total distance. If Howard's hit was still going up when it left the Stadium 350 feet from home, the total distance would have been at least 580 feet.

Series shots—That may actually have been the *second* ball Frank hit over the roof that Ruth built. Yankee shortstop Tony Kubek told Phil Wood and other writers in Baltimore several years ago that in the first game of the 1963 World Series, Howard, then with the Dodgers, hammered one of Whitey Ford's serves over the roof. Again the umpire said foul. Tony said he and second baseman Bobby Richardson exchanged looks as if to say, "That ball was fair." Today Richardson can't remember it, "but if Tony says so, it's true."

Howard's Dodger teammates shake their heads no. It went into the upper deck, says pitcher Johnny Podres. It hit the facade, according to outfielder Wally Moon. This time no newspaper, in Los Angeles or New York, mentioned it at all. So the report must go into the books with a tantalizing question mark.

Frank's own favorite memory came in the fourth game of that Series. His single and home run were the only Los Angeles hits off Ford as the Dodgers beat Whitey, 2-1, to sweep the Series. It was a line drive into Dodger Stadium's upper deck, Podres recalls; before the outfielders could turn their heads to look, it had already bounced back onto the field.

Despite his immense strength and ominous nickname, Hondo was a soft-spoken guy who was always thinking of others. "He was a big ol' pussy cat," says Williams. "A lovable guy, the other guys all liked him."

Frank would miss a turn in batting practice rather than leave a reporter's questions unanswered. And when he hits fungoes these days, he's careful not to give the infielders any short hops that could embarrass them.

"He was a down-to-earth guy," says Menchine. When the Senators called up their farmhands for a cup of coffee each September, Frank would take each of the kids out to dinner. "Can you imagine a guy doing that today?"

Menchine wishes Howard were in his prime today. "It sounds chauvinistic, but look at the pitching back then—Jim Palmer, Mike Cuellar, Catfish Hunter, Vida Blue—almost every team had great pitching."

"And there's a big difference in the baseballs today

from thirty years ago," adds Steve Ridzik, another Senators hurler. "Back then the ball was a little deader than it is today. Today they're hitting homers to the opposite field; you never saw them hit those that far then."

"Frank hit balls 600 feet," Hannan declares. "One distance you can measure was in Anaheim." Before the second deck was added in the outfield, "in back of the bleachers was a paved area, then the big "A" sign on a pylon, then a chain link fence about 600 feet away. He hit the fence. He didn't clear the fence, he hit it on the fly."

In January, 1962, in the finals of the Puerto Rican playoff, Frank hit one off the Orioles' Jack Fisher that was measured at 536 feet. It broke the old 1940 mark, an estimated 525 feet, by an earlier Washington legend, Negro Leaguer Josh Gibson. (In 1995, Juan Gonzalez hit two tremendous drives there, but neither was as long as Hondo's or Josh's.)

San Juan fans called Howard "Condo," because he was as big as one.

"It felt like an earthquake when he ran," says Avants. Comedian Phil Silvers claimed that Frank was so big, "fans in left field complained that he was blocking their view."

He swung a 45-ounce bat. "It felt like one of those lead bats that hitters used to swing in the on-deck circle," says Minnesota third baseman Ron Clark.

How much?—The encyclopedia says Hondo packed 255 pounds on a six-foot-eight frame, but many question that.

"Weight was a big bone of contention all the time," Williams says. "I'd say, 'Frank, how much do you weigh?' He'd say, 'Oh, about 262, Skip.' I'd say, 'Get on the scales for me,' and it was always ten-twenty pounds more than he told me."

"He weighed 305," Bosman declares. "I saw him on the scale." Dick concedes that a few years earlier Frank may have been lighter, perhaps 280 or 290, or even 260 when he broke in in 1958 at the age of twenty.

Howard reported each spring at 255, his roomate, pitcher Joe Coleman says, but his size grew as the season wore on. ("He loved to eat and drink his beer," Menchine smiles.) But big Frank needed the extra pounds, because he would sweat off ten pounds a game in the Washington humdity.

Gil Hodges, Williams's predecessor as manager, had Hondo on a strict 260-pound limit. "I was pushing 265," Frank grins. "It was going to cost me some money if I didn't make it. I came in Saturday morning, got on the scale at 261. I'm trying to get with the program," he said with his sincerest grin. "That might I went out, I was breaking into all the donut shops after closing. Sunday morning our trainer wants me to weight again. I was 274, so you can imagine what kind of binge I was on in one night."

The Senators' scales went only to 275, Hannan says. But the Redskins in the adjoining locker room had a freight scale. They pushed Frank onto it and blinked as the needle stopped at 315.

Frank preferred to eat in his room, so no one could see how much he was packing away. "You hungry, Roomie?" he asked Hannan one night, picking up the phone. "Hello, room service? How about steaks? Three, medium rare. Yeah, potatoes, too. Got any dessert? Okay, strawberry shortcake with cream." Then he looked at Hannan. "Jim, what do *you* want?"

Hannan remembers breakfast in the Chicago airport. "Do you have poached eggs?" Howard asked the waitress. "I'll have a dozen. And toast, please—but make it dry, I'm on a diet."

What if Howard had known about Creatine as McGwire does today? "Creatine?" smiles Wood. "He didn't even work out! The heaviest thing he lifted was one of those big sandwiches."

Williams nods. "He'd come out early, work his ass off, but he'd put it all down the sewer when the game was over, making a bee-line to a beer joint he knew and drink half a case of beer."

The Yankee Stadium megablast was unusual, Hannan says, because Hondo seldom hit balls down the line. "His power was to center and left-center."

He also hit line drives as often as high flies. "He could hit the ball lower and farther than anyone I ever saw," says Ridzik, a long-time Virginia resident now living in Florida.

Menchine remembers one liner. "It left the bat and hit the wall in an instant. Looked like it was going to go right through the wall—kaboom, it was off the wall."

"I know how to pitch to Howard," lefty Tommy John of the White Sox boasted. "Work him outside."

"Frank hit one off John at RFK," Hannan recalls. "John started to jump for the ball, and it actually broke a seat in centerfield and came back between the outfield and second base."

"Tommy Agee in center field started in," Senator outfielder Fred Valentine adds. "It was like a two-iron, it just kept rising and rising. They painted another seat."

A year later Dennis Bennett, who had joined the Red Sox from the National League, was shaken by the sight of the painted seat in deep center. "I'm just throwing changeups and curves," he vowed. "He's not going to see a fastball from me."

Bennett got big Frank out three times with soft stuff, then he got cocky. Shaking off repeated signs for curves, he uncorked a fastball, and Howard hit it several rows beyond the Tommy John seat.

Tiger shortstop Ray Oyler jumped for another Hondo homer. "It's a good thing he didn't catch it,' says Wood, "it would have carried him into left field."

Howard threw fear into the pitchers and infielders.

"He hit bullets through the box," winces Ridzik. "I even hated to pitch batting practice against him."

Baltimore's Hall of Fame third baseman Brooks Robinson said the only time he was really scared in baseball was when Howard came to bat.

Ron Clark says Hondo "tore the damn webbing off my glove." With trembling knees, he approached the pitcher, lefthander Jim Kaat. "Why don't you pitch him over the middle of the plate more?" Ron suggested.

"Why would I want to do *that*?" Kaat replied.

Once, however, Jim apparently did do it. The result, Menchine says, was "a low-trajectory laser shot" over the head of center fielder Ted Uhlaender. "Ted didn't even move. As he turned his head, it hit him on the chest on the way back."

Big Hondo was a good bunter and sometimes dropped base hits in front of third basemen who were playing in left field.

"Howard owned those good lefthanders—Kaat, John, Ford, Mickey Lolich, Sam McDowell," Wood chuckles.

A homer binge—In 1968 Howard went on a record binge, bashing ten home runs in six games.

Number one came in Washington against Detroit's Lolich (17-9 that year). Number two was against righthander Fred Lasher (5-1). "It was a rising ball," Bosman gulps. "We were in the bullpen, and we couldn't get out from under the awning fast enough— it was already up there! Must have broken the seat."

Number three, in Boston, "nearly tore a hole through the net atop the fence," Minot wrote. Number four landed eight rows into the Fenway center field bleachers. The next day Frank socked number five against Boston's righthander Jose Santiago (9-4).

Numbers six and seven came in Cleveland against strikeout king Sudden Sam McDowell (15-14). Both were "monstrous shots," said Bosman, pitching coach for the Texas Rangers. The second one landed in deep left-center field. Ten feet to the right, and it would have been the only ball ever to reach the bleachers. An usher retrieved it 523 feet from home.

"I don't think I hit either one flush," Frank apologized.

The next night, in Detroit, he smashed his eighth homer in five games to erase Babe Ruth's record.

In his sixth game Frank faced Lolich again and blasted two more. The first one went into the right field upper deck.

On the second, Bosman remembers: "Lolich tried to sneak a fastball by him, didn't get it in enough. The ball hit on the back of the roof and went out there." The roof is 94 feet high. They estimated the blow at 550 feet.

However, Coleman, Anaheim's pitching coach, thought the ball went farther than that. It went out above the 365-foot sign, and the roof was set back about 40 feet beyond that for a total distance of about 405. Coleman says the ball hit the front of the roof, which tilted forward. If the ball had been coming down, it would have bounced back toward the field. Frank's blow glanced off the roof and kept right on going. That would make it as far as the Yankee Stadium blow.

Williams recalls another time against Yankee righthander Mel Stottlemyre in Washington. "Frank swung from the ass and hit a low fastball on a line to center field that could have split a rock." Ted grabbed the bullpen phone. "Hold that ball for me," he barked, "I want to look at it."

Memories—My own vivid memory of Howard is not his home runs but his strikeouts. I remember him waving futilely at righthanded curves; despite his long arms, his bat seemed to be six inches too short to reach them.

"That means he was fooled," Ted says. "He walked about 40 times a year, struck out about 125. He wasn't getting a good ball to hit. If you're fooled by pitches, you've got to take them, up to two strikes."

However, Orioles righthander Jim Palmer usually got Howard out pitching inside, under his elbows. As Jim tells the story:

"Ted Williams had told Frank to move back off the plate."

Williams nods. "The easiest thing in the world is to defend yourself against the inside pitch. Stay only as close as you have to to protect the outside corner. History is made from middle-in."

Anyway, Palmer says ruefully, "I threw my 'seventh-inning fastball' over the corner, "only it wasn't inside anymore. He hit it into the third deck, headed out of Memorial Stadium. Luis Tiant was the only man who ever got hit out of the stadium [by Frank Robinson]. The only thing that kept me from joining Tiant was a little chain link fence that kept people from falling out of the third deck." Frank's drive hit the fence.

Hondo's friends remember not only his big blasts but his self-deprecating "aw shucks" demeanor. When his family was away, he roomed with youngsters Bosman and Coleman, sort of their father figure, Coleman says. Big Frank gave the kids the beds while he bunked down in the living room.

At card-signing shows, Menchine says, some players won't even look at the people shuffling up to their tables—just sign and keep the line moving. "Frank is just the opposite. He's friendly, talks to everyone." The promoters almost hate to have him in the shows, because it takes so long to move the line. "You just have to love the guy."

"A Flesh And Blood Frank Merriwell—That's Wesley Ferrell."
New York World-Telegram, *July 23, 1935.*

The Wes Ferrell Story

Dick Thompson

Several years ago I became involved in a discussion regarding potential candidates for Baseball's Hall of Fame. I'm not usually interested in this subject, but I did offer my opinion that Wes Ferrell was a worthy player whose greatness has long been overlooked. My contention was uncomplicated. Ferrell was a six-time 20-game winner and arguably the greatest hitting pitcher of all time. The counter-argument was just as simple, Ferrell had more career walks (1,040) than strikeouts (985) and had a career ERA of 4.04. Both were legitimate points that I couldn't argue, at least at the time.

I spent the next two years looking at the box score of every major league game that Ferrell appeared in. I searched out dozens of articles in *The Sporting News* and reviewed the huge stack of newspaper clippings that made up Ferrell's file at the National Baseball Library at the Hall of Fame.

Wes Ferrell appeared in fifteen major league seasons but really played only ten. His first two seasons, at ages nineteen and twenty, were brief September call-ups, and his last three seasons, 1939-1941, were futile comeback attempts following what was essentially career-ending elbow surgery in the fall of 1938. In between, Ferrell matched Lefty Grove and Carl Hubbell, generally viewed as the two greatest hurlers of that generation, win for win as a starting pitcher.

In this article I compare Ferrell to many of his contemporaries. I had initially planned to use Lefty Gomez

Dick Thompson *would like to thank Bill Deane, Wes and George Ferrell Jr., Scott Flatow, the late Jack Kavanagh, Kerry Keene, Ray Nemec, Pete Palmer, Dave Smith, Lyle Spatz, Dixie Tourangeau, and the SABR-L gang for assistance with this article.*

as Ferrell's yardstick, but quickly determined that Grove would be a better contrast. My intent isn't to claim that Ferrell was the same pitcher as Grove, but rather to show Ferrell's value in its truest light. What better way to do that than to compare him to the best?

Early days—Wesley Cheek Ferrell came into the world in Greensboro, North Carolina on February 2, 1908, the fifth of seven sons born to Rufus and Alice Carpenter Ferrell. The family patriarch was a railroad worker who, as his family grew in number, settled into the life of a rural dairy farmer in Guilford, North Carolina. The two oldest Ferrell brothers, Basil and William Kermit, were content to follow farming as a career choice,[1] although Basil, according to family legend, was the best hitter in the family.[2] The remaining brothers, George Stuart, Richard Benjamin, Wesley Cheek, Isaac Marvin, and Thomas Ewell, all became obsessed with the national pastime.

Richard's career needs little mention. Rick Ferrell's lifetime association with the game, including eighteen big league seasons, resulted in his 1984 selection to the Hall of Fame.

George, born in 1904, also made a career of professional baseball. While never appearing in a major league game, he accumulated over 2,800 minor league hits.[3] He later managed in the minors and scouted for the Detroit Tigers. George's son, George, Jr., played in the Tigers and Red Sox chains in the late 1950s and early 1960s.

Marvin, born in 1911, pitched in the minors 1931-1940. His highest professional classification came in 1931, the same year George reached his top level.

Marvin played with Milwaukee in the American Association, while George was with Buffalo in the International League.

First cousin Beverly "Red" Ferrell played for the Baltimore International League club in 1934.[4] A decent hitter in the lower minors, Red hit .338 in the Georgia-Florida League in 1936. First cousin Dewitt "Charley" Ferrell played professionally for a decade. He caught in the International League in 1945 and 1946. There were so many Ferrells playing in the 1930s that even professional baseball found it hard to keep track of them. *The Sporting News* reported in 1932 that a confidence man, claiming to be a Ferrell brother, was arrested in Minneapolis as an impostor.[5]

Wes attended Guilford High School and the Oak Ridge Military Academy, a prep school[6] in North Carolina, where a Cleveland scout named Bill Rapp spotted him. When Wes went off in 1927 to play for the East Douglas, Massachusetts team in the Blackstone Valley League, a strong semipro circuit on the Massachusetts-Rhode Island-Connecticut border, he promised Rapp he wouldn't sign with any other major league team before first speaking with him.

A number of major leaguers played in East Douglas, the most prominent being Hank Greenberg. In his autobiography Greenberg wrote:

> The town revolved around the Schuster Woolen Mills and its owner, Walter Schuster. I don't think there was a square inch of East Douglas that Mr. Schuster didn't own, and I'm including the churches and the school. The town was a fiefdom, and Mr. Schuster was the king, but a benevolent one. Baseball was his only outside interest. He once promised Lefty Grove $1,000 in advance and $100 a strikeout to pitch against the East Douglas team in an exhibition game. Grove struck out 17 and collected $2,700, the most, as far as I know, that anyone at that time had ever been paid to pitch in an exhibition game.
>
> "Mr. Schuster developed ballplayers like Gene Desautels and Bump Hadley and Wes Ferrell, and when I first went up there, the lineup was so tough that I couldn't even break in.[7]

Greenberg mentions Ferrell several times in his book. His take on Wes was direct and to the point:
"He should be in the Hall of Fame. Why his name has been overlooked I'll never understand, but his record measures up to anybody's."[8]

1927—Ferrell pitched well enough in East Douglas to attract the attention of both the New York Yankees and the Detroit Tigers. Frank Shaugnessey, Detroit's New England scout, said, "I was doing my turn around the New England colleges in the spring of 1927 when I spotted a big fellow who could fire the ball, on a mill team near Providence. His name was Wes Ferrell."[9]

Shaugnessey brought Ferrell to Fenway Park for a tryout when the Tigers were in Boston. There Ferrell witnessed a brawl between Tigers manager George Moriarty and his infielder Marty McManus. The incident didn't sit well with Ferrell and he told Shaugnessey he wouldn't sign with Detroit.[10]

Yankee scout Paul Krichell had noticed Ferrell when he signed pitcher Ben Shields from the Oak Ridge school. Krichell lost interest when Wes developed soreness in his throwing arm, but he arrived back on the scene in 1927 and was willing to top Cleveland's offer. Cleveland wired Rapp and told him to get up to New England as fast as possible.[11]

True to his word, Wes took a train to Cleveland when he heard from Rapp.[12] There he signed a two year contract worth $3,000 a year. He also received a $3,000 signing bonus with another $3,000 promised if the Indians retained him after the first two years.[13] His major league debut came in Fenway Park on September 9. He gave up three earned runs while pitching the last inning of the game.

1928—Ferrell was dazzling in the Indians spring camp in New Orleans in 1928. Roger Peckinpaugh, Cleveland's new manager, was impressed enough to take him north when the major league season opened. Cleveland coach Grover Hartley, who had caught for the New York Giants when Christy Mathewson was still at his peak, said: "He looks more like Matty than any young pitcher I ever saw. He's got the same simple, easy motion Matty had. He just goes up like this and comes down like this and lets the ball go without any effort, but when he lets it go it's got plenty on it. He's a big, swell-looking kid, and the way he's put together he couldn't be anything but a pitcher. They turned him over to me, so's that I could teach him something about pitching, but nobody has to teach him much. He was born with it, I guess, just like most really good pitchers are. Now and then, of course, I have to tell him something, but I have to tell it to him only once."[14]

Ferrell was sent to Terre Haute before he could could get into a game and he spent the season pitching in the Three-I League. His 20 wins topped the circuit. Recalled to the majors after the Three-I playoffs concluded, Wes made two late September starts in which Cleveland was shut out. On September 28, he lost a 1-0 game to the Red Sox. The Tribe managed just six hits, and the only one for extra bases was Ferrell's own triple.

1929—Ferrell's breakthrough season came in 1929 and by the end of the year he was the toast of the

American League. Working mostly in relief and as a spot starter, his record stood at 6-7 on July 10. At the same time (July 12), Lefty Grove was cruising along with a 15-2 mark and an ERA of less than 2.00. At that point Grove broke down, probably from overuse. Ferrell took off. Over the last three months of the season it was Ferrell, not Grove, who dominated the American League. Here are Grove's and Ferrell's first half, second half, and final numbers in 1929.

		W-L	Inn.	ERA
Grove	1st half	15-2	157.0	1.83
Ferrell	1st half	6-7	85.2	4.31
Grove	2nd half	5-4	118.2	4.10
Ferrell	2nd half	15-3	157.0	3.21
Grove	Total	20-6	275.2	2.81
Ferrell	Total	21-10	242.2	3.60

Beginning on July 15, Ferrell ran off a 9-0 mark in ten starts (he also went 1-1 in relief), including two complete game wins each against Philadelphia and New York. In his first ten appearances that season versus those two American League powerhouses, he was 6-0 with a 2.83 ERA. Writer Sam Murphy noted: "Ferrell is one pitcher whose skill on the mound has won the admiration of Miller Huggins and Connie Mack. Al Simmons, the mighty hitter of the Philadelphia outfit, says he can't seem to get a hold on anything that Ferrell pitches. In eleven times the righthanded Quaker slugger has faced the young Indian pitcher he has dented the ball for one lone hit, a puny average of .091."[15]

Simmons went on record that winter as saying he, "would rather bat against any other pitcher in the American League."[16] Another clipping from that period said: "Yankee players are enthusiastic about this young pitcher, and the same holds true of the A's. The Athletics say he was the best man they faced during the trip."[17]

Ferrell was also impressing opponents with his bat. He hit his first major league home run off Washington's Bump Hadley on July 10. On July 19, he hit a pinch-hit triple against New York, then repeated the trick four days later against Philadelphia.

Ferrell didn't go unnoticed in the post-season award voting. Grove topped *The Sporting News* All-Star pitcher balloting with 174 votes.[18] Burleigh Grimes was second with 37 votes and Ferrell was seventh (the third rated American Leaguer) with 20 votes. Carl Hubbell, who won 18 games in his second major league season, managed just a single vote.

MVP awards in 1929 and 1930 were unofficial and followed the same rules as the 1922-1928 American League Award: each voter had to name one player from each team. Both Grove and Ferrell were shut out in the BBWAA's voting, which Ferrell's teammate Lew Fonseca won. Three Athletics, Jimmy Dykes, Al Simmons, and Mickey Cochrane, received votes.

The *Sporting News* MVP went to Simmons, and while Grove was shut out in the voting, Ferrell finished eleventh, one vote shy of Lefty's teammates, Dykes and Jimmie Foxx.

Grove's season stands a little more scrutiny. He was a two-team pitcher, going 12-1 with a 2.37 ERA against Cleveland (5-0) and the last place Red Sox (7-1) who managed just 28 home runs during the season. Against the three best offensive teams in the American League that year, (Philadelphia, New York and Detroit—the only AL teams to top 100 homers), Grove, aided by not having to face his own club, went 4-1 in 70.2 innings of work while Ferrell went 11-4 in 112.2 innings. Grove pitched almost as many innings against the Red Sox (60) as he did against New York (33.1) and Detroit (37.1) combined.

Mack started Grove 37 times in 1929, the most starts Lefty ever made in a season. During the pennant-winning era of 1929-1931, Mack experimented with his aces (Grove, Earnshaw, and Walberg), and at various times all three suffered from those practices. Early in 1929 he started Grove on consecutive days, and later in the year, after Lefty began breaking down, Mack let him pitch a seventeen-inning game in which he allowed 20 hits. Surely Mack's first-half experimentation caused Grove's second-half arm woes and undoubtedly was the real reason that Grove did not start a World Series game that year. Grove pitched less than six innings in 12 of his 37 starts, and the Philadelphia bats, as evidenced by Grove's 11 no-decisions, saved Grove from a number of losses in 1929. Lefty received no-decisions in seven starts in which he left the game with his team trailing.

1930—The leading pitchers in the American League in 1930 were:

	W-L	ERA
Lefty Grove	28-5	2.54
Wes Ferrell	25-13	3.31
George Earnshaw	22-13	4.44
Ted Lyons	22-15	3.77

Grove led the league in wins, ERA, and strikeouts. Ferrell was second in wins and ERA, and fourth in strikeouts. Conventional wisdom is that Grove was the best pitcher of 1930. Ferrell, however, faced much tougher competition than Grove, and he did it with a inferior team behind him.

The Athletics played over .600 ball without Grove's won-lost record while the Indians were a sub-.500 club without Ferrell's contribution. Grove had Foxx, Simmons, and Cochrane, while Ferrell's best offensive teammate was Earl Averill.

Mack went into the season with a preconceived notion of how many wins it would take to win the pennant. His theory was that any pitcher could be cannon fodder for the Yankees' bats, but pitching Grove against the weaker teams was a sure win.

The top three American League teams in 1930 were Philadelphia (102-52), Washington (94-60), and New York (86-68). Washington, skippered by Walter Johnson, had the best pitching. With Ruth, Gehrig, and Lazzeri all with over 100 RBIs, the Yankees were an offensive powerhouse with a mediocre hill staff. Ferrell's Cleveland club (81-73) rounded out the upper division.

George "Rube" Walberg was the A's designated whipping boy in 1930. A decent lefty, he had won 16, 17, and 18 games for Mack in the three preceding years, and would win 20 and 17 in 1931 and 1932. His 13-12 record for the 1930 Philadelphia club certainly looks aberrant.

Walberg made 16 of his 30 starts that year against Washington and New York (eight starts each), while Grove made just seven of his 32 starts versus the same teams, five against Washington and two against the Yankees. While Grove and Earnshaw started five times each against both the tail-end White Sox and Red Sox, Walberg didn't start at all against Boston and only three times versus Chicago.

Grove started twice against New York in 1930. He beat them with a complete game on April 15, then allowed six earned runs in 2.1 innings on April 22. The clubs met an additional 20 times that season. Grove never started again.

The following table shows the workload of Ferrell and Grove against the top three American League clubs in 1930.

	Starts	Inn.	W-L	ERA
Ferrell				
v. Phil.	7	54.1	5-2	2.98
v. Was.	4	36.0	4-0	0.75
v. NY	6	45.0	3-3	6.20
Total	**17**	**135.1**	**12-5**	**3.45**
Grove				
v. Phil.	0	0	0	0
v. Was.	5	46.2	2-1	2.31
v. NY	2	16.2	1-0	4.86
Total	**7**	**63.1**	**3-1**	**2.98**

Ferrell and Grove finished the season with 23 starting victories apiece. At the end of August, Ferrell was 23-9 and Grove was 22-5. Grove pulled away by going 6-0 in September, three wins coming in relief, while Ferrell went 2-4, losing a 2-1 decision to Ted Lyons and a game each to the Yankees and Athletics. During the last two months of the season Grove went 6-0 versus the last place Red Sox, picking up three of those victories in relief.

Ferrell's record stood at 11-9 when he woke up on the morning of July 9. He then ran off 13 consecutive complete-game victories, during which time his ERA was 2.48. Included in the streak were two wins each against the Yankees and the Athletics. The next year Grove put together his famous 16-game winning streak, in which he didn't have to face the best team in the league (his own) and never started against the Yankees.

Ferrell's streak ended on September 6, when he lost a 2-1 decision to Ted Lyons and the White Sox. Lyons remembered the game years later:

"I'll tell you a story about Wes Ferrell. There was a real fine pitcher. He'd battle you all the way. He kept you busy, all right. Well, one time Wes and I had each won 10 straight games. He came into Chicago, and we were going to pitch against each other. Now Wes was superstitious about having his picture taken on the day he was going to pitch, and I knew that. I knew, too, that if there was one way to upset a ballplayer, it was to monkey around with his superstitions."[19]

Lyons, with the help of a Chicago photographer, was able to cajole Ferrell into having their picture taken.

"I'm sure that it was on his mind the whole game. I beat him, 2-1. Well, there was a big potbellied stove in the clubhouse, and he went in and pretty near tore that thing up. He stomped around in there for about an hour, steaming and snorting.

"I saw Wes in Florida a few years ago, and I reminded him of that game. Did he remember it? Need you ask?"[20]

By September the fans were screaming for a Ferrell-Grove match-up and it loomed for mid-September before a little skullduggery on the part of Mack or Grove, or maybe both, threw a monkey wrench into the works. Ed Bang, *The Sporting News'* Cleveland correspondent, wrote:

Wesley Cheek Ferrell of Cleveland and Robert Moses Grove of Philadelphia will not meet in a pitching duel this season. The last possibility that the brilliant young Indian righthander and the veteran Athletics southpaw would engage in battle vanished last Saturday under circumstances that sank the Philadelphian to the very nadir of unpopularity with the Cleveland fans. Strangely enough, the resentment of the customers has not been directed at Connie Mack, the general public apparently deciding that the tall tactician merely was carrying out the wishes of Grove in avoiding the duel with Ferrell.

The facts of the case are these. After three weeks of agitation for a Grove-Ferrell contest, during which Billy Evans, Roger Peckinpaugh, and Ferrell himself, were openly favorable to the proposition and Mack was unwilling to pin himself to a definite declaration. Philadelphia came to Cleveland last Saturday for the first of a two-game series. The Cleveland management announced that Ferrell would pitch Sunday's game, leaving the issue clearly with Grove and his manager.[21]

George Earnshaw started the Saturday game against Cleveland. He had a 5-2 lead, but did not come out of the dugout to start the fifth inning. Grove did.

It is not difficult, then, to imagine the gasps of amazement and justified indignation that went through the crowd when the official announcer megaphoned the startling news that no one but Robert Moses Grove had relieved Earnshaw. With Cleveland trailing by three runs, there was no point in placing Ferrell in the game, so the youngster had to sit in disgust while Grove set down his mates without a run and only one hit in the five innings he worked.

There was, of course, no apparent reason for the shift. Earnshaw certainly was in no imminent danger of defeat, and the theory advanced earlier in the week—that Mack, with the pennant not yet clinched, might prefer to save Grove for a game which he would almost be certain to win—could not seriously be advanced, because here was a game that was practically won already. Incidentally, if Grove hoped to better his season's record by the afternoon's work, he was disappointed, for the official scorer ruled that Earnshaw was entitled to the decision.[22]

While *The Sporting News'* box score did give Earnshaw the win,[23] Grove's official pitching sheet credits him with the victory.[24]

Was Earnshaw relieved because of some physical ailment? Well, he tossed a complete game the next day and beat Ferrell. Was it a psychological ploy on Mack's part to derail the temperamental twenty-two-year-old, who to that point in his career was 9-2 with a 2.73 ERA against Philadelphia?

Bang continued:

Consideration of the season's records only tends to support the opinion of the fan flock that Ferrell is a better pitcher than Grove. True, the Athletic slabster has registered 26 victories while suffering five defeats, and Ferrell has turned in 24 wins while dropping 12 decisions. But whereas Grove has been supported by a team of champions, Ferrell has

been forced to rely on a makeshift combination that will do well enough if it retains fourth place until the season is ended.

It has also been pointed out by those who like to delve into the records that two of Ferrell's defeats have been effected by Ted Lyons, brilliant Chicago slabster, whom Grove, for some reason, has not faced at all this season. Ferrell has met the veteran on three occasions and has won one verdict. Ferrell has also worked six times against New York, splitting even, while Grove has been used only once against the dangerous Yankee bludgeoneers. It has also been observed that Grove, whose work against New York was limited to a single afternoon, has been sent against the lowly Red Sox for seven of his victories.[25]

One other clipping in Ferrell's Hall of Fame file confirms this opinion.

Robert Moses Grove won seven straight games for the Athletics versus Boston in 1930 without a loss. Six of them came in the last two months of the campaign and three of them within four days, September 3 to 6, inclusive.

Seven victories and no defeats in one season against a single club is the biggest one-man record of 1930, but the facts are not to be overlooked that the victim was the league's trailing club, and that Connie Mack picked spots that helped to make Grove's record.[26]

One more take on this question. "Mickey Cochrane was asked one day who was going to pitch against the Red Sox and he promptly answered that 'all the boys would be in shape for the series.'

"There are no sore arms when the Red Sox are to be met,' explained Cochrane, with a grin."[27]

The *Sporting News'* 1930 MVP award went to Joe Cronin who received 52 votes. Ferrell finished tied for fifth place with Lou Gehrig with 29 votes. Grove was next in line, tied at seventh place with Babe Ruth with nine votes. Ted Lyons, who won 22 games for the seventh place White Sox, drew 30 votes and finished fourth.[28]

The Associated Press' MVP voting followed a similar pattern. Lyons finished fifth, Ferrell sixth, and Grove ninth.[29]

On January 1, 1931 *The Sporting News* announced its 1930 All-Star Team, which had been selected by a vote of 228 members of the BBWAA. Only ten players, encompassing both leagues, were selected, one for each position plus two pitchers. The hurlers were Grove, who received 218 votes, and Ferrell, 163. Other slabsters who received more than two votes were Lyons with 41, Dazzy Vance with nine and Earnshaw with seven.

1931—Ferrell celebrated his twenty-third birthday before spring training in 1931. At an age when Grove had yet to reach the major leagues, Wes had already turned in a 46-23 record in his first two full seasons and was considered the best righthander in baseball. Grove, despite his 108-36 record with Baltimore in the International League 1920-1924, had a much tougher time, at a more mature age and playing for a better team, adjusting to the major leagues, going 23-25 over his first two seasons.

Noted sportswriter Joe Williams penned this article on Ferrell. It came from a rainy day interview with Roger Peckinpaugh.

About this Wes Ferrell that everyone is calling a second Mathewson? What makes him tick?...

"I'll tell about Ferrell," volunteered Peckinpaugh. "To begin with, he's got a lot of stuff. I mean a fine fast ball and a good curve, and he seems to know what it is all about. But what makes him stand out is that he knows he can throw the ball...."

It was suggested that practically everyone in the American League knew precisely as much.

"He's another Cobb when it comes to self-reliance," continues Peckinpaugh, "He likes to pitch, and there isn't any team he doesn't think he can't beat. He's at his best against the big hitters you fellows write about.

"Any time we have a tight ball game and some one else is pitching Ferrell will come around and say, 'If things get tough, send me in there. I'll stop 'em!' Get that! Not 'I'll try to stop 'em,' but 'I'll stop 'em!' What makes this important is that when you send him in he does stop 'em.'[30]

Can 1931, then, be looked at as crossroads on the journey toward fame? Grove had what is generally considered the finest season ever by a left-hander. Ferrell had arguably the greatest hitting season ever by a pitcher. For Grove, in a historical sense, that meant distinction. For Ferrell, it spelled oddity. In reality, it meant Grove played for a better team and again avoided pitching against the Yankees.

Ferrell got off to a quicker start than Grove did and by the end of April was 4-1 with a 2.03 ERA. Grove was 3-1 with a 3.00 mark. Wes ended the month by tossing a no-hitter versus the Browns on the 29th. At the plate that day, he doubled, homered, and drove in four runs.

Baseball experts were agreed that young Mr. Ferrell handed the Browns plenty. Billy Evans, general manager of the Indians, who beat the Browns behind Ferrell's superb performance, 9 to 0, declared Ferrell to be one of the greatest pitchers he had ever seen in action...

Billy Evans said last night that Addie Joss was one of the greatest pitchers he had ever seen and that even the Joss fastball, which was the best pitch of the famous righthander, was no better than the fast one Ferrell tossed yesterday.

And furthermore, Evans said Ferrell's curve far surpassed the Joss curve and that all Joss had superior to Ferrell was that accomplishment of "hiding" the ball from the batter until it was too late to swing effectively.

This from the general manager of the Indians whose big job each spring is to convince Wesley Ferrell that the Cleveland club has offered him everything in the way of salary it can afford. Even the prospect of another salary duel with Ferrell next spring could not restrain Evans from giving Ferrell the praise his experience and judgment prompted.[31]

Ferrell's no-hitter didn't come without cost. In his next three starts he gave up 25 hits and 18 earned runs in just 8.1 innings of work. Twice, against Boston on May 8 and five days later versus Washington, he walked off the mound of his own accord in the middle of an inning. In early June he announced that he had been suffering from a sore arm since the no-hitter and hadn't been able to throw a true fastball in that span.

Boston, June 3.—Wesley Ferrell, pitching ace of the Cleveland Indians, has given up struggling along with a right shoulder that has been sore since his no-hit performance of April 29.

Ferrell, who has been battered freely since his history-making game, finally admitted that his shoulder is painfully sore. Manager Roger Peckinpaugh prescribed a trip to the dentist today, and if that fails, treatment by a specialist in baseball arms and shoulders.[32]

Ferrell's best pitching in 1931 came against the second-place Yankees, the greatest run-scoring colossus in baseball history. He held the Bronx bombers, who averaged close to seven runs a game that year, to a single run in three of the four games he started against them. On one occasion the lone run was unearned.

He won a 2-1 duel from Herb Pennock on July 17, in which he allowed just three hits, one to Bill Dickey and two to Babe Ruth. Ruth hit a home run in the fifth inning to erase a 1-0 Cleveland lead, but Ferrell, undaunted, homered himself in the seventh for the game winner.

With Philadelphia wrapping up the pennant by late August, the only goal the New Yorkers had was to overtake the Senators. New York did that with a fast September rush, but not before their ten-game winning streak was snapped on September 21 by Ferrell, who beat Red Ruffing, 5-1. Said writer Will Wedge:

> Ferrell made the Yanks atone for their temerity in tearing off a ten-game winning streak so late in the season.
>
> There are Bronx spectators who think Ferrell should spell his name Ferule, like the old-fashioned flat ruler with which teachers used to chastise naughty children across their upraised palms. The Yanks had their hands raised for that second-place money. But what they got was a good, sharp rap over the knuckles from Mister Ferule. Wes slapped the Yanks down just when it looked as if they were getting someplace.
>
> But it was nothing new in the line of punishment that the Yanks have had to take from Wondrous Wes. He has been getting them used to that treatment all year. It made Ferrell's record for 1931 against the Yanks 4 won and 1 lost. The one game he dropped was back in June, when he went in to relieve [Willis] Hudlin.
>
> Twice this year Ferrell turned in three-hit jobs in downing the Yanks, in one of those games he copped a decision over Pennock by settling the game himself with a home run.
>
> Personally we are inclined to rate Ferrell as the year's best righthander in the league. Though it's hard to say that with Earnshaw to consider. Earnshaw twice this year came within a whisker of a no-hit game. Ferrell actually accomplished one, but the circumstances hung over him as a hoodoo for nearly a month.
>
> But considering that for a good part of this season Ferrell has labored under the handicap of a lame arm, yet has nevertheless hung up twenty-one victories, his work rates to stand alongside of Earnshaw's.[33]

Ferrell beat Washington, 3-1, on June 21, with his own seventh-inning homer breaking a 1-1 deadlock. He was next scheduled to make a start in a four-game series with Boston, which opened on June 23. Instead, he was held back to pitch against the Yankees on June 27.

Lou Gehrig hit a grand-slam off Wes in the first inning and New York scored an additional run in the next frame. Ferrell then tossed seven scoreless innings while his teammates came back to win the game.

Contrast that with Grove's August 29 start versus the Yankees. Beginning in Detroit on July 17, Grove completed all but two of his remaining regular-season starts. Both of those games came against the Yankees, one August 29, the other September 27.

The Athletics had given Grove a 7-0 lead in the August game but Mack immediately pulled Grove when he allowed a Gehrig grand-slam in the sixth inning. The September game was Lefty's last regular-season appearance. It may have been a World Series tune-up, but if it was, it wasn't much of one. Lefty allowed five earned runs and eight hits in just three innings and took his fourth loss of the season.

Mack wasn't known as the "tall tactician" for nothing. During his pennant-winning seasons, Mack made certain that Grove's psyche wasn't dealt too harsh a blow. Mr. McGillicuddy made sure there was no repeat of 1928, a season in which Grove went 23-2 versus the rest of the American League but 1-6 against the Yankees. Grove hurled just 17.2 starter innings against the Yankees in 1931, the second season in a row in which his fewest-opponent-innings came against New York.

The following table represents the number of innings that Ferrell and Grove worked as starters against opposing teams, ranked in order of cumulative team won-lost records, in 1930 and 1931. If I ranked them in order of runs scored, New York would be at the top of the list.

	Grove		Ferrell	
Philadelphia			99.2	18.1%
Washington	95.0	18.5%	82.1	15.0%
New York	29.0	5.7%	80.0	14.5%
Cleveland	79.0	15.4%		
Detroit	95.0	18.5%	71.2	13.0%
St. Louis	69.1	13.5%	78.0	14.2%
Chicago	75.1	14.7%	86.1	15.7%
Boston	69.2	13.6%	52.1	9.5%

Ferrell was as dominant as Grove in 1931 against five of the teams they faced that year. The biggest difference was that Lefty mastered the Detroit Tigers and Ferrell did not. The following table shows how they pitched, in a starting role, against Boston, New York, Chicago, Washington, and St. Louis.

	GS	CG	W-L	IPs	ER	ERA
Ferrell	24	20	19-3	189.2	58	2.75
Grove	21	18	18-3	179.2	34	1.70

This is how they hit in those same games.

	AB	R	H	2b	3b	HR	RBI	BA
Ferrell	75	19	26	3	1	7	24	.347
Grove	70	5	12	1	0	0	7	.171

Whatever ground Ferrell lost to Grove in pitching ability he gained right back with his bat. Adding in Detroit put Grove at 23-3 as a starter while Ferrell was 21-6.

The best way to judge the impact of Ferrell's hitting is to compare him to his teammates. Here is how Cleveland batters with at least 75 at bats performed in the 35 games Ferrell started in 1931. Wes always batted ninth.

	G	AB	R	H	2b	3b	HR	RBI	BA
Morgan	30	105	26	47	7	3	6	20	.448
Ferrell	35	106	24	37	6	1	9	29	.349
Hodapp	29	112	19	39	3	1	1	21	.348
Averill	35	148	37	50	11	0	7	35	.338
Vosmik	33	130	17	39	9	3	5	29	.300
Burnett	22	89	14	25	5	0	0	10	.281
Kamm	25	87	13	24	5	0	0	14	.276
L. Sewell	26	104	10	26	4	0	0	15	.250

Why was Grove a better pitcher statistically than Ferrell in 1931? Well, in addition to ducking the Yankees, Grove also didn't have to face his own teammates. Ferrell was unable to handle the reigning world champs, going 0-5 with a 6.41 mark. Grove went 4-0 with a 3.05 E.R.A. against Cleveland.

Grove and Ferrell met three times that year. The scores were 4-3, 4-3 and 6-3. None would be remembered as classics. Earnshaw, additionally, beat Wes, 4-2.

Ferrell won just once in the eight head-to-head meetings he had with Grove over the course of their careers. Lefty came out on top in all six of their confrontations while he was with the Athletics, a single run deciding three of the games.

On the other hand, Tommy Bridges was the one guy who hated to see Ferrell, either as a pitching opponent or as a batter. Ferrell and Bridges met five times 1931-1936 with Bridges managing just one win, a one-run decision that came in their last meeting. Wes hit five home runs off Bridges, one each in four of their pitching match-ups and one as a pinchhitter.

Bridges surrendered 181 career home runs. Here are the guys who kissed him the most.[34]

Player	Homers
Jimmie Foxx	16
Hal Trosky	10
Bob Johnson	7
Ben Chapman	6
Zeke Bonura	5
Bill Dickey	5
Wes Ferrell	5
Joe Kuhel	5
Babe Ruth	5

1932—The 1932 season started with Ferrell again being compared to Christy Mathewson. After Wes pitched against the Dodgers in spring training, Brooklyn manager Max Carey said, "Ferrell is another Christy Mathewson. That means he is one of the greatest pitchers I have ever seen. He has the same stuff that made Matty well-nigh invincible, and if his arm does not go back on him he ought to develop into the best right-hander that the American League has ever produced. The secret of Ferrell's success is that he knows how and what to pitch to each hitter."[35]

Ferrell came out of the starting gate as he had in the both 1930 and 1931, going the route and winning consistently. He opened the season with an eleven-inning, 6-5 win in Detroit on a frigid April day. By the Fourth of July he was 15-5, completing 16 of his 19 starts.

His bat, while not as lethal as it had been the previous season, continued to be productive when it mattered. On June 3, trailing 1-0, he hit a two-run homer off Tommy Bridges in the fifth inning of a 3-1 win over the Tigers. Four days later he helped himself with two doubles in a 4-3 decision over the Athletics. On June 30, he had three hits and three RBI in a 7-4 victory over the Tigers, driving in two runs in the seventh inning that produced the winning margin.

Other season highlights included a one-hit shutout against Boston on August 6 in which the lone hit was a bad-hop single.

> With two down Alexander hit what appeared to be an easy chance toward Cissell. That was when the ball left the bat. Just as Bill was set to make the play, the ball hit a pebble or something, took a freak hop and instead of hugging the ground, bounced high in the air. Cissell made a last dying-gasp stab at the ball, succeeded in blocking it and it rolled a few feet away.
>
> Had it not been for the last fractional part of a second bad hop it would have been an easy chance. None of the baseball reporters, including yours truly, [Ed Bang] who was the official scorer, thought that one was to be the only play of the game that would have a chance to be chalked up as a hit. If so, chances are it might have been scored an error.[36]

Joe Sewell, baseball's toughest man to fan, also had an eventful meeting with Mr. Ferrell. "Wes Ferrell of Cleveland struck out Joe Sewell, July 28, to accomplish a feat no other hurler has achieved this season. The New York Yankee really didn't strike out, but was called out by Umpire [Bill] Guthrie."[37] This was no trivial matter since Sewell fanned only three times that season in over 500 at-bats.

The top winner in the American League that year in

starting wins was Lefty Gomez with 23. Grove and Ferrell followed with 22 apiece.

Grove missed several weeks when he twisted an ankle in mid-June, then reinjured it in an *exhibition* game! Ferrell missed several starts in early September, sitting out a suspension (below).

The run support the three received was about a run different. Gomez got 6.9 runs per start from his mates, while Grove and Ferrell received 6.0 and 5.0 respectively.

Ferrell's frustrations seemed to reach a boiling point in midseason. On July 8, he beat Washington, 6-5, for his tenth consecutive complete game. Two days later Philadelphia came to Cleveland to play the famous 18-17 game in which Athletics reliever Eddie Rommel went seventeen innings to pick up the win.

Peckinpaugh waved Ferrell into the game in the seventh inning, and, despite just a single day of rest, left him in to pitch the remainder of the game—11.1 innings. Wes was tagged with the loss when Eric McNair doubled home Jimmie Foxx in the eighteenth. What isn't generally known is that Wes had the game won in regulation. With two outs in the ninth, Ferrell induced Jimmy Dykes to hit a slow roller to Eddie Morgan, the Indians' first baseman. Morgan pulled a Bill Buckner and the Athletics eventually scored two unearned runs.

In his next start the Yankees knocked Ferrell out in three innings. He then shutout Boston before losing a one-run game to the White Sox in twelve innings. Again pounded by the Yankees, he followed that with a 1-0 loss to the Athletics. Next came consecutive shutout wins against Boston and Detroit.

As Ferrell said: "Now, that was just a little relief stint, those eleven innings. A few days later I'm taking my regular turn, against the Yankees in New York. I go out there, and I don't have anything on the ball. They beat me. I'm sitting in the clubhouse after the game, and Peckinpaugh comes over and says, 'Hey, why didn't you bear down out there?'.

"'What the hell are you talking about?' I said. I was steamin'. 'I've been winning twenty games a year for you and pitching out of turn whenever you needed me, and you ask me why I wasn't bearing down? I always bear down. I just didn't have anything to bear down with today.'"[38]

A feud had been simmering between Ferrell and Peckinpaugh since the spring when Wes, responding to a question about the American League pennant race, answered that the Yankees had the edge because they had the best manager in Joe McCarthy.[39]

That obviously didn't sit well with Peckinpaugh. Ferrell claimed he was misquoted but the flames were fanned when McCarthy returned the compliment by saying: "Why, this Ferrell is another Matty! I realized last year that he was a great pitcher, but not until Saturday, when he shut us out after the second inning, did

I appreciate the mental side of his skill. That young man knows how to pitch. The way he maneuvered to make each batter hit the ball where he wanted him to increased my admiration twofold."[40]

By mid-August the rumors were flying. Ferrell was going to the Yankees even up for Gomez.[41] Ferrell was headed to Philadelphia for Earnshaw *and* Walberg.[42] Sportswriter Joe Williams frequently wrote about Ferrell coming to the Yankees. He guaranteed that Wes would be in pinstripes for the 1933 season.

> Mr. Wesley Ferrell is to be given an opportunity next year to pitch for the man he says is the best manager in baseball…
>
> My insider tells me that if the Yankees haven't already been offered Ferrell for Lefty Gomez they can have him at a moment's notice and the further dope is that the Yankee management is more than interested…
>
> The Yankees, I am told, figure that physically Ferrell is a better pitcher than Gomez and that mechanically it is about even…
>
> From what I hear the Yankees are under the impression that Gomez is a playboy. His romance with that Broadway gal has done him no good in the front office. On the other hand they know Ferrell is strictly a plugger. All he cares about is being a great pitcher.[43]

Ferrell dropped a 4-2 decision to the Yankees on August 26 that left his record at 20-12. Four days later Peckinpaugh relieved Ferrell in the first inning of a game in Boston. Wes was irate and didn't want to leave the hill. His argument was that he was well capable of working out of an early jam, especially as he had allowed the Red Sox only two earned runs in 27 previous innings that year.

When the team got back to Cleveland, Ferrell learned he had been suspended for ten days and would lose $1,200 in pay. Peckinpaugh said that Ferrell, "apparently had not been trying to win some games." Wes quickly retorted: "If anybody can prove that I ever laid down, I'll be willing to pitch a whole season for nothing. I'd pay to pitch, in fact. Nobody can say I'm not in shape and haven't kept in shape. I know some games I didn't pitch well, but I was trying. My arm was sore, that's all."[44]

The Sporting News chipped in on the state of Ferrell's arm: "That's another story—that sore arm. Ferrell says he doesn't like to mention it because he doesn't want to alibi. But he gives it as an explanation of his weakness against the heavy hitting clubs this season. Peck says he has no way of knowing when Ferrell's arm is sore. He adds that he has always been willing to give the slab ace a rest from his regular turn when it was requested."[45]

The situation was blown out of proportion. Peckinpaugh, who had been at the Indians' helm for five seasons, was bringing the team home in fourth place for the third consecutive season. His job was on the line. Ferrell's intense desire to win had been misconstrued by the press many times, but the players on the field understood his nature: "He talks but little and is not much of a mixer. Some think he is swell-headed. He knows he is a great pitcher but it is his reserved disposition that gives this impression."[46]

That didn't stop them, however, from backing Peckinpaugh. The fans were also on Ferrell's case and they let him know it with a chorus of boos when he took the mound in League Park.

Ferrell's initial anger subsided and he took the suspension as gracefully as possible. Cleveland President Alva Bradley and GM Billy Evans reiterated that Ferrell was neither for sale nor on the trading block. Writer Sam Murphy interviewed Ferrell regarding the incident:

> "They are kicking me around a little lately," said Ferrell, in discussing his suspension. "I guess I can take it. I suppose I got sore when the Red Sox started to beat me, especially as they could not touch me the last time I pitched against them. I have been trying hard to win my twenty-first game, and I suppose I did overstep the mark.
>
> "I tell you I can beat any team in the country when my arm is right and I can beat a lot of them even when it is ailing. Sometimes my arm is heavy, but when you get the call to the mound you go in there and pitch.
>
> "That talk of me laying down is nonsense. I make a living at pitching, and I always try and do my best. For four straight years I have won twenty games. That shows I am not loafing."[47]

Peckinpaugh never held it against Ferrell. In 1973 he said, "He was a fine pitcher, but he had a temper. He never wanted to be taken out of a game. He would be mad, not at anybody else, but mad at himself. Because he didn't think anybody could get a base hit off him and when they did he would get mad. He wasn't mad at a manager for taking him out of a game, but at himself."[48]

Luke Sewell, Cleveland's regular catcher, also realized that Ferrell's temper was part of his competitive make-up and played an essential role in his pitching. "Ferrell has that will to win. He has that intense desire to get that ball over the plate and by the batter. That's why you see him out there acting mad if he's not right, pawing the ground and cussing himself. Some fellows when they get mad are nervous and they go to pieces. When Ferrell gets mad he works all the harder. It makes him actually cooler. And he pitches even better. When he rares up and lets that ball go with all his weight behind him and with his heart in it, boy, he's tough to hit."[49]

Ferrell finished his suspension and still had time to toss three complete game victories before the season ended. The first, a 5-4 decision over the Yankees on September 11, snapped rookie Johnny Allen's ten-game winning streak.

Wes's final tally in 1932, again with a fourth-place team behind him, was 23-13. He had the most trouble with the first-place Yankees and second-place Athletics, going a combined 3-8 with a 5.27 ERA. Against the rest of the league he was 20-5 and 3.00.

The Yankees had overcome the gap between themselves and the Athletics, so Mack no longer had the luxury of picking Grove's spots against New York. He faired no better against the Yankees in 1932 (5.49 ERA. in 41 innings) than Ferrell did (5.48 ERA. in 42.2 innings).

As a matter of fact, looking just at the teams they mutually faced in 1932, there was hardly any difference at all between them. Evidently the voting sportswriters felt the same way. Grove received nine votes and Ferrell five in the MVP balloting. Neither finished in the top ten.

	Starts	CG	W-L	IPs	ER	ERA
Grove	24	21	21-7	234.0	78	3.00
Ferrell	30	24	22-9	246.2	94	3.43

	AB	R	H	2b	3b	HR	RBI	BA
Grove	85	6	11	0	0	3	10	.129
Ferrell[50]	95	11	25	2	2	2	15	.263

Hot stove rumors continued in the off-season. One had Wes going to the Athletics for Mickey Cochrane.

> In this connection the name of Gordon Cochrane, Philadelphia catcher, comes to mind. There are insistent rumors that Connie Mack would part with the hard-hitting Irishman if he received the right offer. Few clubs in the American League have men they would give for Cochrane who would be acceptable to Mack. The veteran catcher will come high, that's a certainty. If Cochrane leaves Philadelphia, it will be in exchange for a near-record amount of cash or for a player who ranks near the very top of the club ratings.
>
> But Cleveland obviously could use a catcher of Cochrane's proven talent and Philadelphia could easily find a place for Ferrell. With one thing and another, including the well-known depression, it is not asking too much of the imagination to conceive some kind of deal in-

volving the pair, even if both club owners stoutly deny the possibility.

No other club other than Cleveland has Wesley Ferrell, however. The big righthander certainly would make any owner feel inclined to propose a generous bargain. He has an amazing record, he has youth, he can hit as well as pitch. And he is—or was, at least—involved in unpleasantness with his manager. Apparently that breach has been healed. If not, there is just a chance, Bradley's statement to the contrary notwithstanding, that the Indians would consider parting with Ferrell.

No one in Cleveland would want to see him go. In spite of criticism that resulted from one or two of his temperamental outbursts last season, Ferrell ranks high with the fan flock. After all, the won and lost column is the last criterion of a pitcher's value, and Ferrell leaves nothing to be desired in that connection.[51]

1933—Wes Ferrell never met Christy Mathewson but it's easy to imagine how flattered he was by the frequent comparisons to the legend that many considered the greatest pitcher who ever lived. It's doubtful he felt that way in 1933.

Wes left late for spring training in New Orleans due to stalled contract negotiations. He was still at home when misfortune struck the family.

"Greensboro, N.C.—Ewell Ferrell, 20, youngest of the famous family of baseball playing Ferrell brothers, died from a bullet wound in the head, supposedly self-inflicted, March 6. The tragedy occurred at the home of Marvin Ferrell, pitcher for the Baltimore club of the International League, where Ewell was visiting. Marvin told police he heard a shot in another room of his home and upon investigation found his younger brother lying on the floor fatally wounded, a small pistol at his side. Marvin called the police, who sought to determine if the bullet was fired accidentally or with suicidal intent. Like his brothers, he played baseball and was supposed to be preparing to embark on a professional career. He was a pitcher and did fine for the Guilford High School team. No reason could be ascribed for the tragedy."

The Mathewson family had suffered a similar tragic event in 1909 when Matty's younger brother Nicholas took his own life.

On January 15, 1909, Nick stopped by an elderly friend's house and presented him with two sizable pickerels he'd just caught. 'You were always good to me when I cut your lawn and you paid me well,' Nick said to his friend. With that, he went down the road to the Mathewson house. Walking into the back of the barn, he scrawled a few incoherent lines onto a sheet of note paper, climbed up onto the hayloft, and shot a bullet into his brain. He was not 20 years old.[53]

There were no additional stories in *The Sporting News* on the Ferrell tragedy, and I wouldn't want to speculate on the sad and coincidental demise of the younger brothers of Wes and Matty other than to say both young men were reported to possess extraordinary pitching ability. Trying to live up to legendary older brothers may have been too much of an emotional challenge for them to overcome.

By 1933 the Depression was in full swing. Ferrell, who was paid $20,000 in 1931, for which he produced 22 victories, was cut to $18,000 in 1932. His reward for winning 23 games was another cut, this time to $12,000.[54]

Wes held out through the off-season. He wanted $18,000 and the team was offering $15,000. Wes wouldn't budge until after his brother's death. When he agreed to terms, the Indian's $15,000 offer turned out to be $12,000 guaranteed with a $2,000 bonus for 20 wins and $1,000 more for 25. Having no other choice, Wes signed on March 18.[55]

Ferrell's first appearance of the season was on April 16 in St. Louis. He was cruising along enroute to a 7-1 win when he threw a curveball to Jack Burns in the seventh inning. Ferrell felt something pop and immediately grabbed his shoulder. He was done for the day. St. Louis team physician Robert Hyland examined Ferrell and prescribed rest.

Followers of the Cleveland Indians are interested these days in an entirely new aspect of the famous Arm Case. The Arm Case, the casual reader will remember, has to do with one Wes Ferrell, the first pitcher in all baseball history, to win 20 or more games in each of his first four seasons in the big show. Intermittently, Ferrell complained of soreness in his right arm virtually since he joined the Tribe. Rival batters were inclined to dismiss the matter with the observation that "If this fellow has a sore arm, it's a good thing for us it isn't broken." Nevertheless, there is no question that the big fellow has had a most distressing time with his salary whip. Early in the training session he admitted the trouble was still there. Arthritis was the official diagnosis.[56]

At least one big league star had detected a flaw in Ferrell's delivery and predicted that Wes would develop arm trouble. Back in 1929, Herb Pennock had laid out a timetable that was right on the money: "A pitcher of undoubted talent; a great fast ball and a flair for striking out a lot of batters. But he hasn't a free-sweeping motion. He doesn't bring his arm all the way back in his swing. He jerks and snaps it from the shoulder. That type of delivery is likely to wear out his arm. In three or four years I think he will find he has a badly lame arm."[57]

Ferrell tried to downplay the injury. As he had done in the past, he would try to pitch through the discomfort. "Feels fine." he said, "I actually believe there was an adhesion of ligaments in my shoulder. I know my arm seemed to be pulling tight on every pitch this spring. Now it feels stronger. My movement is absolutely unrestrained. I think I have remedied my ailment."[58]

Wes returned to the hill just eight days after the injury. Favoring the arm, he still managed to pitch effectively through the end of June at which time his record stood at 8-4 with an ERA of 2.20. Once it got around the league, however, that there was no longer a Ferrell fastball, and the batters started sitting on the curve, it became a different story. Over his next ten starts Wes went 0-7 with an ERA of 7.50. He fanned fewer than two batters in 19 of his 26 starts in 1933.

> Wes Ferrell, Cleveland's young righthanded ace for four straight seasons, is said to have virtually admitted he thought his arm was gone. Ferrell began having arm trouble last summer and early this season something snapped while he was throwing the ball. The doctor who examined his arm said that adhesions had pulled away and that his wing would be as good as ever after a rest, but soreness still affects his speed.[56]

By the middle of August Ferrell had gone six weeks without a victory. While unwilling to blame his inability to win on his arm, he nevertheless approached manager Walter Johnson, who had replaced Peckinpaugh as Indians skipper in early June, and asked for a trial in the outfield. Johnson told writer Ed Bang that Ferrell would be fine after the proper rest. "Sure, Wes and I have talked about it," he said, "but I haven't given up on him as a pitcher. I've been watching him closely for some time and I think he would make good as an outfielder. But as badly as we need a hard-hitting outfielder, I won't make Ferrell one until I'm convinced he can't win consistently as a pitcher. And I'm not ready to make that admission."[60]

Wes started to pitch a little better, beating Boston, Washington, and Chicago in succession in late August.

His last pitching assignment came on September 8. The next day he made his debut as an outfielder. He appeared 13 times in left field and while not a flop in the field, he also did nothing to distinguish himself. Never again in his major league career would he appear in the field at any position other than pitcher.

> No matter what success Ferrell has as an outfielder, however, it is difficult to believe he will surpass his great pitching record. Wes deserves credit for trying to make the switch, instead of sitting idly by, bemoaning the fate that stripped his once-powerful right arm of its mastery over American League sluggers.[61]

Ferrell's bat, outstanding when he was pitching, also lost its luster when he was an outfielder. Johnson initially had Ferrell hitting fifth, but soon dropped him to sixth and eventually seventh in the batting order. Here is a breakdown of Ferrell's hitting in 1933.

	AB	R	H	2b	3b	HR	RBI	BA
P	78	19	23	4	0	7	19	.295
OF	48	6	13	3	0	0	6	.271
PH	14	1	2	0	0	0	1	.143

1934—Cleveland's contract offer to Ferrell in 1934 contained another cut, this time to $5,000. The Tribe offered a bonus that would pay him $14,500 if he reached 25 victories.[62] Wes refused to sign.

There was a lot of speculation over the winter about Ferrell's arm. Walter Johnson believed that it would bounce back. Connie Mack felt just as strongly that Ferrell was washed up. Joe McCarthy and Joe Cronin, whom Cleveland offered Ferrell to, were unsure. McCarthy's indecision may well have cost the Yankees an unprecedented six consecutive pennants. In retrospect, it is not unreasonable to imagine Ferrell turning in between 50 and 60 victories for the Yankees in 1934 and 1935.

As Ferrell's holdout went deeper into the spring, Cleveland decided to wash their hands of him. Browns skipper Rogers Hornsby turned him down because he didn't feel he could top Cleveland's offer. The White Sox were also reportedly interested. Cleveland GM Billy Evans remarked: "In the last few months I have offered as many as four starting pitchers to the New York club. I would give Ferrell to McCarthy for an old man and a bench warmer."[63]

Cleveland opened the regular season without Ferrell.

> Cleveland, April 27.—Billy Evans, general manager of the Cleveland Indians, made no comment today as Wesley Ferrell, the club's pitcher holdout, was suspended under the rule

which automatically suspends any player who does not report to his club within ten days after the season opens.

"We had nothing to do with the suspension and have not talked to Ferrell or heard from him in months." Evans said.

At his home in Greensboro, N.C., Ferrell said he doesn't intend to do anything about the suspension until May 5, "when I'll be on the voluntary retired list for the year."

Ferrell has refused to accept the $5,000 salary offered to him by the Cleveland club. To become reinstated, he must appeal to the club, the league, and to Commissioner K. M. Landis.[64]

Boston—Wes was determined to sit out the season and probably would have if it weren't for his brother Rick. During the winter Rick had worked out with Wes and knew that he had regained his arm strength. He convinced Boston manager Bucky Harris to talk to Tom Yawkey. The new millionaire owner of the Boston club wasn't shy about spending money. He had already acquired Grove from Connie Mack and now was placing Wes in the same rotation. Joe Williams wrote: "Wesley Ferrell, who refused to accept a $5,000 contract from Cleveland, learned the tyranny of baseball was something more than a phrase smacking of old Russia. The big pitcher would still be down on the farm in North Carolina mooning over the box scores if the young and wealthy Tom Yawkey hadn't come along and bought him for the Red Sox."[65]

On May 25 Boston sent pitcher Bob Weiland, outfielder Bob Seeds, and $25,000 to Cleveland for Ferrell and outfielder Dick Porter. Wes saw his first action on May 30, and six days later picked up his first Boston win by tossing 5.2 innings of two-hit, shutout relief against the Yankees.

Wes won his first three starts, prompting Williams to write:

It would be somewhat ironic, wouldn't it, if it should develop that the Indian's failure to deal with Ferrell in the spring cost them the championship? I happen to know that Walter Johnson, the manager, didn't exactly relish the idea of letting him go.

"Ferrell is still a great pitcher," Johnson told me at the baseball writer's dinner last winter. "He would make the Yankees a sure pennant winner, and he'd help any club that can pay him what he thinks he is worth."

Johnson spoke not only from close critical observation but from actual clinical experience. He had warmed up with Ferrell just before the season closed, and the pitcher had shown him most of his old-time stuff.[66]

Ferrell's record stood at 9-1 on August 1. He finished the season at 14-5 for the fourth-place Red Sox who broke even at 76-76. Included in Wes's five losses were a 1-0 decision to Chicago, a 3-2 game to Cleveland, and an extra-inning loss to Washington.

Wes's bat, like his arm, was also back.

- On June 10, in his first start of the year, he beat Washington, 4-3. His only hit of the day was an RBI double, but with one out in the bottom of the ninth he hit a long fly that drove in the winning run. Without a clear sacrifice-fly rule, this was just an at bat, an out, and no RBI.
- On July 7, the Red Sox scored four runs in the bottom of the ninth to overtake the Athletics who entered the inning with a 10-7 lead. Wes's pinch-hit double off the center-field wall produced the tying and winning runs.
- On July 13, Wes beat the Browns in St. Louis, 7-2. He hit two home runs and accounted for 4 RBI. The Browns scored two harmless runs in the bottom of the ninth.
- On August 22, Wes beat the White Sox, 3-2, at Fenway Park. Trailing, 2-1, in the bottom of the eighth, Ferrell hit a Les Tietje pitch over the left-field wall to tie the game. The contest remained deadlocked until Wes' next at bat which came with two outs in the bottom of the tenth. He hit another home run, this time to center field, for the game winner.

Despite the fact that the Red Sox had played 43 games of their schedule before Ferrell made his first start of the season, Wes finished eighth in the American League MVP voting. Jimmie Foxx, who drove in 130 runs for the Athletics, and Al Simmons, who hit .344 for the White Sox, finished tenth and eleventh.

Wes was unable to keep his temper in check for the whole season. On September 18, he was tossed for arguing a called third strike he took as a batter.

Chicago, Sept. 20—The Ferrell brothers, Wesley and Rick, of the Boston Red Sox, were suspended and fined yesterday by President Will Harridge of the American League, for conduct detrimental to the best interests of baseball. Wesley was suspended for five days and fined $100 and Rick drew a three-day suspension and a $100 fine.

The action taken against the Ferrell brothers resulted from an argument with Umpire Louis Kolls on a called third strike on Wesley in Tuesday's game between the Red Sox and Browns in St. Louis.[67]

Wes's argument was that the pitch, which came on an 0-2 count, could not possibly have been a strike because no Browns hurler would risk throwing a pitch anywhere near the plate in that situation. Hornsby had a standing fine in place for any pitcher who didn't waste one on a 0-2 count. Bobo Newsom, the pitcher who fanned Wes, recalled the story years later. In Newsom's recollection, the umpire is different.

> I had two strikes and no balls on Wes and I decided I might sneak a fast ball past him, if I could cut the corner of the plate with it. Wes knew Hornsby's rule and he didn't even swing at the ball. Umpire Bill McGowan called, "Strike three," and then things started to happen.
>
> Wes jumped at McGowan. "That wasn't no strike," he yelled. "He's not allowed to throw a strike on a two-and-no count because Hornsby will fine him." Rick Ferrell joined in the argument and McGowan threw both of them out of the game. Later on, they were fined for the rumpus they caused, and I was fined for throwing the strike, despite the fact I got him out.[68]

Wes came off the suspended list in time for one last start. He beat Washington, 1-0.

1935—Ferrell opened 1935 as he had closed 1934, with a 1-0 shutout. This time it was against Lefty Gomez on opening day in Yankee Stadium. Wes allowed two singles and faced just 29 batters. He neither walked nor fanned a single one. Joe Cronin, Boston's new skipper, had given Wes the opening day assignment over Grove, an honor that was significant to Wes. All his life, Wes would refer to this as his greatest game: "My greatest thrill came on opening day in '35. In spring training Joe told me I'd pitch the opener at Yankee Stadium. All spring I kept getting cuffed, but he never wavered in his confidence in me."[69]

"Wes had everything against those Yankees," said Rick Ferrell, his catcher brother, who was behind the plate on Tuesday. "He was faster than he had been in three years, and, as you know, his control was perfect. He could put that ball anywhere he wanted to.

In the Yankee dugout Lou Gehrig was Ferrell's most ardent booster, "He looked like the Ferrell of four years ago. He wouldn't give anybody a fat ball to hit at. And how many times was he behind the hitter all afternoon?"[70]

This was Ferrell's greatest season. He won 25 games for yet another fourth-place team and was Boston's most productive hitter whenever he was in the lineup. He also delivered clutch pinch hits all season long.

Tom Yawkey continued to spend money on his new toy. With his first pennant still more than a decade away, Yawkey had already embarked on the rebuilding process. While the core of the 1946 team was composed of players who came to Boston from the minor leagues, the 1935 version, with player-manager Joe Cronin the major addition, was stocked with established big league veterans.

The 1935 Red Sox were not a very good team. With the exception of the last place Athletics, Boston scored the fewest runs in the league. They hit only 69 home runs, fewest in the league next to the Washington club. The Red Sox also made the most errors in the league.

What the Red Sox had in 1935 was a Hall of Fame shortstop, albeit a somewhat shaky fielding one, and the two best pitchers in the league, Grove and Ferrell, who both had notorious tempers and felt that the game was their own personal battleground. Pity the poor teammate who screwed it up.

Poor Joe Cronin!

On April 26, Grove lost his second start of the season to Washington, 10-5. Just two of the ten runs Grove allowed were earned as the Red Sox committed five errors, three by Cronin. Two days later, in his third start of the season, Ferrell opened the top of the ninth with a 3-1 lead over the same Washington team. Cronin made two errors as the Senators scored four unearned runs to beat Ferrell, 5-3.

Cronin had the satisfaction of watching Lefty and Wes dominate the rest of the league, and in the world of baseball, domination means respect. On the other hand, as a poor-fielding shortstop, despite being their manager, he had a long way to go in order to earn the respect of Grove and Ferrell.

Putting Wes on the field as often as possible was an easy decision for Cronin.

- In his second start of the season, Wes beat the Senators, 4-2. At the plate he went four for four with a double, a triple and two runs scored.
- In his sixth start of the year, on May 13, Cronin watched Ferrell's seventh-inning homer break a 1-1 tie in a 2-1 win over the Browns.
- In his next start, on May 17, Cronin watched Wes beat Chicago, 2-1, in thirteen innings. Wes had three hits.
- Wes beat Alvin Crowder and the defending league-champion Tigers on June 11, 5-2, allowing just a single earned run. He had a home run and two RBIs.

- On June 19, Wes had four hits and two RBIs while hurling a complete-game win over the Browns.
- On June 23, Wes lost a 4-2 game to Ted Lyons and the White Sox. Wes had two hits, scored one of Boston's two runs, and knocked in the other.
- He tossed a two-hit shutout against the White Sox on July 10. He homered and drove in two.
- On July 18, Ferrell lost an 8-0 game to Schoolboy Rowe. Cronin made two of the three Boston errors that led to six unearned runs for Detroit.
- On July 20, Ferrell entered the game as a pinch-hitter for Rube Walberg in the bottom of the seventh. Wes delivered an RBI double as the Red Sox wiped out a 5-1 deficit. Ferrell got tagged with the loss when he allowed Detroit a ninth-inning run.
- On July 21, Detroit took a 6-4 lead over the Red Sox and Grove into the bottom of the ninth but Ferrell hit a three-run pinch-hit homer to give Lefty and the Sox the win.
- On July 22, he hit a homer in the bottom of the ninth for his second consecutive walk-off homer as he tossed a complete-game, 2-1, win over the Browns.
- On July 27, Ferrell went one for four and scored one of the two Boston runs as he defeated the Athletics with a 2-0, three-hit shutout.
- On July 31, Wes beat Bobo Newsom and the Senators, 6-4. Wes went the route. His three hits included two home runs and four RBIs.
- On August 4, Wes downed Philadelphia, 7-6, in ten innings. He opened the bottom of the tenth with a single and eventually came around to score the game winner.

While Ferrell has historically taken a back seat to Lefty Grove, 1935 allows us to take a closer look at the two, now healthy and playing for the same team.

Here is how they did as starting pitchers.

	Starts	CG	W-L	IPs	ER	ERA
Ferrell	38	31	25-11	316.1	119	3.39
Grove	30	23	18-11	261.0	80	2.76

Now let's add in their hitting production while in the role of starting pitcher.

	AB	R	H	2b	3b	HR	RBI	BA
Ferrell	119	22	42	2	1	6	23	.353
Grove[71]	87	5	7	1	1	1	5	.080

Wes's bat influenced Grove's record as well as his own. Without Wes, Grove's 18-11 starting mark may have been 15-14. On August 3, Grove beat the Athletics, 5-4, in ten innings. Wes delivered an RBI single in the eighth inning as the Red Sox overcame a 3-1 deficit. Without Ferrell's hit Grove would have lost the game in regulation. On September 15, Grove gave up five earned runs to St. Louis in the first inning. Boston came up with a big sixth-inning rally in which Ferrell, batting for Grove, delivered an RBI single.

Most famously, on July 21, Grove received credit for a complete game, 7-6, win over Tommy Bridges and Detroit. It was a close game and Grove took a 4-3 lead into the top of the ninth but, as *The Sporting News* recorded, "Grove had quite an explosion in the recent Red Sox-Detroit series, when Cronin insisted on an intentional pass for Hank Greenberg, filling the bases. Goslin and Rogell followed with singles. Mose was ripping mad, hurled his glove into the grandstand, smashed a bat on the edge of the dugout, and ripped his uniform blouse."[72]

In the next half-inning, though, Ferrell hit a three-run pinch-hit homer to give Grove the win instead of the loss. Wes recalled: "So we all rush into the clubhouse, laughing and hollering, the way you do after a game like that. And here's Lefty, sitting there, still thinking he's lost his game. When he saw all the carrying-on, I tell you, the smoke started coming out of his eyes.

"'I don't see what's so funny,' he says. 'A man loses a ball game, and you're all carrying on.'

"Then somebody says, 'Hell Lefty, we won it. Wes hit a home run for you.'

"Well, I was sitting across the clubhouse from him, pulling my uniform off, and I notice he's staring at me, with just a trace of smile at the corners of his mouth. Just staring at me. He doesn't say anything. I give him a big grin and pull my sweat shirt up over my head. Then I hear him say, 'Hey, Wes.' I look over and he's rolling a bottle of wine to me—he'd keep a bottle of one thing or another stashed in his locker. So here it comes, rolling and bumping along the clubhouse floor. I picked it up and thanked him and put it in my locker. At the end of the season I brought it back to Carolina with me and let it sit up on the mantel. It sat up there for years and years. Every time I looked at it I thought of Old Left (sic). He rolled it over to me."[73]

Writer Dan Daniel penned a comprehensive column on American League pinch-hitting shortly after the season ended.[74] The Red Sox, led by Bing Miller's nine and Ferrell's eight RBIs, topped the league with 20 tallies from substitute batters. Wrote Daniel: "Wesley

Ferrell had a remarkable record as a pinch hitter as well as a pitcher. Ferrell's emergency hits won four games for the Red Sox. Wes had the distinction of hitting one of the pinch homers seen in his circuit during the season. Ralph Winegarner got the other one.

"Boston pinch hitters accounted for a dozen games, five of which went to the credit of Lefty Grove."

In addition to the pinch-hit homer on July 21, Ferrell won an additional game from the soon-to-be World Champion Tigers on September 18. Deadlocked, 3-3, in the bottom on the ninth, Wes delivered the game winner with a pinch-hit single off Schoolboy Rowe.

As with 1931, the best way to judge Ferrell's impact as a hitter in 1935 is to compare him to his teammates. Here is how Ferrell stacked up to his teammates with at least 75 at bats in the 38 games he started. Remember, Ferrell always batted ninth.

	G	AB	R	H	2b	3b	HR	RBI	BA
Wes Ferrell	38	119	22	42	2	1	6	23	.353
Roy Johnson	34	143	23	48	9	3	0	23	.336
Joe Cronin	35	142	22	45	16	2	5	28	.317
Rick Ferrell	37	138	13	42	11	2	0	17	.304
Oscar Melillo	24	90	15	27	2	2	0	9	.300
Mel Almada	36	153	25	44	8	0	0	17	.288
B. Dahlgren	38	133	21	37	5	1	0	12	.278
Bill Werber	32	124	23	34	9	1	3	15	.274
Dusty Cooke	24	82	12	22	2	1	2	9	.268

Ferrell's season was not overlooked in postseason award voting. Despite playing for a fourth-place team, Ferrell finished second in the American League MVP voting (BBWAA) behind Hank Greenberg of the World Champion Detroit Tigers. In *The Sporting News* American League MVP voting, Wes finished fifth, topping all pitchers. Grove did not appear among the sixteen players who received votes.[75]

In *The Sporting News* All-Star team voting,[76] Dizzy Dean and Carl Hubbell were the top vote-gathering pitchers. Ferrell and Grove, third and fourth in the overall voting, topped the American League.

Ferrell didn't make the midseason All-Star team although Grove did. Dan Daniel noted that with the game still in its infancy, it was a matter of league supremacy.

Well, the League picks the players, and there is Lefty Grove on the team again, while guys like Wes Ferrell and Ted Lyons are not even mentioned. This does not sit well with the customers but there is a good reason for picking Grove…

…the power of the National League is left-handed. So the American League says we gotta have two crooked-arms to shoot at Terry, Vaughn, Ott, Moore, and Paul Waner.[77]

1936—The 1936 Red Sox were a major disappointment. Tom Yawkey's money had brought Jimmie Foxx and Heinie Manush to Boston. In addition to having an above-average third baseman in Bill Werber, and adding Doc Cramer to the outfield, Cronin could now field a team that included future Hall of Famers at first base, shortstop, catcher, and left field. And he still had the two best pitchers in the league in Grove and Ferrell.

So what went wrong? How did this team end up in sixth place with a 74-80 record? Well, after Lefty and Wes, there was no pitching depth, and Cronin and Manush were both out of the lineup for extended periods with injuries. Beyond that, the veteran team had little respect for manager Cronin.

Cronin had married into baseball royalty, taking as his bride the neice of Senators owner Clark Griffith, and Tom Yawkey had paid $250,000 for his services. With the nation in the middle of a depression, the Red Sox players knew Cronin had the proverbial golden spoon protruding from his mouth.

Cronin, still not yet thirty years old, only the fourth-best player on his own team, had a hard time proving himself to this bunch. His already poor fielding was worsening. Appearing in 57 of the 76 games Ferrell started for Boston in 1935 and 1936, Joe committed 20 errors (Cronin made a total of 63 errors in 220 fielding games in 1935 and 1936). The players felt that Eric McNair, not Cronin, should be the everyday shortstop. Cronin got so nervous that he began dropping to one knee to field routine ground balls, causing Boston second baseman Oscar Melillo to quip, "For Christ sake, Joe, if you're going to miss 'em, you might as well stand up and miss 'em like a big leaguer."[78]

Washington scribe Shirley Povich wrote early in 1936: "It was one day last summer that Joe Cronin patted Ferrell on the back in Fenway Park and sent him to the mound to start a game—it was during a series in which Cronin had lost two consecutive games by his own errors. 'All right, Wes, let's win this one,' said Cronin. Ferrell looked at Cronin steadily for a minute, and said, 'All right, Joe, but first tell me which side you're playing on today.'"[79]

Shortly after the 1935 World Series, Yawkey gave an interview to J. G. Taylor Spink: "Interviewed in Chicago, Yawkey cut loose with some interesting information. Early in the series, a rumor started that Yawkey had decided to pay off Cronin. Tom laughed at this yarn. 'As long as I am connected with the Red Sox, and Cronin likes me, there can be nothing to any such nonsense,' said Tom. But Yawkey did indicate that Cronin would never be seen at shortstop again. Joe has slowed up around short. He picked up a lot of weight. And the wrist break he suffered last year did something to his throwing. Cronin will play first base, unless Yawkey gets Foxx. Joe will perform at third, unless Yawkey buys Higgins. But Cronin will not play short and that is as definite as the fact that Joe will remain as manager of the Red Sox."[80]

Ferrell again got the opening day assignment from Cronin and beat the Athletics without much trouble, 9-4, collecting a couple of hits and an RBI. In his second start of the year, on April 19, Wes again put down Philadelphia, this time by the score of 2-1.

Grove had opened his season with a duplication of Ferrell's 1935 opener, a two-hit shutout of the Yankees in the Stadium on April 17. In the first month of his season Grove was untouchable, going 7-1 with an ERA of 0.85 in eight starts. Four of the six shutouts he tossed that season came in April and May.

The Red Sox were in the race until midseason, sitting in third place on July 13 with a 52-44 record. From then until the end of the season they went 22-36.

The American League, with an ERA of 5.04, was a hitter's paradise in 1936. The leading pitchers were:

	W-L	ERA	Team
Tommy Bridges, Det	23-11	3.60	2nd
Vern Kennedy, Chi	21-9	4.63	3rd
Johnny Allen, Cle	20-10	3.44	5th
Red Ruffing, NY	20-12	3.85	1st
Wes Ferrell, Bos	20-15	4.19	6th
Monte Pearson, NY	19-7	3.71	1st
Schoolboy Rowe, Det	19-10	4.52	2nd
Jimmie Deshong, Was	18-10	4.62	4th
Lefty Grove, Bos	17-12	2.81	6th

Based on ERA, Grove appears to have dominated the American League in 1936, but his fast start was the only thing that really separated him from the pack. Here is how Grove and Ferrell performed in 1936 as starting pitchers:

	GS	CG	W-L	IPs	ER	ERA
Ferrell	38	28	20-15	298.1	138	4.16
Grove	30	22	17-10	237.2	76	2.88

However, here is how they pitched in the first month of the season as starters.

	GS	CG	W-L	IPs	ER	ERA
Ferrell	8	5	4-3	59.0	28	4.27
Grove	8	7	7-1	63.2	6	0.85

Here is how they pitched during the rest of the season in a starting role, which in Ferrell's case began on May 20, and for Grove, May 23.

	GS	CG	W-L	IPs	ER	ERA
Ferrell	30	23	16-12	239.1	110	4.14
Grove	22	15	10-9	174.0	70	3.62

Now let's factor in the offensive contribution of the two in games they started.

	AB	R	H	2b	3b	HR	RBI	BA
Ferrell	116	20	36	6	1	5	21	.310
Grove	74	5	11	4	0	0	5	.149

Again, whatever ground Ferrell lost to Grove on the mound he made up for at the plate. On May 3 he got two hits while shutting out Tommy Bridges and the defending World Champion Tigers on two hits. On May 26 he got two hits and beat the Yankees and Red Ruffing, 5-4. On June 3 Wes beat Johnny Allen and the Indians, 6-2, without allowing an earned run. He had two hits off Allen, one of which, in the seventh inning, drove in the tying and winning runs. On June 17 he beat Ted Lyons and the White Sox, 9-4. One of Ferrell's two hits off Lyons was a home run. On June 24 despite his own eighth inning homer, Wes lost, 7-6, to Bridges and the Tigers. On July 17 Ferrell beat Ivy Andrews and the Browns, 2-1. Trailing 1-0 with one out in the ninth, he banged a double of the left field wall, his third hit of the day, to start the winning rally.

On August 12 Wes beat Hod Lisenbee and the Athletics, 6-4. Trailing 2-0, Wes hit a two-run homer and a grand slam in successive innings to account for all of Boston's scoring. On September 6 Wes had three hits, including a home run, as he and the Red Sox trounced the Yankees, 14-5. On September 11 Wes had two hits and three walks in five plate appearances as he beat the Browns, 6-2.

In 1935 Ferrell was Boston's most productive hitter. In 1936 he took a back seat only to Jimmie Foxx. Here is how the Boston hitters, with at least 75 at bats, fared in the games Ferrell started in 1936.

	G	AB	R	H	2b	3b	HR	RBI	BA
Jimmie Foxx	38	146	31	59	8	2	12	36	.404
Rick Ferrell	34	115	19	38	9	1	1	13	.330
Wes Ferrell	38	116	20	36	6	1	5	21	.310
Doc Cramer	38	162	22	50	6	0	0	14	.309
H. Manush	21	79	12	24	4	0	0	12	.304
Dusty Cooke	26	87	17	25	5	0	1	6	.287
Eric McNair	32	124	18	34	4	1	0	12	.274
Bill Werber	36	130	16	34	6	1	3	24	.262
Joe Cronin	22	88	6	20	4	1	0	13	.227

Ferrell's problem in 1936, not unexpectedly, was his temper. Wes followed up his two-hit shutout of Detroit on May 3 with a 9-6 win over the Browns. Booed by some of the Fenway fans as he walked off the field, he responded by thumbing his nose.[81]

The Sporting News's page one headline on August 27 screamed in big black type:

WES FERRELL WALKOUT DOOMS HUB CAREER.
The "Golden Rule" of the Red Sox is over and the "clubhouse" players may now get ready to walk the plank. For retribution has

come big Wes Ferrell's way at last, and drastic punishment that might have saved this Boston team from landing ingloriously in the second division had it been meted out earlier, sounds an eleventh hour warning to malcontents, who may have been inclined to side with the temperamental pitcher. When Ferrell, in one of his frequent moods of peevishness, abruptly walked out of a game at the Ruppert Stadium, August 21, leaving his team without a hurler ready to replace him, this action brought to an end manager Joe Cronin's toleration...

The outbreak by the great right-hander was the culmination of a series of offenses which had gradually served to destroy the popularity of a baseball idol. Weeks ago, nettled by the joshing of the fans, he thumbed his nose at the grandstand occupants at Fenway Park and escaped with a mild censure in the newspapers...

A fortnight later, during a stormy first inning at the Boston park, he objected to Fritz Ostermueller starting to warm up in the bullpen and told his manager that he would quit the rubber then and there unless the young southpaw ceased pitching...

Then came the outbreak at Fenway Park in August, when he quit the game as the Senators got to him in the eighth inning, forcing play to be momentarily held up while Jack Russell, without any chance to warm up, had to be sent in to replace him...

Though Ferrell insists that he did not leave the box of his own accord and went only because he thought that Oscar Melillo had signaled to the bullpen for a relief pitcher, the latter vehemently denies this and the majority of the Red Sox are stringing along with Cronin.

Ferrell, who reportedly threatened to punch Cronin, was fined $1,000, but his intended suspension was rescinded because the team needed him. The brawl never took place, as Wes usually cooled off fast once he left the field. As both George[82] and Rick[83] Ferrell had done some semiprofessional boxing in North Carolina, it's not unreasonable to imagine Wes inflicting damage if he had come to blows with Cronin.

Ferrell finished the season by going 5-1, his only loss a 3-2 decision to the White Sox, one of five one-run losses he sustained from July 30 through the end of the season. In his first game after the incident Wes tossed a five-hit shutout against Detroit.

Following his late-season suspensions in 1932, 1934 and 1936, Ferrell returned to post a cumulative record of 9-1, with a 1.94 ERA. Ferrell's pitching record, his temperament, and his desire to win at any cost, were tied together. Off the field Wes Ferrell was as polite a gentleman as possible. Once he crossed the line though, he became a ferocious competitor, one who could hold his own with the most tenacious characters the game has ever seen.

Noted Washington scribe Shirley Povich painted a great picture of Ferrell's personality:

The news dispatches from New York which relate that Wesley Cheek Ferrell was fined $1,000 and indefinitely suspended by Manager Joe Cronin yesterday, also quoted Mr. Ferrell as being "amazed." If Ferrell is, indeed, amazed, then he constitutes a minority of one.

Because fans throughout the circuit and all of Cronin's rival managers for several weeks had anticipated the day when Cronin would crack down on the Red Sox's mean-tempered maverick of the mound. Ferrell had been asking for it with great persistence and even the patience of Cronin was nearing its end...

The pitcher who had been a storm center with the Cleveland club and who had been unable to curb his temperament with the Red Sox never has been able to take adversity in stride, but his actions were making a full-fledged sucker out of Cronin, who was supposed to be the boss of the team...

Except to those who know Cronin as an extremely patient and forgiving individual, the wonder is that Cronin did not crack down on Ferrell weeks ago...

He really isn't a bad guy, this Ferrell—just temperamental. His zeal to win is exceeded by that of no other player in the big leagues but he has never learned to temper it with reason...

When he failed to win a place on the 1936 American League all-star team as did a hundred and fifty other big leaguers, Ferrell took it sorely to heart. Despite the fact that he lived only five minutes' walk from Braves Field, the scene of the game, he refused to attend it, declaring, "If I'm not good enough to play with those guys then damned if I'm gonna watch 'em...."

Ferrell's fierce desire to win does not confine itself to the baseball field. On the golf course a $10 No. 1 wood represents only something to be shattered across the nearest tree when Ferrell misses a shot. He probably holds all international records for club-heaving at which he gets greater distance than on many of his drives.

It was down in Florida before the 1936 training season began that Ferrell probably gave his greatest display of temperament. He was playing with Paul Waner, of the Pirates, and on the last tee still had a chance to square the match and save his $4 bet.

Ferrell addressed his ball, swung, and in great dismay saw it skid off toward the rough only a dozen feet from the tee.

Whereupon Mr. Ferrell heaved his club after the ball, sat down on the tee and banged his head a half-dozen times against the iron tee-markers.

Then suddenly bethinking himself, he desisted. Without pausing to rub his head, he looked up at Waner and said: "Say, Paul, if I kill myself, you'll find enough money to pay the bet in my righthand hip pocket."[84]

Long-time Boston sportswriter Harold Kaese, author of the Putnam Series volume on the Boston Braves, remembered the 1936 game in which Wes accounted for all of Boston's offense.

Against the Athletics on Aug. 12, in the first game of a doubleheader, the talented but tempestuous Ferrell hit two homers over the left field fence off Hod Lisenbee.

The first was in the third inning, with his brother, Rick, on base.

The second was in the fourth inning, with the bases full.

Ferrell won the game, his 15th victory, 6-4. His two homers knocked in all six Boston runs.

He was very angry before he hit those homers, because he made two boo-boos in the second inning. First, he played a squeeze bunt home too late to get the runner. Then he gave the A's another run by picking up a topped roller when it was rolling foul.

When Ferrell got mad, something had to give. It might be his glove, a bat, a clubhouse door, a chair, a water bottle, or even his wrist watch.

But fairly often, as it was in this case, it was the ball game. Ferrell was a mean, ornery, unrelenting, hotheaded, ferocious competitor —but he was also a shrewd, clever adversary.[85]

The Red Sox brass realized that Ferrell's biggest problem was channeling his energy. While getting to the major leagues may be the result of God-given abilities, achieving star status has a lot to do with the inner man. Ferrell's desire to win wasn't viewed as a negative thing.

The coming shifts will not include any change in Wes Ferrell's status. He has learned his lesson, although this was given him only

after he had tried Joe Cronin's patience until it reached the breaking point. No statement has as yet been given out by the Red Sox administration as to that $1,000 fine having been lopped from the pitcher's pay, but it is generally believed that the cut was restored to him. It was hinted when the fine was imposed that restitution might be made in the event that Ferrell dropped his peevishness and followed orders. Ferrell swung into line, mended his way, and as he was allowed to go home a week before the schedule closed, it is only reasonable to assume he patched up his differences with the front office and left the club eminently satisfied.

Pitchers who can win 20 games in a season are not acquired every day, or picked up for extravagant prices in the minor leagues. Ferrell is temperamental, is inclined to show exasperation when he or one of his teammates is guilty of a boot, but he is out to win and his heart is in the game. So, he is looked upon as one of the mainstays of the Red Sox hurling roster for 1937.[86]

1937—The Red Sox didn't move Ferrell during the winter of 1936. Management realized, as had Cleveland following his 1932 suspension, that Ferrell's on-field value outweighed his temperamental outbursts.

Both Mickey Cochrane and Bucky Harris went on record as saying they were interested in Ferrell.

If the Red Sox try and dispose of Ferrell in the open market, it is certain that Detroit will not acquire his contract without opposition. Bucky Harris, for one, would see to that. The Washington manager handled Ferrell for one season in Boston and more than once has disagreed with those who charged him with being hopelessly incorrigible.

"I always got along with Wesley," said Harris one day last summer when everybody else was talking about the pitcher's action in leaving the box in Yankee Stadium without authority.

Harris would like to have the veteran right-hander under his command again and would eagerly join negotiations with the Boston owners."[87]

Ferrell was on fire when the season opened, but, unfortunately, it was his bat and not his fastball that was smoking. Wes beat Philadelphia, 11-5, on April 20 in his third consecutive opening day assignment. Boston gave him a 10-1 lead before he eased up in the latter stages of the game. He scored two runs and knocked in another with a double.

After his first five starts Wes was hitting .571 with two doubles, a home run, and five RBIs. Opposing hitters, however, were teeing off on almost every pitch he threw. On June 10 Red Sox GM Eddie Collins sent the Ferrell brothers and Mel Almada to Washington for Buck Newsom and Ben Chapman. The deal had been in the works for several weeks, and while the Red Sox were eager to unload Wes, they weren't as keen to move Rick, whom Washington insisted on. Quipped *The Sporting News*: "If restoration of harmony in the Red Sox family is supposed to be assured through the acquisition of Newsom and Chapman, then someone may have missed his guess."[88]

Ferrell and Grove spent three full seasons as teammates, from May 1934 through June 1937. They contributed the following pitching and hitting statistics to the Red Sox. Grove had a significantly lower ERA, which is how most people rate pitchers, but is there any real doubt which man was more valuable to the Red Sox?

	G	GS	CG	W-L	IP	ER	ERA
Ferrell	118	110	81	62-40	878.2	401	4.11
Grove	94	76	53	46-33	665.2	245	3.31

	AB	R	H	2b	3b	HR	RBI	BA
Ferrell	396	64	122	17	2	17	82	.308
Grove	215	11	25	6	1	1	13	.116

Why had Ferrell's early 1937 form deteriorated so badly from 1936? Ferrell, twenty-nine-years-old and the winner of 20 games in six of his eight big league seasons, lost his stuff because Joe Cronin did not know how to handle a pitching staff.

Wes rarely started games on short rest before 1935. During his stay in Cleveland he started on less than three days' rest just five times: once each in 1930, 1931, 1932, and twice in 1933. In 1935 and 1936, Cronin started Ferrell with two days' rest eleven times, five times in 1935 and six more in 1936. Here is how Cronin used Ferrell and Grove in 1935 and 1936. Just for comparison, I've included Greg Maddux's and Tommy Glavine's use patterns in 1998 and 1999.[89] Draw your own conclusions.

Days of rest between starts

	0	1	2	3	4	5	6+
Ferrell	1	0	11	36	19	4	3
Grove	0	0	1	27	11	9	10
Maddux	0	0	0	2	45	17	3
Glavine	0	0	0	1	48	16	3

Cronin had a two-step pitching plan. The first step was Ferrell and Grove. The next step was Grove and Ferrell. In charge of one of the greatest pitching duos in all baseball history, Cronin pitched Lefty and Wes,

especially Wes, into the ground. Koufax and Drysdale, or Maddux and Glavine, at peak value and in context of time and place, had nothing on Grove and Ferrell.

Both pitchers came into 1935 with a history of arm problems, yet Cronin often let them work deep into extra innings. In 1935, Grove lost complete-game efforts of 13.1 and 14.2 innings. In 1936, he lost a game after tossing 12.2 innings. Ferrell twice went 13 innings in 1935.

Ferrell was on pace to make forty starts in both 1935 and 1936. A turned ankle in 1935 kept him out of action for a week in August. He was allowed to leave for North Carolina with a week remaining in the 1936 season. He pitched well on two days' rest in 1935, but the difference was noticeable in 1936. His ERA was 6.36 in the six starts he made on two days' rest, but 3.76 in his other starts.

Ferrell made 18 starts by July 1, 1935. In 1936 he made 20. In 1938, without Ferrell around, Cronin put 17 starts on Grove's 38-year old arm by July 1. Is it any surprise that Lefty broke down shortly thereafter?

Ferrell, of course, was just as responsible as Cronin for pitching on short rest. His competitive nature compelled him to take the ball as often as possible. After defeating Philadelphia in the first game of a doubleheader on May 30, 1935, and sitting around for several hours, Wes delivered a pinch-hit RBI double that tied up the second game in the eighth inning. Cronin left him in to pitch. He worked two scoreless innings before allowing five runs in the eleventh. If Ferrell hadn't doubled in the tying run, he would not have taken the loss. Cronin stuck with Ferrell longer than he should have in hopes of getting him—the team's best hitter—to the plate again. This manager was clearly not concerned about the arm strain on his ace. He was just concerned about winning the game, tomorrow be damned.

Grove, on the other hand, had no problem telling Cronin where to shove his two days of rest. Ted Williams, even as a rookie, noticed it. "Joe Cronin had little power to discipline his big name players. To Yawkey, Grove became Mose, his idol and dinner companion. Mose was a cranky old geezer. He would scream at Cronin for making an error behind him and there was nothing much that Cronin could do about it. Not when Old Mose could rip him apart to the boss a couple of hours later over the drink."[90]

Here are a couple of other quotes from 1936 that explore the Grove-Yawkey-Cronin relationship. The first one may explain some of the Ferrell-Cronin problems in 1936. If Cronin allowed Grove to decide for himself when he could leave the game, why shouldn't Cronin's other ace, Ferrell, feel he also had the same right? If there was a problem here, it seems Cronin created it himself with his inability to handle Grove.

"Joe Cronin saves Bob Grove the embarrassment of

waving him off the mound when he loses his stuff by allowing Mose to walk out of the box on his own volition."[91]

"In order not to miss the broadcast of the Schmeling-Louis fight, owner Tom Yawkey and Lefty Bob Grove preceded the arrival of the Red Sox at St. Louis, June 19, flying down from Chicago in the afternoon, while manager Joe Cronin and the others arrived at 10:15 at night by train."[92]

Elden Auker pitched for the Red Sox in 1939. He told Tom Yawkey he would rather retire than work a second season under Cronin. At the 2000 SABR convention in West Palm Beach, Florida, Auker told me that Grove hated Cronin and wouldn't talk to him if he approached the mound during a game. "Lefty pitched when Lefty wanted to pitch, not when Cronin wanted him to pitch," said Auker.

SABR member and former Red Sox first baseman Tony Lupien made a similar observation about Cronin. "I don't want to malign the man, for he was a fine gentleman, but I don't think he was a very good handler of pitchers. I don't believe he understood the rotation of pitchers. When he began his managing career with Washington, he had some older heads like Clyde Milan to help him run the club while he played shortstop; then with Boston he had veteran pitchers like Grove and Walberg who pitched when they wanted to and how they wanted to…He either didn't understand or just didn't use the method of choosing a rotation and staying with it no matter who we played."[93]

Washington—Once Wes arrived in Washington, his pitching form suddenly reappeared. His first three starts, totaling 29 innings, resulted in three wins in which he allowed but five earned runs.

With the exception of three starts he made sandwiched around the All-Star Game, Ferrell was as good as ever. On July 4, 10, and 16, Wes got clobbered twice by the Yankees and once by the Indians. Here are his totals in those three games.

GS	CG	IP	H	ER	W-L	ERA
3	0	9.2	24	23	0-3	21.41

Here is how he pitched in the rest of his Washington games in 1937. Six of these ten losses were by one run.

G	GS	CG	IP	H	ER	W-L	ERA
22	21	21	198	190	68	11-10	3.09

Here are the highlights of Ferrell's season in Washington.

- June 12: beat the White Sox, 6-2, allowing just four hits while putting two on the board himself.

- June 15: drove home two with a pinch-hit double in the bottom of the ninth as Washington rallied for seven to tie the game.
- June 16: beat the Tigers, 2-1, in twelve innings.
- June 30: beat the Red Sox and Bobo Newsom, 6-4, in first meeting after trade. Washington came from behind with three runs in the eighth for the win. Wes drove in the tying run.
- July 20: lost, 4-2, in 10 innings to Thornton Lee and the White Sox. Only two of Chicago's four runs were earned.
- July 29: lost, 2-0, to Thornton Lee and the White Sox.
- August 3: contributed an RBI double as he beat the Tigers, 3-2, in twelve.
- August 4: delivered the winning run in both games of a doubleheader with the Browns, both times as a pinch hitter. In the first game, with the score tied, 5-5, in the ninth, Wes, sent a long fly to the outfield scoring Buddy Myer from third. In the second game, with the score again tied, 5-5, Wes delivered the winning run with a seventh-inning single. The game winner in the opener, clearly a sac fly by today's standards, was credited as an at-bat and no RBI.
- August 7: Rudy York of the Tigers hit a three-run homer in the seventh inning to beat Wes, 3-2.
- August 15: beat Grove and the Red Sox, 8-3.
- August 19: despite getting two hits off Red Ruffing, loses, 4-3, to the Yankees in twelve. Only one of the Yankees runs was earned.
- August 24: beat the Browns, 9-6, driving in three runs on three hits.
- August 28: lost, 3-2, to Ted Lyons and the White Sox.
- September 6: lost, 6-2, to Grove and the Red Sox. The game was a 2-2 duel until Wes surrendered four in the eighth.

1938—This season marked the beginning of the end for the four greatest pitchers of the 1930s. Carl Hubbell's season ended with elbow surgery in August.[94] Grove's season, although he did pitch a few times in August and September, effectively ended on July 14 when he lost the pulse in his arm in the middle of a game.[95] Ferrell and Dizzy Dean limped through the season relying solely on their one remaining pitch, the "nuthin'" ball.

Ferrell came into 1938 having worked harder than any other major league hurler over the three previous years. By the end of the campaign it seemed clear that the workload had taken its toll.

1935-1937

	Starts	CG	Innings
Ferrell	111	85	904.1
Newsom	104	59	802.0
Bridges	103	67	814.1
Hubbell	101	67	868.1
Lee	99	55	783.0
Blanton	97	52	732.2
Derringer	96	45	781.2
Dean	95	74	837.2
Harder	95	43	745.2
Gomez	94	50	713.0
Ruffing	93	66	749.1
Grove	92	66	788.1
Warneke	92	51	741.0

Ferrell opened the 1938 major league season before President Roosevelt in Washington on April 18 with a 12-8 win over the Athletics. In his next two starts he topped Lefty Gomez in Yankee Stadium on April 23, 7-4, and then the Athletics, 7-2, on April 28.

From that point on his season was a roller-coaster ride. He tossed an occasional good game, but got hit harder and harder as the season progressed.

	G	GS	CG	IP	H	ER	W-L	ERA
April	3	3	3	27.0	31	12	3-0	4.00
May	7	6	3	45.2	55	29	4-3	5.71
June	6	6	2	35.0	50	26	3-2	6.68
July	5	5	1	31.1	43	23	2-2	6.60
August	5	5	1	31.2	50	26	3-2	7.39
Sept.	2	1	0	8.1	16	9	0-1	9.72

The Sporting News reported early in the season that Ferrell was having trouble rounding into shape due to neck and shoulder problems.[96] Despite the bad arm, and despite again being saddled with a team that would end the season in fifth place, Ferrell continued to take his regular turn. And as long as he was in the rotation, he was among the league leaders in victories. It may have been smoke-and-mirror time, but Ferrell, with virtually nothing left in his arm, was still a master craftsman.

At the All-Star break, he was one of five American League hurlers who had won ten games. By August 4 his 13 wins trailed just Grove and Ruffing, who each had 14. Even as late as September 1, by then pitching very little, Wes's 15 wins were bettered by only Ruffing (19-4) and Bobo Newsom (16-12).

Ferrell's season, and for that matter his mettle, may best be summed up in a game played with Detroit on June 12. Wes, as he had in recent years, handled the Tigers fairly easily in 1938, beating them three times without a loss. In this particular game the Senators had given Ferrell an 11-1 lead as Detroit came to bat in the top of the sixth. The Bengals, after a long rain delay, eventually won the game, 18-12. Charlie Gehringer and Hank Greenberg both remembered the game years later. Greenberg recalled: "So we sat around for about an hour with the rain coming down and jeered at Ferrell, who was pacing in the dugout. He couldn't wait to get back in action. Finally the rain let up a little bit, though it was still drizzling.

"After the game resumed, we scored seven runs and Ferrell got yanked from the game.

"Ferrell went into the dugout; we were all yelling at him from across the field. I noticed he sat down in the corner of the dugout where none of the other players were even close to him. Pretty soon he started picking at his glove. He was tearing his glove apart, just ripping away at it. He couldn't tear it fast enough. It was a difficult thing to do, but he was so annoyed and so unhappy and the more he ripped his glove, the more his teammates moved away from him, and the more we gave him hell: 'Go get 'em, Wes.' 'You can do it, Wes.' They told me that he went into the clubhouse before the game was over and tore his uniform to shreds. He took his watch out of his pocket and jumped on it and smashed it to smithereens."[97]

Said Gehringer: "Wes was one of your toughest competitors. He just hated to lose...

"I happened to be the first man he faced after the delay, and I hit a home run. That started it off. We began hitting and didn't stop until we tied the score. Bucky Harris was managing Washington then, and for some reason he left Wes in. Well, the next inning we get two more runs. That finished Wes. He went over to the bench, sat down, threw his glove disgustedly to the dugout floor, clamped down on it with his spikes and gritted his teeth and reached over and just started pulling that glove all to pieces, tearing up the fingers, the webbing, the stuffing, the whole thing."[98]

Washington released Ferrell on August 12, with a statement from Clark Griffith that Wes, despite his team-leading 13-8 record, wasn't helping the club. Tight with a buck, Griffith wasn't happy when Ferrell, while waiting outside a railroad station, reportedly said, "This club is so cheap it won't even pay cab fares."[99]

Wes had never been one to underestimate his value. Early in his career he had said that he had two goals, one was to win 250 games and the other was to make $250,000. True to his convictions, Wes had been a tough negotiator when contracts were sent out in January, 1938.

Washington, D.C.—One important player in the Senators' cast, Wesley Ferrell, already has announced that he has found unsatisfactory the terms offered and has fired the papers back to headquarter here, although Griffith indignantly denies this.

While no one officially connected with the Senators will say anything, there is good reason to believe the other big shots on the playing roster have done likewise, or are preparing to follow Ferrell's example…

With a pitching staff in such a sorry plight, the Senators must have Ferrell in order to put up any kind of a respectable front in the impending campaign and nobody knows this better than Wesley Cheek of North Carolina and points south. But this time, the former Indian and Red Sox hurler will be up against a tougher proposition than he has ever encountered for Griffith is not easy to deal with.[100]

New York—Ferrell planned to head home to North Carolina to mull over his options, but before he had time to go anywhere he received a call from Joe McCarthy. On August 14, just two days after his release from Washington, Wes was a member of the New York Yankees.

His first start in pinstripes came on August 18. He beat the Senators, 5-4, in eleven innings. As Wes had received ten days severance pay from Washington, he took great pleasure in this victory.

The Yankees had little need for Ferrell in the last six weeks of the season. It's not hard to imagine that McCarthy, long an admirer of Ferrell, was hoping that the former ace still had a little mileage left in the arm. It may be a little harder to imagine, but had Ferrell remained with Washington, or signed with a team that made regular use of him, he would have had, despite his ERA, a chance at 20 wins.

Now presented with the opportunity for some World Series exposure, Wes's arm was in no condition to meet the challenge. Dizzy Dean, on the other hand, with a bad arm that limited him to just ten starts for the Cubs that year, watched his fame grow by fooling the Yankees for seven innings in the second game of the World Series (he didn't fool them in the eighth). Wrote *The Sporting News*: "The spectacle of a sore-arm pitcher, who has lost his speed and was forced to throw a 'nothing' ball most of the time, hurling back the attack of the heaviest-armed battalion in baseball history for seven innings will linger long as a heroic saga of the diamond…"[101]

When he signed with New York, the Yankees offered him a $7,500 bonus if they retained him for 1939.[102] Just days after the World Series ended the Yankees picked up that option and Wes went under the knife.

Spurgeon Chandler and Wesley Ferrell, Yankees pitchers, were in St. Elizabeth's Hospital today, mending after operations on their arms. Dr. Robert Emmett Walsh, club physician, who performed the delicate surgical jobs, said that Spud and Wes had come out of the ether in fine shape and after ten days in bed could go home.

"I removed two chips from Ferrell's arm and one from Chandler's," said Dr. Walsh, "Those chips show up big in the x-ray pictures, but actually are only half as big as a split pea. I cannot see why both pitchers should not be better than ever next season."

Ferrell was quite excited over the interest shown in him by Joe McCarthy and the Yankee front office. As a matter of fact Wes, who won only one game after his release by Washington and immediate signing by the Bombers, had expected to be set free right after the Series.[103]

Ferrell didn't get much ink in spring training in 1939. Most of the Yankees news dealt with the unexplained deterioration of Lou Gehrig. Once the season began, Wes appeared three times in May before being released on May 28. We can only speculate on what a tremendous force he would have been if he had spent any significant time with New York while his arm was still sound.

Wes worked out briefly with the Giants but was soon home in North Carolina contemplating his future.

Hollywood is the goal of Wesley Ferrell, recently released by the New York Yankees, both for a job in the movies and with the Hollywood Stars of the Pacific Coast League, he revealed in Charlotte, N. C., June 6. Ferrell was recently chosen as the "handsomest major league player" in a poll of feminine fans conducted by Dick Farrington of *The Sporting News*. Wes has adopted a novel means of curing the arthritis in his pitching arm, which was responsible for his release by the Yankees. He catches honey bees from flowers, holding them to his arm until they sting him, and his arm swells to twice the normal size. "It's the only way that you can get the arthritis out of your arm when it's sore," he explained.[104]

Ferrell made two more comeback attempts. Because teams were allowed to carry thirty players until May 15,[105] Wes was able to make the Dodgers squad coming out of spring training in 1940. Leo Durocher used Wes once in relief before releasing him.

Early in 1941 Wes wrote to the Boston Braves requesting a tryout. He hadn't played since his release from Brooklyn and felt sure the long rest would help his arm. He again pitched well enough to make the club in the spring.

Ferrell revived his old days of glory, April 17. Wes was sent to the hill in the sixth with two on and two out and the tally 5-4 in favor of the Phils. Ferrell quelled the uprising by disposing of Joe Marty, and held the Quakers runless the last three frames, permitting only two hits. As a fitting climax, he flailed a homer into the left field stands in his only trip to the plate, in the ninth.[106]

Four days later, Wes beat Philadelphia, 8-1, tossing a complete game and chipping in an RBI single. It was his final career victory. The Dodgers and Cards knocked him out early in his next two starts and Casey Stengel released him on May 8.

Still only thirty-three years old, Wes knew he still had some baseball left in him. Several weeks later he turned up managing the Leaksville team in the Bi-State League. In his first game there he picked the opposing player-manager off base. That base runner was his brother George.[107]

Wes continued to manage in the minors during much of the 1940s, but his arm was gone. After being such a dominating major league hitter, he had little trouble hitting minor league pitchers. His lifetime minor league batting average was .349 and he copped two minor league batting titles, one in the Virginia League in 1942 and a second in the Western Carolina League in 1948. His 31 home runs in 1942 also topped the circuit. Here are his offensive numbers in the only three minor league seasons in which he batted at least 200 times.

Yr	Lg	AB	R	H	2b	3b	HR	RBI	BA
1941	Bi-State	253	58	84	13	2	20	70	.332
1942	Virginia	410	92	148	18	9	31	99	.361
1948	W. Car.	381	99	162	30	14	24	119	.425

Wes had little connection with professional baseball in the 1950s, but the lure of the game called him back in the 1960s.

He has been named manager of the Rock Hill entry in the Class A Western Carolinas League. This is Ferrell's first managerial position in Organized ball since piloting Tampa in '49.

"I am mighty glad to be active in baseball again," admitted Ferrell, who lives just outside the Greensboro city limits on a 40-acre fisherman's paradise which includes five lakes.

Ferrell has no financial problems prompting his return to the game. He's independently wealthy through investments. He has a beauti-

ful home with relics of his baseball past everywhere.[108]

Ferrell spent the final years of his life commuting between North Carolina and Florida. He passed away on December 9, 1976.

"He should've been in the Hall of Fame," say many of his friends.

He may still make it, but now he'll never know.

They're burying Wes Ferrell in Greensboro, N.C. Monday.

Ferrell died Thursday evening at the Sarasota Memorial Hospital. He had gone there for kidney cancer surgery. He was 68 years old.

Ferrell's wife had passed away five years earlier.

A son, Wes, Jr., who bears a striking resemblance to his father, moved to Bradenton two years ago from Greensboro.

Wes, Jr., recalled how his dad "was coming to this area since 1935."

Wes, Sr. lived in Sarasota, Lake Placid, and was renting in North Port Charlotte at the time of his death.

"He was one of the best snook fisherman you'll ever see," said his son. The senior Ferrell was a mighty fine golfer, too. He was club champion at Placid lakes Country Club a couple of years ago, just after his 65th birthday…

A.C. Doc Davis, who is owner-manager of Martin's Restaurant in Port Charlotte, was a longtime golf-playing buddy of Ferrell's.

"He sure didn't look 68," says Davis. "He was about as handsome a man as he was a good pitcher. He was still playing golf right up to the time of his death. He went out a week ago and he shot an 82."[109]

Wes Ferrell has been dead for close to a quarter of a century, yet baseball historians have never truly defined his place in baseball history. He finished with 193 victories, and while many consider 200 the minimum standard of pitching greatness, Dazzy Vance (197), Rube Waddell (193), Lefty Gomez (189), Sandy Koufax (165), and Dizzy Dean (150) all finished their careers with similar or lesser totals. While all five, despite ranking below Ferrell in *Total Baseball's* Total Player Ranking (TPR) system,[110] are in the Hall of Fame, Ferrell remains outside the sanctum. Why is that?

Earned Run Average—Ferrell finished his career with an ERA of 4.04. How, you ask, can we possibly enshrine that number in the Hall of Fame? Context and judgment. Wes Ferrell, like every true superstar of the game, was concerned with one, and only one thing: Baseball games won.

Baseball historian Bill James wrote: "For the same reason that Babe Herman's .324 lifetime batting average doesn't prove that he was a Hall of Famer, Wes Ferrell's 4.04 ERA doesn't prove that he wasn't. He pitched in a high-run era and pitched almost all of his career in parks that favored the hitter (League Park in Cleveland, then Fenway Park), so in context, a 4.04 ERA is quite good."[111]

In seven of his first eight seasons, the exception being the 1933 season when he hurt his arm, Ferrell finished among the top ten ERA qualifiers in the American League. Ferrell's ERA of 3.72 from 1929-1936 was among the best of his era in his league. He took a big career hit by pitching with a deteriorating arm in 1937 and 1938.

Grove, Gomez, Bridges, and Ruffing had a great advantage over Harder, Ferrell, and Lyons. They played for the teams with the best batters, so didn't have to face them. That, given the way baseball was formatted in the 1930s, had an effect it wouldn't have today. Greg Maddux, Roger Clemens, Pedro Martinez, or Randy Johnson don't pitch 50-plus innings against a single team in a given year.

Here are how the 17 pitchers who recorded 20-win seasons in the American League from 1929-1938 compare in ERA, first from 1929-1936 and then from 1929-1938.

	20-Wins Seasons	ERA '29-'36	ERA '29-'38	+/-
Grove	6	2.90	2.93	+0.03
Gomez	4	3.36	3.22	-0.14
Bridges	3	3.66	3.79	+0.13
Allen	1	3.69	3.61	-0.08
Harder	2	3.70	3.78	+0.08
Ferrell	6	3.72	4.03	+0.31
Rowe	1	3.83	3.96	+0.13
Ruffing	3	3.94	3.78	-0.16
Lyons	1	4.05	4.02	-0.03
Stewart	1	4.08	4.08	0.00
Crowder	2	4.13	4.13	0.00
Weaver	1	4.17	4.32	+0.15
Walberg	1	4.23	4.32	+0.09
Newsom	1	4.28	4.57	+0.29
Kennedy	1	4.29	4.64	+0.35
Whitehill	1	4.29	4.52	+0.23
Earnshaw	3	4.34	4.34	0.00

The Ball—When we evaluate major league statistics from the 1930s we must take into account that the National League used a different and considerably less resilient ball than the American League did throughout most of that decade. A review of *The Sporting News*

during the 1930s yields a number of editorials and stories regarding the differences between the balls. These first two are from 1931.

> For the moment there is distinctly a ball game of two different types in the major leagues.
>
> In the best light of all the information that we have been able to obtain, and after we have heard of the results of the analyses that have been made by the most competent authorities in baseball, it seems to us that the slightly thicker and heavier cover on the NL ball, as modest as it seems to be, is the reason for this.
>
> The AL ball is identical with that of 1930 except that the stitching is raised, and not countersunk, as was the case last year. The late president [Ernest] Barnard of the AL thought, after consultation with his club owners, that their change was enough for this season.
>
> The NL went a little farther. It called in the president of one of the principal firms which makes baseballs and explained to him what its members had in mind and asked him if he would have a sample ball made which carried out their ideas. He produced the sample ball with its raised stitches and with its thicker cover and told them what he thought it might do. They like the change he made and adopted the ball.
>
> The curiously interesting fact, most prominent in all of this discussion is that the balls are identical, except as to the cover. It is also quite obvious that very little need be changed in a baseball to alter results.[112]

> National League teams have scored more than 1,000 fewer runs this year than they did last season, which condition is attributed by President John A. Heydler to the new ball with raised stitches and a heavier coat. The National League president favors the continuation of the new ball next season and it is believed the American League will also adopt the heavier cover to make it uniform throughout both major leagues."[113]

Sportswriter Bob Broeg, long a Ferrell supporter, penned a column on Joe Cronin and Wes when the pair were in St. Louis for the fortieth-anniversary reunion of the 1933 All-Star team.

> I was surprised when Ferrell, tall and still handsome at 65, thought that, whether hand-sewn in Chicopee or Haiti, the ball now is livelier than the one used when Wes came up

to Cleveland in '29.

Cronin agreed. "When Wes and I played in Boston, a ball rarely went into the center field section at Fenway Park," he said, "but now it's a common occurrence."

Although Spalding has made the major league ball for years, there was a difference at least until 1934, Cronin recalled, when the stitches of both the American and National League balls were standardized red. Previously, the N.L. ball had red and black stitching, the A.L. red and blue.

"I know the ball in '33 was different," said Cronin, "because we alternated balls in both the All-Star Game and the World Series, and the National League ball had higher seams, favoring the curve-baller."[114]

The redoubtable Rogers Hornsby felt the American League ball needed to be deadened. The Sporting News headline on July 9, 1936, read, BROWNIE MANAGER ASKS FOR SLOWER BALL.

Rog Hornsby, who broke more pitchers' hearts, when he was in his heyday in the National League than perhaps any other batter, now is a-gin' the sluggers. The iconoclastic Hornsby is a-gin' 'em because he believes so much pitching is being sacrificed on the altar of boom-boom explotation [sic] that the game is beginning to suffer.

In short, the Rajah feels that something must be done to slow down the ball and give the throwers a chance, not for the salvation of the Browns, but for the game, presented as a major league attraction...

"Personally, I think major league baseball, as it is going, is verging on bush league stuff, because the pitchers, as represented by the present crop, cannot match the hitters," exploded Rog...

"Why under present conditions a manager can't play for a run," says Rog. "He can't sacrifice unless he is a run behind and it is a late inning. He can't hit-and-run, or try to hit behind the runner, if he is trying to measure the fact that his own pitcher is likely to be slugged for nine runs the next inning."

Early in 1938 over 500 baseball execs, players and writers gathered in Baltimore to watch a batting demonstration with the new balls that were to be used during the upcoming season. Jimmie Foxx, Chuck Klein, and Charlie Keller were on hand as hitting representatives for the AL, NL, and IL, respectively.

Baseball's mid-winter party in frigid Oriole Park, January 10, established two points regarding the dead ball, as adopted by the National League, and the lively ball, as retained by the American and International Leagues. Both will travel over the fences when hit properly. However, the National League ball has a distinctly "dead" sound coming off the bat, compared to the livelier American League ball.[115]

Control—Detractors point to Ferrell issuing 100 or more bases on balls in seven different seasons, and finishing his career with more walks allowed than strikeouts. To the uninformed it appears that Ferrell had poor control. Nothing could be further from the truth. Ferrell walked a lot of batters only because that was the standard for American League hurlers of his day.

Between 1929 and 1939, American League pitchers walked 49,336 batters. During that same span, National League hurlers walked only 38,567, an average of about 1,000 fewer free passes per season. American League hurlers recorded at least 100 walks on more than 70 occasions while National Leaguers did so fewer than 20 times. This might lead us to assume that National League pitchers had better control. But if we look at the All-Star Games for 1933-1939 and the World Series 1929-1939, we see just the opposite. National Leaguers issued 253 free passes to American League hitters while American Leaguers walked just 131 National League batters. Can anyone really doubt that the National League used a deader ball than the American League?

Wes Ferrell was a control pitcher. When he came to the major leagues he had a curve ball and an excellent fastball. He quickly learned that the key to success at the major league level was changing speeds. Writer Sam Murphy noted after Wes had scored his fourteenth victory in 1929: "The finest change-of-pace pitcher in the country today! That's what players say of Wesley Ferrell of the Indians."[116]

Wes told writer Gordon Cobbledick in August of that same year: "I like to pitch against the free swingers, fellows like Simmons and Foxx. I find that a change of pace bothers them a lot. But when you try to change up on the weaker hitters they just poke the ball over the infield for base hits."[117]

Ferrell was a master who studied the finer points of his profession. His nephew, George Ferrell, Jr., recalls years of family conversations between his father and uncles where they talked for hours on pitching strategy and how to set up batters.

In an unidentified and undated newspaper clipping in Ferrell's Hall of Fame file, writer H. G. Salsinger noted:

"When Willis Hudlin saw four successive singles made by Detroit in the seventh inning yesterday, he looked toward the bench to see Mr. Roger Peckinpaugh beckoning him. The relief pitcher was Mr. Ferrell. He came from the bullpen and proceeded to warm up from the pitcher's box. After he had thrown more than 15 balls Mr. Will McGowan, the umpire, called a halt. He said it was enough. Mr. Ferrell said it was not. Mr. McGowan was right and Mr. Ferrell was temperamental. Mr. Ferrell had pitched 15 successive strikes and any pitcher who can deliver 15 successive strikes is hot enough for any opposition."[118]

In October, 1935 an unidentified teammate, in discussing Wes's return to the top of the pitching pile, said: "Oh, his arm was really sore all right. It isn't as strong now as it was, but Wes has gotten smart. And he has just about perfect control. He can throw that ball right through a knothole all afternoon."

How about his speed?

The player chuckled.

"Well, I'll tell you. He's not as fast as he was, but he's a lot faster than the hitters think he is. He kinda sneaks that fast one by 'em unexpected like."[119]

J. G. Taylor Spink wrote a column in *The Sporting News* issue of October 3, 1935 pertaining to the paper's All-Star team. About Wes, he said:

"Wesley Ferrell…The man with a smirk for Fate…Hard-to-handle Wesley…A really great pitcher, with the perfect pitching psychology …Make 'em hit at the bad ones, is his policy, his secret of success…He antagonizes the hitter…He antagonizes his own teammates …Bullheaded, but bright…Reticent, sure of himself, somewhat good looking…Student of the stars…He went daffy about astrology while in Cleveland and would not pitch unless assured that the stars were in the right places and the zodiac said "go."

Shirley Povich wrote:

He learned the art of pitching after he lost the burning fast ball that was his greatest asset when he broke in…

Unlike Lefty Grove, Fred Marberry and the dozens of other fire-balling pitchers who neglected to learn how to throw a slow curve and thus prolong their earning ability in the big leagues, Ferrell grimly set himself for the task and emerged last season as the cleverest pitcher in the league.

When he was out there for the Indians fog-ging the ball past the hitters, he was not great shucks at control. But the new Ferrell now gets by, and very nicely, too, thank you, on control alone. His ability to pitch to a spot, to pull strings on the hitters, is serving him even better than did his fast ball. Those 25 games he won last year are no myth, yet Ferrell, in the parlance of the game, couldn't break a pane of glass at 50 paces.

Ferrell's walk totals, like his ERA, were directly related to being a 1930s American League pitcher.

Epilogue—Wes Ferrell was unique. He was an impact player in the truest sense of the word. He could dominate a game with either his arm or his bat. He played in a highly offensive league and era, which makes evaluating his raw pitching data difficult. (Conversely, if we accept the argument that the American League was a hitter's haven in the 1930s, we must also make an adjustment for Wes' hitting. That is why this article made such an elaborate effort to show how his hitting impacted individual games.)

Wes Ferrell, although packaging his talent differently, had every ounce of value that Lefty Grove and Carl Hubbell had for ten years. Both Grove and Hubbell were valuable for a longer period of time, but at their peaks they had nothing on Ferrell. It could be said, in a way, that Ferrell, flaming at both ends of the baseball candle, just burned out faster.

The following list compares Ferrell to the other top starters, 1929-1938 (starting stats only). Ferrell is the only one who never played for either a pennant-winner or a second-place finisher.[120]

| Pitcher | W-L | Team Finishes | | | |
		1st	2nd	3rd	4th
Hubbell	182-101	3	2	4	0
Grove	181-65	3	2	1	2
Ferrell	180-114	0	0	1	6
Ruffing	157-104	4	4	1	0
Gomez	148-70	4	4	1	0
Whitehill	136-113	1	0	1	2
French	131-111	2	5	0	0
Dean	130-61	2	1	1	1
Bridges	127-87	2	2	0	1
Warneke	122-68	2	2	3	1
Fitzsimmons	122-95	2	2	3	0

In 1984, eight years after Wes' death, the Veterans Committee elected Rick Ferrell to the Hall of Fame. He didn't forget his brother.

"I guess what I'm doing here, hopefully, is putting up a stick for Wes," said Ferrell…

"Wes would understand," he said.

"We've been putting sticks up for each other for a long time," Ferrell said. "Back when Wes and I and our four brothers were growing up on the farm near Greensboro, we used to go into a field and take hitting practice.

"If one of us hit the ball a long way, we'd go and put a stick up at that point and then if somebody hit it farther, he'd run out and move the stick and stick it into the ground where his ball stopped."

Ferrell said it was just a game. But it became a little more than a game when the brothers were playing on rival teams.

"After we both made it to the major leagues, my team was playing his one day in 1933. I was catching for Boston and he was pitching for the Cleveland Indians.

"Well, I hit a home run off Wes and he was watching me trot around the bases, and when I got to second I yelled to Wes, 'Hey, Wes, go put a stick up for that one.'

"Wes got mad and started to kick the mound. But he came to the plate in the following inning and he hit a home run. As he crossed the plate, he looked at me with a big smile on his face and said, 'OK, Rick, looks like you're going to have to go and move the stick.'"[121]

Notes:

1. *The Sporting News. October 27, 1932.*

2. Telephone conversation with George Ferrell, Jr. May 3, 2000.

3. George's career stats are listed in SABR's *Minor League Stars (Volume 1.)*.

4. *The Sporting News. August 13, 1936.*

5. *The Sporting News. August 18, 1932.*

6. Best described today as a junior college.

7. Hank Greenberg and Ira Berkow. *The Story of My Life,* pp. 15-16.

8. Ibid. p. 100.

9. *The Sporting News. December 14, 1960.*

10. Ibid.

11. Unidentified newspaper column, "Daniel's Dope," Dan Daniel, May, 1931.

12. Donald Honig, *Baseball When the Grass was Real*, p. 16.

13. Ibid. pp. 18-19.

14. Unidentified clipping in Ferrell's HOF file, Frank Graham, April 17, 1935.

15. Unidentifed newspaper clipping in Ferrell's HOF file,1929.

16. American League Service Bureau press release, January 26, 1930.

17. Unidentified newspaper clipping in Ferrell's HOF file, dated July, 1929.

18. *The Sporting News. December 5, 1929.*

19. Honig *op. cit.*, p. 121.

20. Ibid. p. 122.

21. *The Sporting News*, Ed Bang, September 18, 1930.

22. Ibid.

23. Ibid.

24. This is one of five wins in the 1928-1938 period for Grove that were, at best, questionable scoring decisions.

25. *The Sporting News*, Ed Bang, September 18, 1930.

26. Unidentified newspaper clipping in Ferrell's HOF file, Dated November, 1930.

27. Unidentified newspaper clippping in Ferrell's Hall of Fame file, August 22, 1930.

28. Bill Deane, *Award Voting*, SABR, 1988

29. Ibid.

30. New York *World-Telegram*, Joe Williams, June 10, 1931.

31. Unidentified newspaper column in Ferrell's HOF file, 1931.

32. Associated Press release in Ferrell's HOF file, 1931.

33. Unidentified newspaper clipping in Ferrell's HOF file.

34. Data provided by David Vincent and SABR's Home Run Log.

35. Unidentified newspaper clipping in Ferrell's HOF file, Copyright 1932.

36. Unidentified newspaper clipping in Ferrell's HOF file, Ed Bang, February 13, 1933.

37. *The Sporting News*, August 4, 1932.

38. Honig, *op cit.*, pp. 26-27.

39. New York *World-Telegram*, Dan Daniel, May 18, 1932.

40. New York *World-Telegram*, Dan Daniel, June 14, 1932.

41. *The Sporting News*, August 25, 1932.

42. *The Sporting News*, September 8, 1932.

43. New York *World-Telegram*, Joe Williams, August 17, 1932.

44. *The Sporting News*, September 8, 1932.

45. Ibid.

46. *The Sporting News*, November 10, 1932.

47. Unidentified newspaper clipping in Ferrell's HOF file, September 1, 1932.

48. Eugene Murdock, *Baseball Between The Wars*, Meckler, 1992, p.13.

49. Unidentified newspaper clipping in Ferrell's HOF file, April 4, 1931.

50. Ferrell's pinch-hitting totals not included.

51. *The Sporting News*, Ed Bang, December 1, 1932. 3.

52. *The Sporting News*, March 9, 1933.

53. Ray Robinson, *Matty: An American Hero*, Oxford University Press, 1993, pp. 113-114.

54. *The Sporting News*, March 23, 1933.

55. Ibid.

56. *The Sporting News*, April 27, 1933.

57. Unidentified newspaper clipping in Ferrell's HOF file, July 20, 1929.

58. Ibid.

59. *The Sporting News*, August 10, 1933.

60. Unidentified newspaper article in Ferrell's HOF file, August 16, 1933.

61. New York *World-Telegram*, September 14, 1933.

62. *The Sporting News*, March 8, 1934.

63. New York *World-Telegram*, May 22, 1934.

64. Associated Press, April 27, 1934.

65. Unidentified Joe Williams column, probably from the *World-Telegram*, June 5, 1934.

66. New York *World-Telegram*, June 21, 1934.

67. New York *World-Telegram*, September 20, 1934.

68. *The Sporting News*, June 21, 1945.

69. *The Sporting News*, September 22, 1973.

70. New York *World-Telegram*, Dan Daniels, April 18, 1935.

71. Four of Grove's five 1935 RBIs came in the same game.

72. *The Sporting News,* August 1, 1935.

73. Honig, *op cit.,* p. 33.

74. New York *World-Telegram,* October 30, 1935.

75. *The Sporting News,* October 3, 1935.

76. *The Sporting News,* January 2, 1936.

77. *The Sporting News,* Dan Daniels, July 4, 1935.

78. Peter Golenbock, *Fenway, An Unexpurgated History of the Boston Red Sox,* p. 91.

79. Unidentified newspaper clipping in Ferrell's HOF file., Shirley Povich, April 3, 1936.

80. *The Sporting News,* October 10, 1935.

81. *The Sporting News,* May 14, 1936.

82. *The Sporting News,* April 23, 1936.

83. Unidentified newspaper clipping in author's file, Harold Kaese, 1959.

84. Unidentified newspaper colum in Ferrell's HOF file, Shirley Povich, August 22, 1936.

85. Unidentified newspaper clipping in author's file, August 16, 1965.

86. *The Sporting News,* October 22, 1937.

87. *The Sporting News,* October 15, 1936.

88. *The Sporting News,* June 17, 1937.

89. Jeff Bower and Chris Kahrl, *Baseball Prosectus* web site.

90. Ed Linn, *Hitter. The Life and Turmoils of Ted Williams,*1993., p. 306.

91. *The Sporting News,* "Fanning with Farrington," June 11, 1936.

92. *The Sporting News,* June 22, 1936.

93. Harrington E. Crissey, Jr., *Teenagers, Graybeards and 4-F's. Volume 2: The American League,* 1982.

94. *The Sporting News,* January 1, 1940.

95. *The Sporting News, July 21, 1938.*

96. *The Sporting News, May 19, 1938.*

97. Greenberg and Ira Berkow, *op. cit.,* p. 100

98. Honig, *op. cit.,* p. 47.

199. *The Sporting News,* December 25, 1976.

100. *The Sporting News,* January 20, 1938.

101. *The Sporting News,* October 13, 1938.

102. *The Sporting News,* January 20, 1938.

103. Unidentified newspaper clipping in Ferrell's HOF file.

104. *The Sporting News,* June 15, 1939.

105. *The Sporting News,* May 9, 1940.

106. *The Sporting News,* April 24, 1941.

107. *The Sporting News,* June 5, 1941.

108. Unidentified newspaper clipping in Ferrell's HOF file, apparently from Greensboro, North Carolina, paper. 1963.

109. Unidentifed newspaper clipping in Ferrell's HOF file.

110. *Total Baseball. 6th Edition.* Ferrell is the 106th rated player of all time. Vance is 157th, Waddell 197th, Dean 237th, Koufax 315th, Gomez 327th.

111. Bill James, *The Politics of Glory,* p. 330.

112. *The Sporting News,* May 28, 1931.

113. *The Sporting News,* September 3, 1931.

114. *The Sporting News,* September 22, 1973.

115.*The Sporting News,* January 20, 1938.

116. Unidentified clipping in Ferrell's HOF file.

117. Unidentified clipping in Ferrell's HOF file.

118. New York *Tribune,* October 1, 1935.

119. Unidentified newspaper clipping in Ferrell's HOF file, April 3, 1936.

120. Dean and Gomez did not pitch full seasons in all of those years. Dean also played briefly for another pennant winner in 1930. Ferrell pitched 30 innings for the Yankees in 1938.

121. *USA Today,* August 14, 1984.

Careers and career years

What kept Joe Peitz out of the majors? His brother, Heinie, stuck around for 1,234 games over sixteen seasons, with a .271 average. All Joe did in his lone big league try (1894) was tear the cover off the ball. In 26 at-bats over seven games as an outfielder for St. Louis, he hit .423 and slugged .731! He was only twenty-four. He scored ten runs and walked six times. Wow!

His pitching twin was Luis Aloma. Luis probably quit the majors because there wasn't enough of a challenge. In the worst of his four seasons, he was 3-1. For his career he was 18-3 (.857). He was a reliever for all but one of his 116 games. In that one start, he pitched a shutout! I guess he didn't get another chance to start because the White Sox were afraid that He'd be banned. His best year was 1951. He was 6-0 with a 1.82 ERA and he even hit .350 on seven hits in 20 at-bats. What happened to Luis? Did Castro make him commissioner of the Cuban League or did he return to the Daily Planet with Lois Lane?

Another mystery season was Cliff Dapper's 1942 performance. As the third catcher behind Mickey Owen and Billy Sullivan for the second-place Dodgers, Dapper hit .471 and slugged .706 in 17 at-bats. If you're not going to make it back to the majors, those are pretty good stats to be remembered by. Frank Luce did pretty well, too, with the '23 Pirates. As an outfield sub, he was six-for-nine. If he had not gone oh-for-three as a pinch hitter, he would have hit .667 instead of a measly .500. Still, that's not a bad lifetime average. A modern player with a six-for-twelve streak would have it flashed on Diamond Vision.

—Cappy Gagnon

SABR Back Publications Order Form

Baseball Research Journal

The *Baseball Research Journal,* the annual publication of the society, features some of the best member research. Articles range from statistical to biographical sketches, plus nearly every other topic in baseball.

*	1975 (112 pp)	
____	1976 (128 pp)	$4.00
*	1977 (144 pp)	
____	1978 (160 pp)	$4.00
____	1979 (160 pp)	$5.00
____	1980 (180 pp)	$5.00
*	1981 (180 pp)	
*	1982 (184 pp)	
*	1983 (188 pp)	

larger format

____	1984 (88 pp)	
____	1985 (88 pp)	$6.00
____	1986 (88 pp)	$6.00
____	1987 (88 pp)	$6.00
____	1988 (88 pp)	$7.00
*	1989 (88 pp)	$8.00
____	1990 (88 pp)	$8.00
____	1991 (88 pp)	$8.00
____	1992 (96 pp)	$7.95
____	1993 (112 pp)	$9.95
____	1994 (112 pp)	$9.95
____	1995 (144 pp)	$9.95
____	1996 (154 pp)	$9.95
____	1997 (144 pp)	$9.95
____	1998 (116 pp)	$9.95
____	1999 (144 pp)	$12.00
____	2000 (144 pp)	$12.00

SABR's Books on the 19th C

Nineteenth Century Stars
____ 1988 (144 pp) $10.00
Bios of America's First Heroes (Non-Hall of Famers)

Baseball's First Stars
____ 1996 (183 pp) $14.95
More Bios, including the Hall of Famers

Base Ball: How to Become a Player
by John Montgomery Ward *(reprint of 1888)*
____ 1993 (149 pp) $9.95

The National Pastime

The National Pastime features articles by members more general in nature, although some volumes are arranged around a theme, as noted below.

*	#1 Fall, 1982 (88 pp)	
*	#2 Fall, 1983 (88 pp)	
____	#3 Spring 1984 (88 pp)	
	19th Century Pictorial	$7.00
____	#4 Spring 1985 (88 pp)	$6.00
____	#5 Winter, 1985 (88 pp)	$6.00
*	#6 Spring, 1986 (88 pp)	
	Dead Ball Era Pictorial	
____	#7 Winter, 1987 (88 pp)	$6.00
*	#8 Spring, 1988 (80 pp)	
*	#9 1989 (88 pp)	
____	#10 Fall, 1990 (88 pp)	$8.00
____	#11 Fall, 1991 (88 pp)	$7.95
____	#12 Summer, 1992 (96 pp)	
	The International Pastime	$7.95
____	#13 Summer, 1993 (96 pp)	$7.95
____	#14 Summer, 1994 (112 pp)	$9.95
____	#15 Spring, 1995 (156 pp)	$9.95
____	#16 Spring, 1996 (144 pp.)	$9.95
____	#17 Spring, 1997 (144 pp.)	$9.95
*	#18 Spring, 1998 (144 pp)	
____	#19 Summer, 1999 (116 pp.)	$12.00
____	#20 Summer, 2000 (132 pp.)	$12.00

SABR Review of Books

____	Volume 1, 1986	$6.00
____	Volume 2, 1987	$6.00
____	Volume 3, 1988	$7.00
____	Volume 4, 1989	$7.00
*	Volume 5, 1990	

All-Star Baseball in Cleveland
____ 1997 Special Publication (64 pp) $7.95

Baseball for the Fun of It
A pictorial looking at the joy of baseball
____ 1997 (92 pp) $14.95

Cooperstown Corner
Columns From The Sporting News *by Lee Allen*
____ 1990 (181 pp) $10.00

Home Runs in the Old Ballparks
____ 1995 $9.95
Listings of top 5 HR hitters in parks no longer in use.

* - out of print

Biographies by SABR

Lefty Grove: An American Original
____ 200 (315 pp) $12.95
Biography of Hall of Fame Pitcher Lefty Grove written by former Sports Illustrated write, Jim Kaplan

Uncle Robbie
____ 1999 (200 pp) $12.95
Biography of Hall of Fame Manager Wilbert Robinson by Jack Kavanagh and Norman Macht

Addie Joss: King of the Pitchers
____ 1998 (141 pp) $14.95
Biography of Hall of Fame Pitcher Addie Joss by Scott Longert

****

Baseball Historical Review
____ 1981; Best of the 1972-74 BRJs $6.00

The Negro Leagues Book

*	1994 (382 pp, softcover)	
____	1994 (382 pp, hardcover)	$49.95
____	1994 (382 pp, limited edit.)	$149.95

(Leather bound, slipcase, autographed)

Minor League History Journal

*	Volume 1	
____	Volume 2 (54 pages)	$6.00
____	Volume 3 (72 pages)	$7.00

Run, Rabbit, Run
Tales of Walter "Rabbit" Maranville
____ 1991 (96 pp) $9.95

Memories of a Ballplayer: Bill Werber and Baseball in the 1930s
____ 2001 (250 pp) $14.95
   Bill Werber, a premier thirdbaseman, is the last man alive who traveled with the '27 Yankees. Werber's memories of the players, umpires, managers, executives, reporters and fans of the 1930s take us back to an era long gone.

How to Do Baseball Research
____ 2000 (163 pp) $12.95
   A primer on how one goes about researching baseball with ideas, information, advice and techniques that will serve any researcher well

---

Name: _____

Address: _____

City, State, ZIP: _____

Daytime Phone (in case of questions): _____

Send your order to:
University of Nebraska Press, 233 North 8th Street, Lincoln, NE 68588-0255.
Call 1-800-755-1105 weekdays from 8am to 5pm CT
Order on-line at: http://nebraskapress.unl.edu
12/13/00

Book Total	$_____
Shipping charges are $4.00 for the first book and 50 cents for each additional book.	$_____
NE residents, add sales tax	$_____
TOTAL	$_____

Master Card & Visa Accepted

Card # _____

Exp Date _____

Two Poems

Don Zamudio

The Old-fashioned Way

Grandpa
sits
at the kitchen table
listening
to the ball game
on a crackling transistor radio

His eyes closed
His body motionless
His face eased into a grin

Grandpa
sits
among the crowd
watching
a ball game
from box seats on third base line

Opening Day in Chicago

Baseball
season begins
on a cold afternoon
as blankets warm cheering fans and

the first pitch soars across home plate,
stinging our catcher's hand
frozen inside
his mitt.

Dan Zamudio *is completing a masters degree in Library Sciences.
His baseball poems have appeared in "Capper's" and "Baseball Ink."
He is working on an essay about baseball poetry for an upcoming book
entitled "Across the Diamond: Essays on Baseball and American
Culture," from Haworth Press.*